WITHDRAWN

D0936528

THE
DRAMA OF J.M. SYNGE

IRISH STUDIES

IRISH STUDIES

Irish studies presents a wide range of books interpreting important aspects of Irish life and culture to scholarly and general audiences. The richness and complexity of the Irish experience, past and present, deserves broad understanding and careful analysis. For this reason an important purpose of the series is to offer a forum to scholars interested in Ireland, its history, and culture. Irish literature is a special concern in the series, but works from the perspectives of the fine arts, history, and the social sciences are also welcome, as are studies which take interdisciplinary approaches.

Irish Studies is a continuing project of Syracuse University Press and is under the general editorship of Richard Fallis, associate professor of English at Syracuse University.

IRISH STUDIES, EDITED BY RICHARD FALLIS

822
Sy 75zk

THE
DRAMA OF J.M. SYNGE

MARY C. KING

SYRACUSE UNIVERSITY PRESS 1985

Copyright © 1985 by Mary C. King

All Rights Reserved

Published in the United States of America by
Syracuse University Press, Syracuse, New York 13210
by arrangement with
Fourth Estate Ltd, Publishers
100 Westbourne Grove
London, UK

ISBN 0-8156-2337-2

CONTENTS

ALLEGHENY COLLEGE LIBRARY

85-7291

PREFACE

MUCH HAS been written about Synge's use of the folk tradition of the peasant people of Ireland in his plays and about the nature of his dramatic language. There has, however, been no detailed consideration to date of the importance, indeed, the centrality, of the theme of language in his work, or of the relationship between text and world which preoccupied him throughout his life. For a long time, Synge has been assessed within the shadow as well as the light thrown by W.B. Yeats's inspired but partial remarks about the significance for the dramatist of his visits to the Aran Islands. The importance of his familiarity with European literature, philosophy, philology and aesthetics has been obscured or neglected, as has the interest which Synge took in the writings of Herbert Spencer, Charles Darwin, Nietzsche and Marx.

Taking as its context Synge's scholarly acquaintance with nineteenth-century European philology and philosophy, this study attempts an analysis of the theme of language in his work. It relates his preoccupation with the word to its origins in his family background and in the history of his class and seeks to trace and evaluate his exploration of the mediating, symbolic role of language and of art.

In his dramatisation of the relationship between word and reality, between text and world, Synge's use of metalinguistic and meta-dramatic strategies looks forward to the techniques of a modernism which, like the work of James Joyce, engages its audience in the interplay between history and myth.

For his constant advice and encouragement during the preparation of my Ph.D. thesis for the University of Leeds, upon which this present book is based, and for the generous support which he has given me at various stages of the work, I wish to thank Dr William McCormack. I wish to express my gratitude to John Spencer of the Institute of Modern English, the University of Leeds, for stimulating my initial interest in Synge's use of language and for his help with techniques of analysis, and to Dr Loreto Todd for her suggestions about representing features of the grammatical structure and syntax of *In the Shadow of the Glen*.

Special gratitude is due to Dr Bernard Meehan and the staff of the Manuscript Room, Trinity College, Dublin, for their patience and help during my numerous visits to Trinity College, and to the Board of the College as custodians of the Synge Papers, and the Trustees of the Synge Estate, for permission to quote from the manuscripts held in the Library of Trinity College. I am grateful to the Oxford University Press for permission to use quotations from their four-volume *Collected Works* of J.M. Synge. All quotations from Synge's published work are from this edition and references are given in the body of the text. My thanks to Mrs Pauline Greenwood for her efficient typing of my manuscript and not least to my husband, Geoffrey, for his help in reading and checking the typescript as well as for his continuing support of and interest in my work.

Finally, I wish to thank my parents for expecting me at any time and for welcoming me during my comings and goings in the course of my research. Having left my native Wicklow some twenty-five years ago, like Synge, 'I travel for my turning home': I now appreciate the life and the language of that home, and the need for the turning, as never before.

The University of Bradford   Mary C. King
January 1985

THE
DRAMA OF J.M. SYNGE

1.
ORIGINS ARE AS EMBLEMATIC AS
THE RESULTS THEMSELVES

IN 1969, a year before the centenary of the playwright's birth, Alan Price surveyed the field of recent work on John Millington Synge. The exercise, he concluded, confirmed Roger McHugh's judgement that 'the best literary criticism of our modern writers in English has been written by writers outside Ireland'; where Synge was concerned, 'from the Irish there is almost nothing'.[1] During the last decade, several studies have begun to redress this imbalance and to free Synge from the shadow of Yeats, under which for so long his genius was interpreted chiefly as that of a writer of peasant plays. The process of reassessment is part of a larger quest for identity, in which Irish writers have initiated an investigation into the problematic nature of the relationships between the Gaelic, the Anglo-Irish, the English and the larger European dimensions of Irish nationhood and culture. The first book on Synge devoted entirely to a study of his plays appeared in 1975, and in 1979 the much disputed questions of the authenticity of his dramatic idiom and his debt to the Irish language received detailed consideration from a scholar fluent in Ireland's two native languages.[2] We must still, however, look outside Ireland for any substantial attempts to locate Synge's work in a European context and to assess his status as a modern writer. In *The Irish Drama of Europe from Yeats to Beckett*, Katharine Worth asks that we see the work of Synge as well as that of Yeats and O'Casey as part of a movement which 'took Ireland into Europe long before the term EEC had been heard' and she argues that the self-conscious theatricality of his plays and the heightened awareness of

1

language as language make him 'in a way one of the most modern of the moderns'.[3]

The discovery of the symbolic nature of words, his realisation that language is a mediator between subject and object, played a crucial role in Synge's development as a creative artist. It was made possible by the fact that he stood historically close to the crossroads of Ireland's complex and contradictory linguistic, as well as her social and political, revolution. It was also facilitated in no small measure by his extensive excursions into European literature, aesthetics and philosophy and by his systematic study of philology and philologically based Celtic studies. European thought in the nineteenth century was deeply affected by a crisis of historicism characterised by the emergence of 'a stage of consciousness in which the problematical nature of language itself has become recognized'.[4] The significance of this recognition for Synge can only be fully appreciated in the context of the peculiarly intense scriptural fundamentalism which dominated intercourse and shaped relationships and identities in the dramatist's family. This fundamentalism made Synge's linguistic journey towards symbolic expression simultaneously liberating and traumatic.

A comprehensive socio-historical investigation into the linguistic beliefs and practices of the Synge household would, no doubt, throw much-needed light on the ascendancy crisis of identity in late-nineteenth-century Ireland. Although such an analysis is beyond the scope of this study, it is, nevertheless, essential to pursue the phenomenon at least as far as Mrs Synge's insistence upon the absolute authority of the Divine Word. In a massive and detailed biography of his uncle, Edward Stephens documents Mrs Synge's uncompromising insistence upon what she regarded as the historical truth of Holy Scripture. He refers repeatedly to the ways in which a dogmatic literalism imbued every aspect of her attitude towards word and deed. 'Mrs Synge', writes Stephens, 'conducted her household by a rule as strict as that of a religious order and supposed that her children would acquiesce without question. She was very well versed in the doctrine to which she adhered and could support every tenet by citing scriptural authority'.[5] This religious fundamentalism inspired frequent homilies about language itself, and even regulated the day-to-day verbal intercourse of the household:

2

His mother had made language one of the special subjects of her religious instruction. She taught that to refer to God in any but a strictly religious manner was a sinful taking in vain of the Holy Name, that to use expletive oaths or curses was a breach of St James's injunction 'Let your yea be yea; and your nay, nay', and that to exaggerate was to lie. Mrs Synge sought divine aid in confining within the closest limits the already restricted speech of the Victorian period, praying fervently, 'Set a watch O Lord, upon our lips' So strict was her rule that it almost paralysed language as an expression of feeling.[6]

This banishment of feeling and exclusion of any scope for ambiguity from the kingdom of the word was not merely a personal idiosyncrasy of Mrs Synge. It was part, also, of a reaction amongst Anglo-Irish Protestants against a growing confusion and disquiet occasioned by their loss of political power and status. Privileged access to the authority of the Divine Word became for some a substitute for the fast-fading privilege of earthly authority. By the mid-nineteenth century the ascendancy was already facing a developing Catholic nationalism, and the birth of an Irish Catholic bourgeoisie, with which facts of history and economics British imperialism was beginning to seek an uneasy and still unconcluded accommodation. Since the ascendancy themselves had become by the nineteenth century 'a predominantly bourgeois social formation', the sense of isolation from history which drove many, like the Synge family, into forms of introverted evangelicalism was, in reality, a very specific and contra- dictory form of alienation from bourgeois rather than from aristocratic roots.[7] They were a Protestant, planted middle class in a country whose emergent indigenous Catholic middle class called into question their identity and even threatened their existence.

Faced with this crisis of identity, the aristocratic pretensions of the ascendancy became increasingly a defensive form of nostalgic, self-perpetuating myth-making. Yeats sought to expurgate his sense of alienation and guilt by striving to create an hierarchic, transcendent community of the aesthetic word. His god-like ambition was 'to make an entire word hitherto unknown to the language', to utter a poetic *fiat* that would break the bitter furies of historical complexity and recall to life the new-old company of the indomitable Irishry.[8] His was an heroic but doomed attempt to convert history into 'a metaphor which has a bearing that is largely aesthetic and stylistic', of which 'very simply, we are told not to take such myths *as* history; they are the myths *of* history'.[9] Although Synge's confrontation of the problematic of self and society shares some of these aesthetic aspirations, he began at an early age to move also in an antithetical direction, particularly in relation to his understanding of the relationship between language and action and between word and deed. The beginning of this awareness preceded his formal philological studies in Europe and had its origins in the remarkable impact upon his intellect and sensibility occasioned by his youthful reading of Charles Darwin's *Origin of Species*. It is to his discovery of Darwin's theory of evolution at the age of about fourteen years that Synge attributes his first experience of 'a chasm between my present and my past and between myself and my kindred and friends' (II, 11). This discovery, he maintains, led to the development of 'a scientific attitude — probably a crude one — which did not and could not interpret life and nature as I heard it interpreted from the pulpit' (II, 11).

Throughout his notebooks and diaries Synge was to return repeatedly, graphically and in words, to this experience, which is explored also in his first play, *When the Moon Has Set*. An early draft of the *Etude Morbide* is illustrated with 'Darwinian' drawings of insects, of a bird's wing compared with a human hand, of composites of a bird, a dog, and a beetle, of a half-animal, half-human Janus figure, and of an insect turning into a stringed musical instrument resembling a violin or a 'cello. In the unpublished text we find the following interesting passage which distinguishes Synge's attitude towards art and science sharply from that of Yeats:

> Blake taught that true imagination was a view of the eternal symbols of Being, but who may know in his own mind or that of others these symbols from mere hallucinations. I am driven back on science — of all names the most abused. If science is a learning of the truth, nature and imagination being a less immediate knowledge of the same, the two when perfect will coincide. The law of evolution is only truly understood by an effort of imagination and a few more such efforts and man will be as god. This then is the task of all who labour to work with transcendental imagination the data no sane instructed being may deny.[10]

Synge's adolescent verse reflects his awareness of the gap between his religious background with its predestinarian emphasis on the doctrine of a fixed and fallen human nature and salvation by faith in the word rather than by works, and his newly acquired 'scientific attitude'. Several youthful effusions allude to the lessons taught by science and history about the changing nature and needs of man. In the following characteristic extract, he is challenging *homo religiosus* in the name of *homo sapiens*:

> You know that sin can be withstood,
> And yet you will not bend your mind
> To relieve our fallen kind.
> Religion is, I fear, the cause
> You think you're right who keep her laws
> And preach an unavailing creed
> *Which history tells us fills no need.*[11]

Another early poem, entitled 'Prometheus', is a thinly disguised profession of atheism which combines a concern for 'those in pain' — identified as the politically overtaxed in one line — with a defiant declaration that man makes himself in, and is made by, history and time:

> Who has helped me 'gainst the Titans' pride?
> Who rescued from death,
> From slavery?
> Hast thou not all thyself achieved
> Thou sacred glowing heart? . . .
> Has not a powerful Time
> Made me a man,
> He and eternal Fate
> Who are my Lords and thine?[12]

The fact that his experience of reading Darwin, some thirty years after the publication of the *Origin of Species*, was so disturbing for the young Synge, and such a powerful cause of alienation from family and friends, testifies to the introverted and censoring character of Anglo-Irish evangelicalism. Yet the acceptance of what appeared to be the equally dogmatic facts of science seemed at first to the young Synge just as constricting as deterministic theology. His fear was real that the inexorable laws of evolution might prove to be a secular equivalent of predestination theology rather than an alternative to it. His allegiance to Darwin was a source of profound tension and anxiety and his ambivalent reactions to it are recorded in his autobiographical writings. From early childhood, helped by his cousin, Florence Ross, Synge had studied insects and birds and the anatomical knowledge gleaned therefrom forced him to recognise the scientific and historical validity of Darwin's exegesis of the book of life.[13] The authority of the evidence and arguments for evolution swept aside at a stroke any possibility of continuing to accept Genesis as literally true. It therefore undermined the naive historicism of Mrs Synge's interpretation of the rest of sacred scripture, bringing down the moral and ethical as well as the linguistic edifice which she had constructed on that foundation: her system stood or fell on its undeviating literalism.[14]

Synge's initial interpretation of evolution, not yet grasped by an effort of imagination, appeared to leave no room for the ethical or moral dimensions of human history. 'My studies,' he wrote, 'showed me the force of what I read, [and] the more I put it from me the more it rushed back with new instances and power . . . It seemed that I was become in a moment the playfellow of Judas. Incest and parricide were but a consequence of the idea that possessed me' (II, 10–11). Affectively at least, it would seem, Synge sensed an affinity between the scientist's imaginative analysis and synthesis of carefully observed and recorded data from the world of nature, and the creative imagination of the artist.

Before he came to appreciate the mediating role of language between the subjective and the objective, Synge turned to music as a means of escape from the theological literalism of his religious background and from the terrifying isolation of the Darwinian vision. It was *the social act of playing in an orchestra*, however, rather than composing or writing poetry, which gave him his first experience of an aesthetic release from the 'real torture in my life' (II, 12). The *Autobiography* concludes with an extended account of this experience and an assessment of its significance:

> The *collective* passion produced by a band working together *with one will and ideal* is unlike any other exaltation . . . No other emotion that I have received was quite so puissant or complete (II, 14, my italics).

6

The music, he recorded, conferred a formal beauty of expression on that 'subconscious avidity of sex [which] wreathed itself in the extraordinary beauty of the movement' (II, 14). Yet Synge's sceptical honesty compelled him to admit that for him, this musical exaltation might have been nothing more than a form of self-indulgent escape into 'the world of magical beauty I dreamed of' (II, 15). The metamorphosis from solitary, tortured composer and painfully introspective soloist into the ecstatic orchestral player has its parallel in the development of the lonely writer of the *Vita Vecchia* and the *Etude Morbide* into the director of the Abbey Theatre and author of *The Playboy of the Western World*. But the author of that play is critically ironic about, as well as appreciative of, the playing of parts. Synge realised — as *When the Moon Has Set* testifies — that a non-verbal art might all too easily become for him a 'perhaps too powerful, too nearly a physical intoxication' (II, 15). Integrity demanded that however intractable those problems might be which *seemed* to be resolved harmoniously in music, but which 'in literature' are 'horrible', he would have to confront them through the medium of words.[15]

If his reading of Darwin forced upon Synge a sudden rejection of the literal interpretation of biblical symbolism and mythology, the epistemological questioning of the status of language itself was more slowly prepared for. It was a part, also, of the changing spirit of the age. Edward Stephens traces the beginning of the linguistic challenge to Mrs Synge's 'language of dead words' to his uncle's acquaintance with Archbishop Trench's *English Past and Present*.[16] Trench's works, *English Past and Present* and *The Study of Words*, provided Synge with his first formal introduction into the world of philology and etymology, arousing his interest in the historical evolution of language. 'From it', Stephens writes, 'John learnt of the process by which languages gradually become dull and meaningless, and of how they may be revitalised'.[17] The Archbishop's etymological excursions had about them little of the systematic profundity or epistemological radicalism of continental philology and biblical criticism. Trench was, in fact, a determined opponent of Darwinism. Indeed, his motives for studying words were eminently conservative and moral and aimed partly at disproving 'the "urang-utang" theory' of evolution by proving that 'God gave man language, just as He gave him reason'.[18] Yet the good ecclesiastic's delvings into 'fossil poetry . . . fossil ethics, or fossil history'

7

were pursued with a delight in the responsiveness of language to social change which quite overrode his moral and conservative purposes.[19] Trench drew his examples of the metaphorical and symbolic behaviour of words, their necessary, but conventionally established, congruities with things, and man's creative delight in their potential for incongruities, from two sources which are of especial interest to a student of Synge's use of language — from the Bible and from the spoken language of peasant people. Stephens calls our attention to a passage from *English Past and Present* which was to throw 'a new light on the value of the curious local dialect to which he was accustomed . . . and using a syntax that was partly English and partly Gaelic in origin':[20]

> A time arrives for a language when, apart from the recoveries I have just been speaking of, its own local and provincial dialects are almost the only sources from which it can obtain acquisitions such as shall really constitute an increase in wealth.[21]

When he went up to university Synge pursued his Celtic and linguistic interests, enrolling for a course in the Irish language. The study of Irish at Trinity, however, had been orientated chiefly towards giving clerical students sufficient knowledge to enable them to carry out their proselytising mission to the natives. It was when he began to study philology at the Sorbonne that he came into direct contact with European scholars whose interests united Celtic philology with the study of Celtic history, politics and culture. Synge began to respond to the far from peripheral or provincial relationship of these to the evolution of Europe's civilisation. He was afforded a perspective, also, on Ireland's political history which was not filtered exclusively through either the Anglo-Saxon or the Nationalist traditions and which gave considerable substance to her claims to independent identity and nationhood.

By the time Synge began his studies, in 1894, the late romantic reaction to the abstract objectivism of classical philology had set in.[22] The development of the romantic trend in philology, of which Humboldt was the master and Nietzsche the apotheosis, was related to the upsurge of nationalism in Germany and of provincial nationalism in France. It had as its intellectual progenitors the philosophers Hamann and Herder. Hamann, at once disciple and reviser of Kant, had taught that we derive all that we know from experience, tradition and speech. Goethe's friend, Herder, argued that we have acquired our thoughts through tradition, speech and external influences. He emphasised the value of both originality and national characteristics in literature and art. Their nineteenth-century disciples placed the emphasis upon national languages rather than the classical study of dead languages, and upon language as the creative activity of the individual psyche. They stressed the affinity, even the identity, of this with aesthetic activity. All linguistic phenomena were individual acts of creativity, analogous to the activity of the artist working in a tradition.[23] The importance of his acquaintance with this movement for Synge can scarcely be exaggerated. Its philosophical orientation, as well as being nationalist, came to the defence of the expression of individual consciousness as the highest aim of language. It thus incorporated into its epistemology *the concept of the word as sign or symbol rather than univocally translatable token or signal* Awareness of the symbolic nature of language was part of that growing interest in the origins of the symbolical which was to lead to the work of Frazer, Freud and Jung as well as to a whole new orientation of biblical criticism. The historical school treated the Judaeo-Christian scriptures as the accumulated literature and mythology of its peoples, to be compared with other, often older, traditions, and to be judged — and exploited — on equal terms for their contemporary relevance. A related phenomenon was the upsurge of the use of ironic, often parodic, biblical allusions in literary, philosophical and polemical writings. In this context it is worth noting Synge's declaration that while 'journalism may be literary, all literature is scriptural'.[24]

The romantic school was critical of what Nietzsche described, with characteristically extreme iconoclasm, as 'a sad story, the story of philology! The disgusting erudition, the lazy, inactive passivity, the timid submission'.[25] Its adherents rejected what they regarded as the passivity of the abstract classical school, approaching language 'from within, from the viewpoint of the person speaking and expressing himself'.[26] But this very theory of self-expression became a prey to solipsistic idealism and was unable to resolve the problem of the objectivity of meaning and its relationship to reality. Founded as it was on a belief in the *a priori* nature of consciousness rather than its evolutionary development, it presupposed that the expressible 'exists first in one form and then switches to another form'.[27] The final stage in this declension of the status of language is the postulation once more of an unbridgeable gap between word and referent. It thus laid the foundations upon which was built a new privileging of the aesthetic intuition and of the *completely*, rather than relatively, autonomous and autotelic poetic word.

The attractions of individualistic subjectivism as an aesthetic and linguistic philosophy were, for Synge, inevitably strong. They find their most direct expression in the play which deals explicitly with his own family and class background — in *When the Moon Has Set*, where the influence of Nietzsche is noticeable. It is when the firmness of social orientation begins to weaken that doubts about the existence of the real world and fears of solipsistic loss of identity begin to call into question the ontological status of the subject-object relationship and with it, the ability of language to relate to reality. In *The Aran Islands* as well as throughout the plays there is evidence of this fear and these doubts. The attempt to take refuge against the sense of loss in fine language for its own sake and in an aestheticised or mythologised nature, and the preoccupation with games and role-playing as a means of both establishing and challenging identity, have also long been noted as features of Synge's drama. These themes, however, are almost always accounted for, in the critical canon, in terms of a simple romantic dichotomy between illusion and reality. Colin Innes's description of *The Playboy of the Western World* as a play which 'remains an assertion, an imposition of romance on reality, which leaves the peasantry ultimately bereft' is typical of a long tradition which sees Synge's plays as an argument that 'the transformation of the real world, the joining together of reality and joy, takes place only *within* the work of art, which by that very transformation becomes alienated from the "reality" on which it is based'.[28] Yet this level of interpretation is an inadequate measure of the complexity of Synge's exploration of the subject-object relationship. It leaves us at what is merely the point of departure, from which the plays take us on a very different journey.

Synge's interest in the evolution of language, and his related concern to understand historical processes, led him to a recognition of the objective rather than illusory nature of the symbolic as a mediating process between object and subject, and between the individual and society. Certainly, once he had visited the Aran Islands, his philological studies did not remain at the levels of either an antiquarian pursuit or an aesthetic exercise. Irish, on the islands, was both an ancient and a living language. It was also a language very obviously in a stage of transition, with increasing pressure and interference from the colonising English tongue. The modernising pressures of an encroaching capitalist economy which made English seem vital to the islanders clashed dramatically with attempts by mainland Nationalists and Gaelic Leaguers to persuade them of the value of Irish and the importance of resisting the processes of anglicisation. Synge came to appreciate, as he listened to the islanders' folk tales, that the folk tradition, like the word, was a living, changing, social activity, not a fossilised repository of a past culture isolated from the impact of the modern world. The islanders' stories and poems, like their language, undoubtedly reflected their past — but these stories and poems were undergoing a continual evolution and transformation which mediated for the people between that past and their present and future. This process of mediation, linguistic, aesthetic, religious and mythical, is explored in the plays. It underlies the references to fine talk, to stories, to games, to rites and rituals and to myth, legend and role-playing. Art becomes both a means of access to the past, and a medium for transforming that past to meet the challenge of the present and the future. That it might equally be a road to an evasion of reality and a mystification of history is never forgotten. Indeed, much of the dramatic tension arises from the conflict between these two opposed — and therefore related — movements. The conflict is at the basis of what we shall characterise as Synge's antithetical vision — an imaginative mode which is, in Kenneth Burke's words, essentially dramatistic, if by dramatism is understood a perspective on language and art which regards them 'primarily as modes of action' rather than as means of conveying information.[29]

Synge's understanding of the contemporaneity of the folk tradition and way of life of the Aran people, and of its relevance to his own historical situation, was an act of imaginative synthesis. It was by no means the result of the happy intuition of the naive romantic imagination rescued in time by Yeats from the decadent pursuit of continental culture. His ability to respond to the significance of the living struggle between Gaelic and English, and to appreciate the effects of bilingualism on the thought-processes of the people, was

11

firmly grounded in his European studies. Although he shared with the late romantics a distaste for the various forms of alienation which he experienced in his own background and observed in the changing conditions of the peasant people, and although he intensely disliked the emergence of the petty-bourgeois 'nullity of the rich', Synge did not subscribe to the atavistic belief in the possibility of returning to a postulated 'past' state of heroic/peasant innocence.[30] He was aware of how history itself becomes mythologised, and was able to acknowledge, if reluctantly at times, that the socio-economic forces which spelt the doom of ascendancy pretensions to aristocratic privilege and leadership were a necessary force for social progress. It is possible to argue that the fact that 'Synge's plays from *In the Shadow of the Glen* to the unfinished *Deirdre* conclude with images of death, of death necessitated and desired as the culmination of life' springs from his imaginative acceptance of the fact that the death of his own hybrid class was historically inevitable — a tragedy, perhaps, for that class, but a part of the larger *comédie humaine*, an entr'acte in the ongoing Rabelaisian Carnival of Life.[31]

Yeats's authoritative — and at times authoritarian — statements have helped to keep the emphasis on the 'primitive' at the expense of the 'civilised' sources of Synge's inspiration and style. In certain respects, his plays are indeed peasant plays but in the sense in which Goethe's *Faust* might be said to be a folk-drama, or the comic epics of Rabelais popular narratives. They draw strength from the historicity of the folk tradition and 'continue the mental and poetic activity of the people'.[32] But his themes also relate the spiritual awakening of the Irish literary revival back to its origins. Synge's acutely perceptive attention to the processes of origination of all ideologies in the dynamic symbolism of the word was the product of a sensibility prepared to respond to and explore the relationships and distinctions between word and deed and between history and myth. For Synge, language and art became available, after his Aran experience, as a form of mediation between the deep contradictions in society, which were the larger reflections and refractions, as well as the source, of his own personal antinomies. Art, and particularly drama, opened up the possibility of transforming these apparent antinomies from a passive condition of social decay and psychic decomposition merely to be suffered into the grounds for symbolic action which gave imaginative life to the necessary dialectic between integrity and alienation. In this context it is right to suggest that

> the settings of Synge's plays — island, dark glen, roadside and isolated pub — should be seen as surrogates for the country-house library of *When the Moon Has Set* or the walled garden of the essay 'A Landlord's Garden in County Wicklow' just as the tramps and travellers of *The Well of the Saints* and *The Playboy* possess the imaginative vision Synge attributes to the middle-class artist.[33]

The maturing of this vision may be traced in the plays. Before Synge mastered the symbolic approach to language and art, aesthetic theory makes an overt appearance in *When the Moon Has Set*. It suffers, in that play, from an undramatic tendentiousness, particularly in the explicitly philosophical passages. In the later works, however, the conflicts and contradictions are bodied forth in the fullness and complexity of dramatic action. To make explicit without destroying in the process what Synge himself called the 'young and therefore fresh and living truths, views, what you will' in his work, which 'have a certain diffidence or tenderness that makes it impossible to state them without the accompanying emotional or imaginative life in which they naturally arise' (II, 347) is a delicate task. It might well have been approached from a Freudian or Jungian perspective, through a study of certain recurring themes and images in Synge's work, or an examination of the plays to establish the treatment of archetypal patterns in plot, characterisation and imagery. Our main objective, although not unrelated, is more modest. It is to try to establish by close textual analysis the significance of language and action, and of language as action, in Synge's drama, to trace its evolution and to show how it relates to the highly self-reflective nature of his strategy and style. To do this, it has been necessary to call provisionally upon critical perspectives which allow for such an analysis but which accommodate also the necessary historical dimension.

Because of the essentially dramatic and antithetical character of Synge's poetic vision and style, and the importance of his appreciation of the evolutionary and objective historical nature of process and change, the perspectives which have proved most valuable for our purposes are those offered by Volosinov's work on the nature and

13

function of the verbal sign, and Kenneth Burke's complementary studies of language as symbolic action. Burke's and Volosinov's analyses of image and word have useful affinities with Synge's socio-genetic understanding of the relationships and interactions between art and society. These affinities are not fortuitous: they have common origins in the development of dialectical modes of thought in nineteenth-century philosphy and aesthetics. The centrality of this understanding to Synge's achievement becomes clear in the context of the relationships between his autobiographical writings, *The Aran Islands* and the themes and techniques of his drama.

Synge's vision repeatedly refuses to grant any *ultimate* privilege to the aesthetic mode, while simultaneously defending the claims of art to be part of historical reality rather than a substitute for living. The strength of Volosinov's approach, which is shared by Burke, lies in the ability 'to see "activity" (the strength of the idealist emphasis after Humboldt) as social activity and to see "system" (the strength of the new objectivist linguistics) in relation to this social activity'.[34] Both Burke and Volosinov share with Synge the conviction that 'all art is a collaboration' (IV, 53). It was this social lesson, above all, that he learnt as his prepared imagination encountered the language, stories, legends, poems and myths of the people of Aran and as he participated in, and sensed his estrangement from, their way of life. He wrote at a time and in a context which made it difficult for formal or stylistic experimentation to divorce itself from engagement with the specific social conditions which gave birth to the experiment itself. Story and play, by sharing in the history of origins, became for him modes of action which explore the relationship between text and world.

NOTES

1. Alan Price, 'A Survey of Recent Work on J.M. Synge', in S. B. Bushrui (ed.), *Sunshine and the Moon's Delight: A Centenary Tribute to J.M. Synge* (Gerrards Cross, Bucks and Beirut, Colin Smythe and the American University of Beirut, 1972), p. 294.

2. Nicholas Grene, *Synge: A Critical Study of the Plays* (London and Basingstoke, Macmillan, 1975); Declan Kiberd, *Synge and the Irish Language* (London and Basingstoke, Macmillan, 1979).

3. Katharine Worth, *The Irish Drama of Europe from Yeats to Beckett* (London, The Athlone Press, 1978), p. 1.

4. Hayden White, *Metahistory: The Historical Imagination in Nineteenth-Century Europe* (Baltimore and London, The Johns Hopkins University Press, 1973), p. 37.

5. Edward Stephens, *My Uncle John: Edward Stephens's Life of J.M. Synge*, edited by Andrew Carpenter (London, Oxford University Press, 1974), p. 28.

6. Ibid., p. 45.

7. Seamus Deane, 'The Literary Myths of the Revival: A Case for their Abandonment', in Joseph Ronsley (ed.), *Myth and Reality in Irish Literature* (Waterloo Ontario, Wilfred Laurier University Press, 1977), p. 320.

8. W.B. Yeats, 'The Autumn of the Body', in *Essays and Introductions* (London and New York, Macmillan, 1961), p. 193.

9. Deane, 'The Literary Myths of the Revival', pp. 320 and 318.

10. Trinity College, Dublin, The Synge Manuscripts (hereafter TCD MS), 4350, f.59v.

11. TCD MS 4371, ff. 31-31v.

12. TCD MS 4364, f. 223v.

13. Florence Ross, Synge's cousin, is described by Robin Skelton as 'the first girl to interest him emotionally': Robin Skelton, *The Writings of J.M. Synge* (London, Thames and Hudson, 1971), p. 9. Florence collaborated with her cousin in the compilation of a nature diary or birdwatcher's journal in November 1882. See TCD MS 4369.

14. In a letter written on March 6th 1922, Synge's brother, The Reverend Samuel Synge, dwells on the family tendency to interpret the Bible literally:

15

ALLEGHENY COLLEGE LIBRARY

> It was also about those closing years of our time at Orwell Park that your Uncle John and I used to have great discussions on theology. I was very conservative in my way of taking or explaining many of the passages, for instance, in the Old Testament. I now see that I should have been far more help to him if I had said to him to take them either way he liked, either as actual historical accounts, or else as parables, so long as he got from them the lessons they were meant to teach.

Samuel's reluctance to make this concession is, however, reflected in his comments, in the same letter, on 'the story of Jonah and the great fish': 'For people to argue, though, that a whale could not swallow a man is foolish. Some whales could not, but plenty of whales could'. Reverend Samuel Synge, *Letters to My Daughter: Being Intimate Recollections of John Millington Synge* (Dublin and Cork, the Talbot Press, 1931), p. 76.

15. TCD MS 4351, f.26.

16. Stephens, *My Uncle John*, p. 46.

17. Ibid., p. 5.

18. Richard Chevenix Trench, *On the Study of Words*, twenty-sixth edition (London, Kegan Paul, Trench, Trubner and Co., 1899), pp. 13 and 14.

19. Ibid., p. 5.

20. Stephens, *My Uncle John*, p. 46.

21. Stephens, p. 46. The quotation is from Trench's second lecture in *English Past and Present*.

22. This account of romantic philology is based upon V.N. Volosinov's analysis in *Marxism and the Philosophy of Language*, translated by Ladislav Matejka and I.R. Titunik (New York and London, Seminar Press, 1973), chapters 1, 2 and 3, pp. 45-98.

23. The influence of this philosophy on Synge is reflected in his insistence that 'all art is a collaboration' (*Collected Works*, Volume IV, p. 53).

24. TCD MS 4393, f.23.

25. Friedrich Nietzsche, *We Philologists*, translated by J.M. Kennedy (Edinburgh and London, T.N. Foulis, 1911), p. 140.

26. Volosinov, *Marxism and the Philosophy of Language*, p. 84.

27. Ibid.

28. Colin Innes, 'Naked Truth, Fine Clothes and Fine Phrases in Synge's *Playboy of the Western World*, in Ronsley (ed.), *Myth and Reality in Irish Literature*, pp. 74-5.

29. Kenneth Burke, *A Grammar of Motives* (New York, Prentice-Hall Inc., 1945), p. xxii.

30. Synge uses the phrase 'nullity of the rich' in *The Aran Islands* to describe the atmosphere which he felt in the town of Galway when he returned there after his first visit to the islands (*Collected Works*, Volume II, p. 103). Yeats took the phrase out of its context and used it in his Address to the Royal Academy of Sweden in 1924 on 'The Irish Dramatic Movement'. In this lecture he continues to propagate the myth that Synge found on the Aran Islands a happy retreat from the modern world. See W.B. Yeats, *Autobiographies* (London and Basingstoke, Macmillan, 1955), p. 568.

31. W.J. McCormack, *Sheridan Le Fanu and Victorian Ireland* (Oxford, Clarendon Press, 1980), p. 265.

32. Georg Lukacs, *Goethe and His Age* translated by Robert Anchor (London, Merlin Press, 1968), p. 160.

33. W.J. McCormack, 'Politics and Dramatic Setting: the Experience of Oscar Wilde and J.M. Synge'. Unpublished paper delivered at the Conference of the British Sociological Association, University of Sussex, Easter 1978, p. 19, Xeroxed copy.

34. Raymond Williams, *Marxism and Literature* (Oxford, Oxford University Press, 1977), p. 35.

2.

SYNGE AND *THE ARAN ISLANDS*:
A Dramatic Apprenticeship

WHILE MUCH has been written about the importance of his Aran experiences for the development of Synge's dramatic idiom, little attention has been paid to the critical interpretation of *The Aran Islands* as a literary text, or to the nature of the relationships between text and world established therein. Although it may have some journalistic characteristics — short sections were published in the *Manchester Guardian, The New Ireland Review* and *The Green Sheaf* — the work is not, as its episodic character might suggest, a loose assemblage of folk materials, descriptive and linguistic essays and personal reflections and reportage. It was conceived and executed as a carefully structured whole, with 'a general plan' (II, 48, footnote No I). Failure to appreciate it as such is partly attributable to a neglect of its genre, that of the confessional autobiography, and partly to the fact that Synge's reputation as a writer of peasant drama has delayed the assessment of its experimental character. If it is attended to as fictional autobiography, Synge's major prose work may be seen as a preparation for and key to the interpretation of his plays 'as symbolic products of the Anglo-Irish ascendancy at the crux of its historical development'.[1]

Before attempting a reading of *The Aran Islands* as a structured whole, it is useful to reconsider the aesthetic importance for Synge of his encounter with the islanders' use of language and their telling of stories and tales. In the *Anatomy of Criticism*, Northrop Frye offers an insight into how this encounter facilitated Synge's transformation into a creative artist. Writing of the value of 'linguistic conflict', Frye argues that 'when people speaking different languages come into contact, an *ideogrammatic* structure is built up out of the efforts at communication'.[2] He further points out that 'this ideogrammatic middle ground between two languages, or between two personal structures of meaning in the same language, must itself be a symbolic structure . . . It brings an *audience* into being, and reinforces the language of consciousness with that of association'[3] The living experience of the linguistic and cultural conflict which existed for the islanders between Gaelic and English, and for Synge, between the restricted English of his family and class and the people's use of words, built up for the writer, and between him and his audience, those symbolic-associative structures which enabled him to make 'the mental leap of metaphor away from the simple "this means that" sign'.[4] The experience broke the literal bond between word and referent insisted upon by his mother's attitude to language. In place of the reified and hypostasised, but absent, Word which condemned the would-be artist to sterility by forbidding recourse to the symbolic, the dynamic which informs and unifies *The Aran Islands* is precisely the creative power of symbolic association. This new-found power was to enable Synge to transform his personal experience into the more universal medium of drama. Synge came to the Aran islands with a mind formally receptive to linguistic structures and processes, and with an intellectual awareness of the symbolic nature of myth and legend, but his associative consciousness was paralysed and censored: his painfully limited ability to express and explore symbolic associations in the language and social context of his class cripples the ascendancy sequences in *When the Moon Has Set*. Through the act of writing *The Aran Islands*, in and through his fictional transformation of his Aran experiences, he establishes, acknowledges and explores the role of language as mediator between subject and object and between self and society. In this respect, *The Aran Islands* is Synge's '*Portrait of the Man as a Young Artist*' and as such, it certainly illuminates the plays.

Generically, then, it should be emphasised that *The Aran Islands* is a fictionalised confessional autobiography, with dramatic characteristics. In it, 'the genre of the written word is being assimilated to that of the spoken one', the speaking voices being those of the author-narrator in several, often antinomic, vocalisations, the island people of Aran, and the islands themselves.[5] Confessional autobiography, Frye reminds us, is a form wherein 'nearly always some theoretical and intellectual interest in religion, politics or art plays a leading role'.[6] All three interests play their part in this work, which is, therefore, in a continuum with Synge's other confessional prose, the *Autobiography*, the *Vita Vecchia* and the *Etude Morbide* or 'Imaginary Portrait', and his incomplete and unpublished novel. As well as the narrative voices of *The Aran Islands* being richer and more dramatic than those of the more explicitly ascendancy writings, the treatment of the political dimensions is more complex, subversive and sophisticated, *pace* Yeats, who, with audacious inaccuracy, described Synge as 'the only man I have ever known incapable of a political thought or of a humanitarian purpose'.[7] The religious, political and aesthetic themes in *The Aran Islands* are carefully contextualised in time and place. They are incorporated into a textual dynamic which establishes a mediated access to history and class through the transformation into art of the day-to-day lives, activities and preoccupations of a community. Confronting and confronted by a defamiliarising culture and language, the thematic ideational content is metamorphosed by and into the historical fiction. The text thus moves away from the hermetic solipsism of the *Vita Vecchia* and the *Etude Morbide* and out towards the mode of dramatic action.

When considering the neglected but important question of the structural form of *The Aran Islands*, the analogy with music is appropriate and helpful. It is appropriate because Synge, who aspired to become a musician and composer before turning to literature, thought of the relationship between art, the activity of the artist, and life itself, in musical terms, and because music, in his earlier writings, is presented as an alternative to, or substitute for, linguistic creativity.[8] The 1907 version of his *Autobiography* opens with the words which Sister Eileen reads at the outset of *When the Moon Has Set* from the writer-composer's aesthetic manuscript: 'Every life is a symphony, and the translation of this life into music, and from music back to literature or sculpture or painting, is the real effort of the artist' (II, 3). The analogy is helpful because *The Aran Islands* employs structural and thematic features which derive from music. Once these are recognised, the apparent diffuseness of the work vanishes, its discontinuities appear as functional and its modernist character, and experimental use of imagetic syntax, begin to reveal themselves. 'In arranging my chapters', Synge wrote, 'I have, of course, used a good deal of freedom, bringing kindred things together and keeping jarring things apart (II, 48, footnote No I).

As well as such features as theme and variation and *leitmotif* acting as unifying and separating devices in *The Aran Islands*, the work as a whole is constructed on symphonic principles Synge, we must remember, was familiar not only with the formal structures of musical composition but also with the musical aesthetics of the nineteenth century, including the debate between Wagner and Nietzsche about the symbolic power of music and its relationships with drama. The text is divided into four main parts, each of which corresponds fictionally to one of four visits to the islands. Each movement concentrates on one of four different but related moods. As is usual with a classical symphony, the first movement, Part I, is the longest and the most complex formally and thematically. In it most of the arguments developed through the work are enunciated and the basic motivic pattern is established which shapes the overall form. This movement also contains almost all of the folk tales, for which, perhaps, *The Aran Islands* is best known. These disappear from Parts II and III, where the text concentrates on presenting the imaginatively transformed historical situation to which the stories relate.

The dominant mood of Part I is one of pleasure at the discovery of an identity, an artistic empathy, with the islands and the island people. The narrator remarks on the people's 'vitality', their 'charm' and his own 'exquisite satisfaction' at finding himself leaving Aran Mor for what he regards as the more primitive island of Inishmaan; he notes that the island artefacts have 'something of the artistic beauty of medieval life' and 'seem to exist as a natural link between the people and the world that is about them' (II, 50-9, *passim*). Contrasting but no less powerful motifs of alienation are, however, present from the outset. The island of Aran Mor, when first seen, is 'a dreary rock', 'desolate', 'naked' and 'lonely' and even on Inishmaan, the favourite topics of the island people are the price of kelp in Connemara and the subject of war (II, 50-60, *passim*). The dialectical movement between integration and alienation is a major theme of *The Aran Islands* where it is explicitly and repeatedly linked with the situation, or plight, of the modern artist. This theme, too, is of major importance in Synge's plays.

21

The short second movement is in a predominantly sombre key, established towards the beginning by the narrator admitting that 'This year I see a darker side of life in the islands. The sun seldom shines, and day after day a cold south-western wind blows over the cliff, bringing up showers of hail and dense masses of cloud' (II, 107). In Part II the mood of alienation dominates, with references to death, emigration, vague depression, storms, graveyards, and epidemics. The movement ends with the dramatic account of the people of the west moving east for the 'celebration' of Parnell's funeral: Parnell, like Synge, was from an ascendancy background; like Christy Mahon, he was both lionised and victimised by the people, whose uncrowned king he became. The almost sinister and politically pregnant synthesis of carnival and wake in this episode acts as a bridge to the scherzo-like Part III. The celebratory character of the third movement is also uneasy and ambivalent. The ambivalence is suggested by the events which surround the narrator's return to the islands. This time he has come from Paris and is resolved to make his home in Aran and find complete identity with the people. The letter announcing his return, however, has failed to arrive. As the curaghs pulled close, his friend, Michael, 'made no sign of recognition' and the people, once they acknowledged him, again wanted to hear about war (II, 126). The very words in which the narrator expresses his initial pleasure at going back to stay with them simultaneously reveal his alienation from the islanders:

> It gave me a thrill of delight to hear their Gaelic blessing, and to see the steamer moving away, leaving me quite alone among them (II, 126).

The scherzo-like theme of celebration, and absence of alienation, is most fully expressed, in Part III, in the account of the islanders' threshing and thatching parties. The narrator writes of the activities in 'our own cottage' (II, 131) and 'our own house' (II, 132). He attributes the 'intelligence and charm' of the people to 'the absence of any division of labour, and to the correspondingly wide development of each individual, whose varied knowledge and skill necessitates a considerable activity of mind' (II, 132). 'Each man', we are told 'can speak two languages' (II, 132). His life on the sea has brought to each 'some of the emotions that are thought peculiar to men who have lived with the arts' (II, 133).[9] The episode which follows, however, reflects,

22

with characteristic paratactic irony, upon this vision, suggesting that it is not shared by, or perhaps appropriate to, the young people of the islands. The narrator, as artist-photographer, overrides the wishes of his young subject to be portrayed in mainland clothes, insisting instead on constructing a 'native homespun' portrait of the youth and thus indulging, perhaps, his own primitivising aesthetic:

> We nearly quarrelled because he wanted me to take his photograph in his Sunday clothes from Galway, instead of his native homespuns that become him far better, though he does not like them as they seem to connect him with the primitive life of the island. With his keen temperament, he may go far if he can ever step out into the world.
> He is constantly thinking (II, 134).

The young boy who tries to resist this deliberate attempt to connect him with 'the primitive life of the island' is the very youth who spends his time reading Gaelic poems and stories to the narrator. This movement, which began with a strong desire to identify with the island life and people, modulates into an elegiac nocturne which contrasts dramatically with the initial 'feeling of festivity that this return procured me' (II, 127). The narrator finds no home in the islands. He becomes, rather, a stranger and Part III concludes with the scripturally ominous words: 'It was getting late, and the rain had lessened for a moment, so I groped my way back to the inn through the intense darkness of a late autumn night' (II, 150).

Continuing the symphonic analogy, Part IV of *The Aran Islands* is of greater length, and also more discursive, than the middle movements. It establishes towards the beginning something of a light, recreative atmosphere, although once more a disturbing and disturbed undertone of conflict is suggested by the opening reference to the nocturnal setting of the narrator's return journey and by the account of the encounter between the steamer and its captain and the passionately angry Claddagh fishermen in their boat. This encounter between industrial might and peasant protest symbolically contextualises the allegorical poems about Ireland's struggle for freedom which appear later in the text. The narrator is invited in the evening to play the fiddle that the islanders may dance, thus becoming once more their playboy artist:

23

Then I struck up the 'Black Rogue' and in a moment a tall man bounded out from his stool under the chimney and began flying round the kitchen with peculiarly sure and graceful bravado.

The lightness of the pampooties seems to make the dancing on this island lighter and swifter than anything I have seen on the mainland (II, 153).

His success as an artist does not last for long: an old man, 'once the best dancer on the island' arrives, but, we are told, 'he did not know the dances in my book, he said, and did not care to dance to music he was not familiar with' (II, 153). In this movement there is a brief return of the folk tale element, with much discussion of the fairies and their activities. Part IV is also permeated by themes and motifs which recur in Synge's plays: we are told of the souls of the dead riding on horses, of the great equestrian feats of Charley Lambert, to be emulated by Christy Mahon in *The Playboy of the Western World*, of island fights over fine words which lead to the dirty deed of the slaying of fathers. As the movement develops, references to dying and to death once more accumulate until mortality itself becomes the dominant theme. The three long poems, political allegories about Ireland's struggle for freedom, act as a counterpoint to the funereal *cantus firmus* of the prose, incorporating and transforming into victory songs the themes of conflict, loss and death. With an abortive reference to a poem entitled 'The Big Wedding', which he declines to retell, a recapitulatory burst of festive music on his fiddle and a valedictory, even dismissive, glance at 'my old men' (II, 184) and their fairy fears, the narrator's departure from the islands brings the work to an abrupt end.

The folk tales which make their appearance in *The Aran Islands* have attracted critical attention chiefly as examples of the materials and language from which Synge developed his 'peasant' plays and dialect. If we accept, however, that we are dealing with a carefully constructed fictional work, it would seem proper to attempt a reading of these tales which reinstates and evaluates them in their textual environment. In order to do this, we need to attend to the effect which the direct, living experience of the folk traditions of the islands had upon Synge's understanding of the nature of art. Prepared as he was by his formal studies, his Aran experience offered him a uniquely favourable opportunity to develop a new insight into the relationships between language, culture and daily life, in a rapidly changing social and

economic context. He discovered on the islands, and particularly in
the islanders' stories, the still-living *transformations* of elements or
traditions of an ancient aristocratic culture which had had to
accommodate to a primitive peasant way of life. This way of life, in
turn, was under threat from a 'mainland' economy, represented for
the island people by England, the United States and the urbanised
areas of the Irish mainland. These historical forces were reflected in
the islanders' accommodation of story and myth to their changing way
of life. Story and myth mediated between the people, their past, their
present activities and their future aspirations, transforming that past
symbolically and releasing them from fatalistic bondage to it. In *The
Aran Islands* the stories and poems of the people are perceived and
presented as part of an active and continuing social process. Theme
and technique are united in ways which invite us to 'attend positively
to the concrete social realities both of the text's historical context and
of our own historical condition as readers'.[10]

When he arrives in Aran, Synge-as-narrator appears at first to
assume the role in which he was cast, retrospectively, by Yeats: that of
a collector of stories and expresser of a life that had never found
expression. Diligently he makes contact with a teacher and story-teller,
an 'old dark man' (11, 50). His half-blind informant is possessed of
impeccable antiquarian credentials: 'He told me that he had known
Petrie and Sir William Wilde, and many living antiquarians, and had
taught Irish to Dr Finck, and Dr Pedersen, and given stories to Mr
Curtin of America' (II, 50). It quickly becomes clear, however, that the
old man's interest in stories — and Synge's interest in the old man — go
beyond the purely antiquarian, dead or alive. It is his informant's
proud boast that

> this gentleman had brought out a volume of his Aran stories in America,
> and made five hundred pounds by the sale of them. 'And what do you think
> he did then?' he continued; 'he wrote a book of his own stories after making
> that lot of money with mine' (II, 50).

The old man's monetary evaluation of his stories is no mere personal or
idiosyncratic expression of pride. It is, rather, symptomatic of an
endemic, even obsessive, preoccupation of the islanders with *price*. On
his first outing on Aran Mor, the narrator was pursued by two boys:

> They spoke at first of their poverty, and then one of them said —
> 'I dare say you do have to pay ten shillings a week in the hotel?'
> 'More,' I answered.
> 'Twelve?'
> 'More.'
> 'Fifteen?'
> 'More still.' (II, 52)

This episode is followed by an account of two further encounters
— with a returned emigrant who 'stopped and asked for coppers' (II,
52) and with 'two little girls' (II, 52) for whom the very island, its flora
and its products have become translated into commodities. They told
the narrator

> how they guide 'ladies and gintlemins' in the summer to all that is worth
> seeing in their neighbourhood, and sell them pampooties and maidenhair
> ferns, which are common among the rocks (II, 52).

References to price recur throughout *The Aran Islands*. For the
inhabitants there is scarcely an object which is not translated into the
terminology of its market value or its equivalent in gold, from the
study of Gaelic to the loss of a father. In Part I alone we are told that
the attraction of Dublin for Pat Dirane was 'all the rich people he was
going to see in the finest streets of the city' (II, 72); that 'in general the
men sit together and talk with endless iteration of the tides and fish,
and of the price of kelp in Connemara' (II, 74); and they 'do not care to
undertake the task of manufacture without a certainty of profit' (II,
77). In the account of the eviction scene, we learn that 'a man of the
name of Patrick has sold his honour' (II, 88). As his pupil prepares to
leave the islands after his first visit, old Pat Dirane can afford no
parting present. He offers his friend the only gift remaining to him
— the opportunity to put a price on his death:

> 'I'll not see you again,' he said, with tears trickling on his face, 'and you're a
> kindly man. When you come back next year I won't be in it. I won't live
> beyond the winter. But listen now to what I'm telling you; let you put
> insurance on me in the city of Dublin, and it's five hundred pounds you'll
> get on my burial.' (II, 102)

Why, we may ask, this emphasis on the islanders' preoccupation with money? The answer is implied in the account of the narrator's return to Galway. As he comes 'out of an hotel full of tourists and commercial travellers', the town, he tells us, 'seems in my present mood a tawdry medley of all that is crudest in modern life. The nullity of the rich and the squalor of the poor give me the same pang of wondering disgust; yet the islands are fading already' (II, 102-3). The islands are not just fading into the geographical distance, or into the distance of memory. They are accommodating to the exigencies of a new economic imperative, dominated by the cash nexus. The way of life to which the narrator-artist has been so powerfully attracted is changing; indeed, the implication is strong that in some of the forms in which it most powerfully attracts him *it may never have existed historically at all.* We should not fail to note, however, that in bowing to the tyranny of money-determined relationships, the poverty-stricken old story-teller, Pat Dirane, has succeeded in transforming that tyranny into a moving expression of kindly human affection, and of concern for his friend's future. Two letters written to the narrator by younger island friends serve as a coda to the theme that the old island life is doomed to pass away. These letters bring into conjunction natural and economic mortality, starkly underscoring the theme of the mortal sickness afflicting the community. The first contains a brief report of the death of an islander:

> Mr. —— died a long time ago on the big island and his boat was on anchor in the harbour and the wind blew her to Black Head and broke her up after his death (II, 103).

The second comes from a boy whose sister 'has come back from America, but I'm thinking it won't be long till she goes away again, for it's lonesome and poor she finds the island now' (II, 104). Since these letters incorporate into the fictional text letters written to Synge by Aran islanders, they insist on the relationship of the text to history and to life.

The stress placed in *The Aran Islands* on the impact of a new economic order on the lives and preoccupations of the people is far removed from the interest of the antiquarian recording a primitive way of life or the romantic in search of an eternal, unchanging rapport with nature. Nor does the emphasis on alienation accord very closely with Yeats's account of Synge as a dilettante writer from 'a very old Irish family' who 'when he found that wild island . . . became happy for the first time'.[11] Once we begin to attend carefully to their contextualisation, it becomes obvious that the folk elements in the text are neither simply a record of the memories of an ancient culture nor a collection of raw materials for future use in the plays. Rather, the stories, poems and anecdotes are presented in such a way that they engage the reader in a fictionalising activity which establishes their symbolic role. If we return to Old Mourteen's boast about the financial success of his stories in America, we discover that this episode is followed at once by the first of many stories about the fairies taking people away, giving them money or goods, or depriving them of these. After several ominous happenings in Old Mourteen's household, including the appearance of a 'dummy' who 'made signs of hammering nails in a coffin', it was discovered that 'the *seed* potatoes were full of blood' (II, 51, my italics). One of his children then

> told his mother that he was going to America.
> That night it died (II, 51).

Shortly after this, we come to the account of the meeting between the narrator and the asthmatic, hopeless man who 'had spent twenty years in America, where he had lost his health and then returned' (II, 52).

This tight but non-linear structuring of the thematic pattern suggests that Synge was very well aware of the symbolic interactions between the tales the people told, the ways they told them, and the social and historical forces at work on their daily lives. However venerable the tales, they were also of functional and urgently contemporary import. America, to the Aran communities, was, by the late nineteenth century, an economic power upon which the survival of their own seemingly pre-capitalist economy had come to depend:

> All eat the flour and bacon that is brought from the United States, so they have a vague fear that 'if anything happened to America,' their own island would cease to be habitable (II, 60).

It was also a place which, through the massive emigration following the potato famines, devoured their seed:

All the evening afterwards the old woman sat on her stool at the corner of the fire with her shawl over her head, keening piteously to herself. America appeared far away, yet she seems to have felt that, after all, it was only the other edge of the Atlantic, and now when she hears them talking of railroads and inland cities where there is no sea, things she cannot understand, it comes home to her that her son is gone for ever (II, 108).

The anecdotes which the people tell about their own dreams and visions, their encounters with fairies and witches and giants, are in a continuum with the more extended tales and ballads. The conversation between the Captain and the hag, in the first story told by Pat Dirane, takes us back to the boys' enquiries on Aran Mor about the price of the hotel:

'For how much will you let me sleep one night in your box?' said the Captain.
'For no money at all would I do such a thing,' said the hag.
'For ten guineas?' said the Captain.
'Not for ten guineas,' said the hag.
'For twelve guineas?' said the Captain.
'Not for twelve guineas,' said the hag (II, 62).

This story — Synge later attempted to dramatise it — tells how 'a little man' gives gold to a farmer's son to enable him to win the daughter of 'a fine rich man' (II, 61). The fairy bond is guaranteed by the traditional pound of flesh. After a deal of trickery by the Captain, who bribes the old hag and steals the wife's rings, the farmer's son is persuaded of his lady wife's infidelity. Pushing her into the sea, he goes away to work as a farm labourer. His wife, however, is rescued by an old peasant woman. Seeking out her husband, she saves him from paying his pound of flesh debt and forces the Captain, at pistol-point, to confess his trickery, whereupon 'the lady O'Conor took the pistol and shot the hag through the body, and they threw her over the cliff into the sea' (II, 64). If we relocate this tale in history, as its contextualisation encourages us to do, it reflects the struggle of the dispossessed to enter into their own. Pat's story is about the historical fate and struggle of Ireland as a nation: it is part of an ongoing, changing, story-telling *activity*, constantly updated by teller-and-audience interaction.[12]

The social criticism in *The Aran Islands'* stories is often expressed within a frame of reference which is superficially, or anachronistically, feudal, but both text and context suggest that a process of euhemerisation is at work, in which the story-tellers are actively translating the mythology of the past into a form of transfigured realism. What we encounter is a constant process of translation of life into art and art into life, which insists on the continuity and the distinctions between these two spheres of human action. The technique of montage which Synge develops in this work has about it a metonymic quality which we shall discover again in the plays. It *enacts* the meaning symbolically, through a process of image-creating contiguity, rather than by making statements or asserting metaphoric identity. This technique is employed with great effectiveness in the eviction scene in Part 1, which is one of the most dramatic, as well as politically most explicit, set pieces in the text. The eviction episode is carefully framed by two stories. The first is a version of 'Jack the Giant Killer'. It tells how the son of a poor widow defeats the giant — and his brother — assumes his armour, and rescues a young princess three times from a sea monster. We should bear in mind that in the eviction scene, the son of the poor widow, Patrick, has been bought over by the state: he is the Patrick who 'sold his honour' (II, 88). In the story, by contrast, the son returned dutifully, in between his adventures, to the labour of looking after the cows. So well did he care for them that 'they found a power of milk in them' (II, 85). In the end of all, we are told, this poor young man won the princess and 'was given all the estate' (II, 87). The tale, therefore, imaginatively reverses what the islanders know is going to happen when the eviction party arrives, rounds up their poor stock of cattle and pigs, and turns indebted families out of their hovels. It offers an alternative happy ending to their sad tale of sorrow, holding out the possibility of freedom and victory. During the eviction, despite their present powerlessness the people score a minor victory over the clumsy police, when two pigs leave 'three policemen lying in the dust' (II, 91). Of such stuff, the text implies, are the dreams and stories of the real magic of the people made: 'It is likely', we are told, 'that they will hand down these animals for generations in the tradition of the island' (II, 91). The story which follows the eviction is a version of the tale of the goose which laid the golden egg. In Pat Dirane's account, peasant and gentleman combine to outwit 'the shopman and his wife' (II, 93). But it is the peasant who takes the prize in the end — by eating the vomit of the shopkeepers who have swallowed the heart and liver of the goose. There could scarcely be a more vivid image of economic reversal of fortune for a people living on the leavings of what middlemen devour.

The set pieces of folk literature virtually disappeared from Parts II and III, to re-emerge with very strong political, even nationalistic, overtones in Part IV, where story yields pride of place to ballads. Two stories appear before this yielding to verse, both of which have fairly obvious links with Synge's plays — one with *Riders to the Sea*, the other with *The Playboy of the Western World*. A young woman is dying on Inishmaan during a typhus outbreak. An old man tells the story of a dead young mother who returned to feed her child and eat potatoes and milk. She tells her people that she has been taken by the fairies, but that they can free her from death. On the night of Oidche Shamhna 'there would be four or five hundred of them riding on horses, and herself would be on a grey horse, riding behind a young man' (II, 159). In *Riders to the Sea* this story is turned on its head. Its plot is reversed when Maurya goes to the crossing to give her son bread, but is unable to do so because of the speed of the riders relentlessly riding away from her forever. The second tale, of Charley Lambert, anticipates Christy Mahon's feats in *The Playboy of the Western World*. A notorious winner of horse-races, Charley is banned from any further competition by an envious community. He risks his life by riding to win a fortune for a 'gentleman' who wants to prove against the English that 'the horses of Ireland were the best horses' (II, 166). This tale is followed by the 'extraordinary English doggerel rhyme' (II, 167) called 'The White Horse' in which a mythical or symbolic horse bears his rider to victory from the day that Adam fell, through a whole series of heroic adventures spanning world history, from Israel, Egypt, Babylon, Troy, Spain and Rome, until they arrive at Ireland, and Brian Boru's victory over the Danes. The Irish adventure continues with Sarsfield and King James. The horse is then ridden 'by the greatest of men/At famed Waterloo' (II, 170) — not, we suggest, the Iron Duke — and then returns to Ireland to bear Daniel O'Connell on his back. Now,

> He's ready once more for the field
> He never will stop till the Tories
> He'll make them to yield (II, 171).

Thus, in a popular ballad, is scripture given symbolic national and historical connotations which would have startled, not to say shocked, Mrs Synge, and which run completely counter to her own method of literal 'historical' exegesis.

'Rucard Mor' and 'Phelim and the Eagle' follow rapidly. Both poems clearly declare their nationalist partisanship and their contemporary symbolic significance. In 'Rucard Mor' the speaker's little horse is stolen from him, leaving 'the old minister in its place' (II, 172). He eventually discovers that it has been slain by an English-speaking hag who is roundly told to

> Keep away from me with your English
> But speak to me in the tongue
> I hear from every person (II, 172).

The poem ends with a lament of a defeated and destitute man, but the English defeat of 'Rucard Mor' is transformed into victory in 'Phelim and the Eagle'. This is the most aggressively political piece of folk literature in the text. The speaker challenges the Eagle, who has stolen his cock, to do battle:

> The Eagle dressed his bravery
> With his share of arms and his clothes . . .
> I and my scythe with me,
> And nothing on but my shirt (II, 177).

Phelim stuns, but does not kill, the Eagle, who tells him that he has 'saved the fame of Eire for yourself till the Day of the Judgment' (II, 177).

We can fairly claim, then, that Synge's presentation of the folk material of the Aran people neither relegates it to the past nor sees in it preserved relics of an ancient culture. In Parts II and III the disappearance of the set pieces and the deliberate concentration on the objective ontological situation from which the folk tales spring break with the magic aura which can lead one 'to obliterate their real historical and social basis and to abandon oneself to a wondrous realm where class conflict does not exist and where harmony reigns supreme'.[13] These central movements are Synge's antidote to, and also his exploration of, the process of fabulation. The structuring of Parts II and III of the text, the techniques of super- and juxta-positioning, the use of montage, and the dislocation and spatialisation of time, anticipate many of the features of modernism, while demonstrating also the availability of such techniques to the historical imagination.

Part II is the shortest and stylistically the most innovative of the four movements. Its two related themes are the threat of emigration to the islands' survival and the pervasive presence and threat of death. The movement opens with a record of Synge's meeting with Michael 'who had left the islands to earn his living on the mainland' (II, 105). 'Michael' is the name of the drowned elder son in *Riders to the Sea* and of the 'kind of farmer has come up from the sea' (III, 41) in *In the Shadow of the Glen*. This Michael is dressed differently for his new role as wage-earner: he wears 'the brown flannels of the Connaught labourer' (II, 105). The two men are joined by 'another Irish-speaking labourer' (II, 105). When the narrator reaches the island he hears that 'Old Pat Dirane is dead, and several of my friends have gone to America; that is all the news they have to give me' (II, 106). The youngest son, Columb — the name reappears as that of the hero in *When the Moon Has Set* — boasts proudly of how he now measures time mechanically, by 'the alarm clock I sent them last year when I went away' (II, 106). The narrator entertains the people, 'who are wearied of the sea', with photographs from the eastern world, 'taken in County Wicklow' (II, 107). The sons of the house 'earn little', and 'two sons . . . have gone away' (II, 107). The letter which arrives from Michael tells of 'his work, and the wages he is getting' (II, 107); the one from his brother in America sends the mother into a trauma of grief at his absence.

The island is storm-lashed and the narrator, who in this section seems to be courting death, wanders in the gale 'till my hair is stiff with salt' (II, 108). He meditates on his own death: 'I might die here and be nailed in my box, and shoved down into a wet crevice in the graveyard before any one could know it on the mainland' (II, 110). Later, fearing imminent death, the people fetch 'the Priest and the Doctor' (II, 111) for a woman in childbirth. The rare recourse to capitalisation here suggests that Synge is thinking of these two as typological representations rather than individual functionaries. Generations, in this sequence, are disrupted and realigned. The baby in the house has been adopted by the old woman 'to console herself for the loss of her own sons' (II, 111); Michael writes from the mainland saying that he is 'getting a forgetfulness on all my friends and kindred' (II, 112). Into the midst of this disjunction and morbidity is introduced a young man who reads — or chants — aloud some of the age-old poems from Douglas Hyde's *Love Songs of Connaught*, but even the poems are absorbed into the past of the island when the old woman takes up the chant. The narrator records his feeling of alienation from the island people: he shares their emotions; they cannot always feel with him. He contains, in part, their history, but he also belongs to a different phase of history as well as a different class. And so, like the village people with Christy Mahon, 'they like me sometimes, and laugh at me sometimes, yet never know what I am doing' (II, 113).

Returning to the north island, he finds there 'the anxiety of men who are eager for gain . . . Even the children here seem to have an indefinable modern quality' (II, 116). He now assumes something, too, of the ascendancy superiority, speaking of 'my crew' (II, 117). His trip in the curagh is violent and dangerous and the lives of all are at risk 'as the life of the rider or the swimmer is often in his own hands' (II, 120). Only in this battle with death does he record any feeling of comradeship, excitement and joy. Abruptly, however, he tells us 'I have left Aran' (II, 121). Landing on the shore at Galway he encounters a drunk who takes him into a dying city, 'in the middle of a waste of broken buildings and skeletons of ships' (II, 121). The drunk throws the writer's bag of books — his collection of words and stories — on the ground and gives vent in broken English to his disappointment that they aren't gold which would enable them to have a 'thundering spree . . . this night in Galway' (II, 122). Briefly he encounters Michael, but the wage-labouring emigrant follows him now like a ghost 'in the shadow' (II, 122), and we learn that 'the work he has here does not agree with him, and he is not contented' (II, 122). This apparently casual reference to Michael's unhappiness is a tentative sounding of the note which is to develop into the elaborate, extraordinary, scherzo-like finale of Part II. This scene of discontent and disorder borders on the riotous. It is both structurally and thematically related to 'Phelim and the Eagle', the last set piece of Part IV. The occasion is 'the eve of the Parnell celebration in Dublin' (II, 122). The *celebration* is, in fact, a *memorial* ceremony to commemorate Parnell's death.

On the surface, Part II of *The Aran Islands* seems to be the most realistic of the four movements, just as *Riders to the Sea* is often described as the most realistic of the plays. But the reality of art is complex and by no means to be identified with a univocal naturalism. Part III of the work opens with two antithetical letters. These express at once the theme and counter-theme of the movement's dialectic. Both are from Michael. The first gives voice, in English, to the disillusion and pain of an exiled labourer. It is the letter which he addressed to the exiled narrator in Paris:

> I am getting good wages from the first of this year, and I am afraid I won't be able to stand with it, although it is not hard, I am working in a saw-mills and getting the money for the wood and keeping an account of it . . .
> I think I soon try America but not until next year if I am alive (II, 125).

The second letter speaks of 'a great Feis' (II, 126) — a festival of music, song, dance and story-telling. It expresses Michael's pleasure at his return to Aran and tells of the destruction of his place of exiled employment:

> I am at home now for about two months, for the mill was burnt where I was at work (II, 126).

In a mood reflecting Michael's elation, and bordering on euphoria, the narrator likewise attempts a return to his adopted home. The mood contrasts completely with the sombre morbidity of Part II — but we are soon to find that the euphoria and the morbidity are related. As he landed on the island he experienced 'a thrill of delight' (II, 126); 'a light haze' gave him 'the *illusion* that it was still summer' (II, 127, my italics). When he returned to the cottage, he claimed it as his own:

> As I sat down on my stool and lit my pipe with the corner of a sod, I could have cried out with the feeling of festivity that this return procured me (II, 127).

His first excursion is by moonlight. The change of tense to the present creates an impression of immediacy, of identification with his surroundings. The description is exotic, rhetorically picturesque: 'the shadows of the clouds throw strange patterns of gold and black'; there

35

is 'a tumult of revelry' and 'the young boys and girls . . . have sport' (II, 127). Under the romanticising moonshine the poor dwelling places have become 'groups of scattered cottages' which remind him 'of places I have sometimes passed when travelling at night in France or Bavaria, places that seemed so enshrined in the blue silence of night one could not believe they would reawaken' (II, 127). But a controlling linguistic irony — which is a characteristic feature of Synge's dramatic writing — is operating here. The picturesque, Loti-like style is deliberately self-referential, unmasking the unreal nature of this 'vision' of the moonlit island. The writer is watching himself gratifying his inclination towards mystification and verbal self-indulgence. 'Though Michael', he tells us laconically, 'is sensible of the beauty of the nature round him, he never speaks of it directly' (II, 128).

The self-directed irony continues in the episodes which follow. It is a Sunday and the narrator entertains the people ceremoniously with 'simple gymnastic feats and conjurer's tricks' (II, 128) — middle class miracles or 'wonders' which some of them immediately associate with witchcraft:

> The older people, who have watched the rye turning to oats, seemed to accept the magic frankly, and did not show any surprise that 'a duine uasal' (a noble person) should be able to do like the witches (II, 128).

Why do the older people proffer and accept the mystifying explanation? The reason we are given is thoroughly scientific and historical: 'miracles must abound wherever the new conception of law is not understood' (II, 128). The conjurer conceals cause from effect in his tricks; as the people cannot make the material connection, the one which they do make is mythical. Yet the tables are turned, shortly, on this scientific self-assurance. When the moon has set and the night is 'quite dark' (II, 129), the narrator begins to imagine that he sees the island through the eyes of its working men. He, however, is *not* an island man. Just as Columb in *When the Moon Has Set* loses the way to his own house and has to be guided by an old peasant, and the Saint in *The Well of the Saints* is fearful of losing his footing on the 'steep, slippy-feeling rocks' (III, 83) so, he tells us,

> When I tried to come home I lost myself among the sandhills, and the night

seemed to grow unutterably cold and dejected, as I groped among slimy masses of seaweed and wet crumbling walls.

After a while I heard a movement in the sand, and two grey shadows appeared beside me. They were two men who were going home from fishing. I spoke to them and knew their voices, and we went home together (II, 130).

This lonely experience of isolation, his inability to come home, is followed at once by the detailed account of the island people engaged in the collective task of gathering, winding and weaving rye-straw for thatching a neighbour's cottage. The ropes of straw twisting and turning from dwelling to dwelling weave a social bond between the people. The work becomes 'a sort of festival'; the cottager 'is a host instead of an employer' and the men 'work with him' (II, 132).

The second set description, in Part III, of the islanders at work is a complete contrast with the thatching party episode. In place of the emphasis on sociability, the theme, once more, is that of alienation and estrangement, followed by a precarious, mediated reconciliation between narrator and people. On this occasion the islanders are selling their stock to a middle-man. 'To-day', the narrator tells us, 'when I went down to the slip I found a pig-jobber from Kilronan with about twenty pigs that were to be shipped for the English market' (II, 137). By contrast with the festive thatching, the shipping of the pigs is a form of labour engaged in by the islanders in response to the demands of the money-based English economy. The scene offers one of the text's most remarkable passages — a key passage in determining Synge's method of representing dramatically and antithetically the ambivalent relationship between the narrator and the island people, who have so recently been described as if they were his own kin. The complexity and tensions of this relationship, and its socio-historical dimensions, are symbolically enacted rather than stated or abstractly analysed. The nature of the symbolism is such that it becomes, like the tales and poems of the people, a powerful form of transfigured realism, exploring and representing, with concrete, sensuous directness, the objective historical and economic roots of the bonds which both unite and divide the people and the writer. In the notebook in which he drafted this sketch, Synge wrote the following inscription: 'To the little Irish pigs that have eaten filth all their lives to enable me to wander in

Paris these leaves are dedicated with respect and sympathy' (II, 138, footnote). Almost the identical words turn up again in *When the Moon Has Set*. In the letter to Columb from his friend and *alter ego*, the 'cellist, O'Neill, they become 'My compliments to the little Irish pigs that eat filth all their lives that you may prosper'.[14] These pigs, we would argue, are not 'just pigs'. In *The Aran Islands* the animals are *quite systematically humanised*. They 'shrieked with almost human intonations' (II, 137); the slip 'was covered with a mass of sobbing animals, with here and there a terrified woman crouching among the bodies, and patting some special favourite' (II, 137-8). The whole scene invites comparison, for its evocation of noisy yet purposeful frenzy, with the description of the crowds moving east to the Parnellite celebration. It is the antithetical expression of Synge's imaginative awareness of the ascendancy dependence upon and exploitation of the Irish peasant. As the pigs are shipped out in the curaghs, all the emotion and power of the remarkable scene are concentrated suddenly not on the animals, but on the narrator as exploiter, in words which suggest a perverse, even evil, communion feast:

> They seemed to know where they were going, and looked up at me over the gunnel with an ignoble desperation that made me shudder to think that I had eaten of this whimpering flesh (II, 138).

As they are carried off by the English ship, the Irish pigs' gaze becomes a mirror which reflects in the artist scion of landlords the centuries of guilt he feels for the cannibalistic exploitation of Ireland by his class.[15] In the sentence which follows, the desolation of an emasculated nation bled of its manhood for the benefit of England is encapsulated:

> when the last curagh went out I was left on the slip with a band of women and children, and one old boar who sat looking out over the sea (II, 138).

Lest we should doubt for one moment with whom the one old boar is symbolically identified, we are told immediately that 'the women were over-excited, and when I tried to talk to them they crowded round me and began jeering and shrieking at me *because I am not married* ' (II, 138, my italics). The narrator has ceased, in this context, to be the person the islanders knew and accepted as their friend; he has become for them the archetypal enemy, the object of their national and class contempt because of his refusal or inability to become consubstantially one with them. *When the Moon Has Set* is preoccupied precisely with this problem of the generational relationship — with all its burden of social, political and religious guilt and fears of illegitimacy — between ascendancy and native people. The narrator finds himself at one and at the same time the target of the people's fury and the butt of their laughter:

> A dozen screamed at a time, and so rapidly that I could not understand all they were saying, yet I was able to make out that they were taking advantage of the absence of their husbands to give me the full volume of their contempt. Some little boys who were listening threw themselves down, writhing with laughter among the seaweed, and the young girls grew red with embarrassment and stared down into the surf (II, 138).

The only way in which he can break from this nightmare of mockery and accusation, equalled in its surrealistic horror by the psychic dream in Part I, is by becoming once again to the islanders a playboy entertainer and maker of images:

> For a moment I was in confusion. I tried to speak to them, but I could not make myself heard, so I sat down on the slip and drew out my wallet of photographs. In an instant I had the whole band clambering round me, in their ordinary mood (II, 138).

Although it may offer a shadowy image of a possible future freed from alienation, the island vision of a labour full of sociability is shown, then, to belong historically to the past. Commitment to this past as a substitute for the present or the future, Synge realised, was a commitment to an unreal and unrealisable utopianism. It was, nevertheless, a myth which had its attractions for ascendancy scion and nationalist patriot alike — because in sentimentalising history, it appeared to resolve its conflicts. The 'psychic dream' episode in Part I, like the episode of the pigs, is a powerful vision of the nightmare into which such a dream can turn. In it the dreamer is made to play a playboy part in the bitter furies of an endless dance.[16] In *When the Moon Has Set* O'Neill, who sends the compliments to 'the little Irish pigs', is described as a 'cellist who cultivates death as a form of art:

> He lives in a low room draped in black from the floor to the ceiling. He has a black quilt on his bed and two skulls on his chimney-piece with girls' hats on them. His matches are in a coffin, and his clock is a gallows.[17]

In the dream sequence from Part I of *The Aran Islands* this pictorial cultivation of death is translated into musical terms. The dreamer finds himself 'among buildings with strangely intense light on them' (II, 99). He then hears 'a faint rhythm of music beginning far away on some stringed instrument' (II, 99). The music is attracting him into a transformed — or mythical — past. As it comes near, it becomes internalised: it 'began to move in my nerves and blood, and to urge me to dance with them' (II, 99). He fights desperately against the temptation to yield to this destructively solipsistic enchantment:

> I knew that if I yielded I would be carried away to some moment of terrible agony, so I struggled to remain quiet, holding my knees together with my hands (II, 99).

As he resists the urge to join in the totally alienated, utterly personal, dance of death, the music increases, 'sounding like the strings of harps, tuned to a forgotten scale' (II, 99). The harp is the national instrument of Ireland; it is also a nationalist symbol. In *When the Moon Has Set*, Sister Eileen plays the harp to Columb, in turn an *alter ego* of O'Neill. The sound like the strings of the harps in the psychic dream is described as 'having a resonance as searching as the strings of the 'cello' (II, 99). Through its association with O'Neill, we may say that the music of the 'cello has morbid connotations for Synge. When the narrator heard it in the dream, the attraction towards it 'became more powerful than my will and my limbs moved in spite of me' (II, 100). At first this seemed 'an ecstasy where all existence was lost in a vortex of movement. I could not think there had ever been a life beyond the whirling of the dance' (II, 100). The ecstasy, however, turns to 'an agony and rage' (II, 100) as the dreamer struggles to free himself from the *Gotterdammerung* celebration. The effort to break free seems only to involve him deeper and deeper in the nightmare of solipsism: 'When I shrieked I could only echo the notes of the rhythm' (II, 100). This rhythm, we remember, is that of his own nerves and blood. In *When the Moon Has Set*, Columb forces a way — apparently — out of a similar nightmare of morbidity, but into a musical requiem, by marrying Sister Eileen. In *The Aran Islands* the dreaming dancer tells us that 'at last with a moment of uncontrollable frenzy I broke back to consciousness and awoke' (II, 100). He dragged himself 'trembling to the window of the cottage and looked out' (II, 100). Back in reality, 'the moon was glittering across the bay, and there was no sound anywhere on the island' (II, 100). The image which the narrator resists in the dream, through an agony of struggle, is founded on images from, or myths of, history, but it is history translated into a potentially *destructive* myth, into moonlit buildings which become the prison-house of a frenzied dance of undying death. The only way out of the nightmare is through facing the present, however unamenable it may be to the desires of the artist at a given moment in, or out of, time.

Immediately after the episode of the pigs in *The Aran Islands* we find the narrator on his way to the most modern and least attractive of the three islands, the south island. As he lands, he notices a few 'hideous' houses 'lately built' (II, 139). He goes to a 'hotel', sees a 'cess collector' at work and finds 'men and boys waiting about, who stared at us while we stood at the door and talked to the proprietor' (II, 139). It is here that he notes for the first time an explicit division of the population along newly-emerging class lines:

> The people of this island are more advanced than their neighbours, and the families here are gradually forming into different ranks, made up of the well-to-do, the struggling, and the quite poor and thriftless (II, 140).

Here, too, we meet the Saxon caricature of the 'stage Irishman', the Irishman who becomes the part the English expect him to act:

> I noticed in the crowd several men of the ragged, humorous type that was once thought to represent the real peasant of Ireland . . . As we looked out through the fog there was something nearly appalling in the shrieks of laughter kept up by one of these individuals, a man of extraordinary ugliness and wit (II, 140).

The ballad-reciter whom he 'fell in with' (II, 140) on this island — the casual expression suggests the looseness and tenuousness of the relationship — has lost the purity of tone of the native tradition. The man's 'pronunciation was lost in the rasping of his throat' (II, 141) and the ballad about emigration is laced with 'English nautical terms' (II, 141). His main interest in his companion is 'whether I am a rich man'(II, 141); he despises the poverty of the islands, and advises the narrator that since he is not married, he ought to return in the summer 'so that he might take me over in a curagh to the Spa in County Clare, where there is "spree mor agus go leor ladies" ("a big spree and plenty of ladies")' (II, 141).

Filled with loathing by the absentee part this debased character would have him play, his return to Inishmaan induces yet again a mood of mythologising euphoria. Once more there is 'a sudden revival of summer' (II, 142). This, together with food and drink, brings on 'a dreamy, voluptuous gaiety' (II, 142). The pull back to the unreal past, by contrast with the unpalatable modernity of the south island, is as powerful as the alluring excitement of the harp-like music in the dream. Once more he begins to indulge his own regressive attraction towards mystification, but the repeated use of 'seemed', running counter to the aetherial abstraction of the style, suggests once again a conjunction of romantic indulgence and subversive irony:

> These men of Inishmaan seemed to be moved by strange archaic sympathies with the world. Their mood accorded itself with wonderful fineness to the suggestions of the day, and their ancient Gaelic seemed so full of divine simplicity that I would have liked to turn the prow to the west and row with them for ever (II, 142).

The intoxicated regression into the past appears to be broken 'when our excitement sobered down' (II, 142) — but the episode which follows shows the narrator being called upon again, this time by Michael, to play yet another historically conditioned part. Like Brecht's Gayly Gay, he is constructed and deconstructed by the social role he is encouraged to assume, and by his own response to it. On this occasion he is taken out shooting by Michael, his closest island friend, even his adopted brother. His friend is now anxious, however, that he should prove himself not as a brother, but as a 'duine uasal', or noble person, effectively as a member of the gentry ascendancy. To prove the legitimacy of his title and position, he must shoot — a rabbit. Michael organises the kill and he applauds the deed *in Gaelic*:

'Buail tu e,' screamed Michael at my elbow as he ran up the rock. I had
killed it.

We shot seven or eight more in the next hour, and Michael was
immensely pleased. If I had done badly I think I should have had to leave
the islands. The people would have despised me. A 'duine uasal' who
cannot shoot seems to these descendants of hunters a fallen type who is worse
than an apostate (II, 142-3).

The strategic, and rare, appearance of the untranslated Gaelic at this
point in the text anticipates certain related strategies used by Joyce in
his striving 'to find forms in which history and technique become a
single problem'.[18] The Gaelic words confront us, as readers, with the
historical process of 'the displacement of one language by another' and
insist, for the text, on 'a dialectical relation to history'.[19] 'Buail tu e' is
not literally translated or translatable by the actor-narrator's claim 'I
had killed it'; the words mean, or may mean, 'You hit him' — and
Michael's Gaelic scream could be interpreted, also, as protest, as
praise, or as both. Also, in Gaelic, a 'duine uasal' is a person of nobility.
The connotations of the title, as well as its denotations, have resonances
in that tongue which make the reduction of its meaning here to that of
an ascendancy scion who proves his title by shooting a rabbit
appropriately subversive.

Lest we should overlook this level of meaning, in an apparently
discrete episode the narrative will shortly refer again to the shooting of
rabbits. The occasion is the one in which the narrator is unable to play
the traditional dance music requested 'in shaking English' (II, 153) by
the oldest and most highly respected island dancer. One of the
islanders reports on the end of a prolonged and frenzied fight in which
the participants' shouts and screams are compared with the noise of 'a
man killing a pig' (II, 152). The talk then turns 'from ordinary music'
to 'music of the fairies' (II, 154). The imminent folk anecdote about a
rabbit is therefore set amongst *leitmotif*-like evocations of music,
dancing, fighting and pigs. The people — there is no single narrator
this time — tell how one of the islanders 'got his gun one day and went
to look for rabbits in a thicket near the small Dun' (II, 154):

He saw a rabbit sitting up under a tree, and he lifted his gun to take aim at it,
but just as he had it covered he heard a kind of music over his head and he
looked up into the sky. When he looked back for the rabbit, not a bit of it was
to be seen.

He went on after that, and he heard the music again.
Then he looked over a wall, and he saw a rabbit sitting up by the wall
with a sort of flute in its mouth and it playing on it with its two fingers
(II, 154).

This time, the music saves the rabbit from death. But who, we must ask
retrospectively, in the context of this further example of folk-based
anthropomorphism, does Michael's 'duine uasal' kill? The question is
not explicitly answered, but it is certainly raised, by the text. [20]

What might well be described as the apotheosis, in *The Aran Islands*,
of the turning of words against The Word occurs in Part III of the
work. The narrator has left the islands and is once again in Galway
city. There he meets an old man who had once 'gone to see a relative of
mine in Dublin when he first left the island' (II, 147). This relative, we
may assume, was very likely the uncle of Synge, Alexander, who
'became the first Protestant clergyman to take up regular duties in the
Aran Islands' and who was possibly also, therefore, the prototype for
the old minister of 'Rucard Mor'.[21] It was, Edward Stephens records,
Alexander Synge's sister, Jane, who 'encouraged [Synge] to study both
languages [Irish and Hebrew] for she remembered how much her
brother Alexander had needed a knowledge of Irish during his
ministry'.[22] The ministrations from which the old man who tells 'his
story'(II, 147) claims to have benefited are anything but those which
would have been intended by a proselytising ascendancy clergyman.
The story is Synge's last ironic tribute in this movement to the
transformational powers of the imagination nourished on the folk
tradition. The man stresses the liberality of 'Mr. Synge' — not with the
spiritual waters of life, but with 'whisky' (II, 147). Twice, he asserts,
Mr Synge offered 'a glass of whisky all round' — and to the old
story-teller he gave 'a book in Irish' (II, 147). Although the man does
not say so — and the omission is itself an indication of the irrelevance of
this to the recipient of the gift — the book will have been an Irish
translation of the Bible. The end result of this act of proselytising
liberality is a complete turning of the tables on Synge's class. The Book
does not convert the man to the Protestant persuasion: it confirms and
strengthens him in his sense of identity as an Irishman. Indeed, it
makes him more Irish than the Irish themselves:

44

I owe it to Mr. Synge and that book that when I came back here, after not
hearing a word of Irish for thirty years, I had as good Irish, or maybe better
Irish, than any person on the island (II, 147).

'I could see all through his talk', comments the narrator wryly, 'that
the sense of superiority which his scholarship in this little-known
language gave him above the ordinary seaman, had influenced his
whole personality and been the central interest of his life' (II, 147-8).
Here, perhaps, are the seeds which were to germinate into Martin
Doul's triumph over the words, water and way of seeing of the holy
father in *The Well of the Saints*, the tinkers' victory over the priest in *The
Tinker's Wedding*, and Christy Mahon's joyful dominion over his father
in *The Playboy of the Western World*.

The ancestral gift of the book to the exiled man of Aran enables the
island man to turn critic after dinner. He criticises Archbishop
MacHale's version of *Moore's Irish Melodies* 'with great severity and
acuteness' (II, 149). But Synge (unlike Moore) does not sentimentalise;
he recognises that the man's view of language is tied to a passing way of
life; although there is an important truth in his association of language
with labour. Synge tells us that

> In spite of his singular intelligence and minute observation his reasoning
> was medieval.
>   I asked him what he thought about the future of the language on these
> islands.
>   'It can never die out,' said he, 'because there's no family in the place can
> live without a bit of a field for potatoes, and they have only the Irish words
> for all that they do in the fields. They sail their new boats — their hookers
> — in English, but they sail a curagh oftener in Irish, and in the fields they
> have the Irish alone (II, 149-50).

The old islander's meditation on the relationship between language
and action, and his comic testimony, in his tale about Mr Synge, the
book, and the whisky, to the ability of story to turn a relationship of
dependence into one of triumphant superiority, together concentrate,
with splendid economy of structure and style, the main themes of *The
Aran Islands*. They are themes which were to preoccupy the nephew of
Aran's first Protestant clergyman, and foster-son of the islands,
throughout his life as maker of plays.

NOTES

1. W.J. McCormack, *Sheridan Le Fanu and Victorian Ireland* (Oxford, Clarendon Press, 1980), p. 265.

2. Northrop Frye, *Anatomy of Criticism: Four Essays* (Princeton, New Jersey, Princeton University Press, 1957), p. 333.

3. Ibid., pp. 333-4.

4. Ibid., p. 334.

5. Ibid., p. 247.

6. Ibid., p. 308.

7. W.B. Yeats, 'The Irish Dramatic Movement': a lecture delivered to the Royal Academy of Sweden in 1924, published in *Autobiographies* (London and Basingstoke, Macmillan, 1955), p. 567.

8. These themes are explored in Synge's first play, *When the Moon Has Set*, where the hero, Columb Sweeny, appears to be familiar with the debate between Nietzsche and Wagner about the relationships between music and words. Synge's readings from Wagner and Nietzsche are recorded in several of his notebooks and diaries.

9. Synge would appear, in these passages, to be drawing upon the writings of William Morris and Karl Marx about art, alienation and the division of labour. He recorded his reading of Marx in his diary for the year 1896, the year in which he met W.B. Yeats. The notes which he made from *Das Kapital* are contained in TCD MS 4379. These are in German, with comments in English and French.

10. W.J. McCormack, 'Nightmares of History: James Joyce and the Phenomenon of Anglo-Irish Literature', in W.J. McCormack and Alistair Stead (eds.), *James Joyce and Modern Literature* (London, Boston, Melbourne and Henley, Routledge and Kegan Paul, 1982), p. 83.

11. W.B. Yeats, *Autobiographies*, p. 568.

12. In 'The Gaelic Story-teller: With Some Notes on Gaelic Folktales', J.H. Delargy examines the way in which this activity develops into a form of collaborative drama. See *Proceedings of the British Academy* (1945), pp. 177-221.

13. Jack Zipes, 'Breaking the Magic Spell: Politics and the Fairy Tale', in *New German Critique*, 6 (1975), p. 116.

14. TCD MS 4351, f.9.

15. This black mass theme reappears, in comic form, in *The Playboy*

of the Western World. See Chapter 7 of this study.

16. In an essay entitled 'Synge's Ecstatic Dance and the Myth of the Undying Father', Jeanne Flood offers a valuable study of this episode from *The Aran Islands.* The essay appears in *American Imago*, Volume 33, Number 2 (Summer 1976), pp. 174-96.

17. TCD MS 4351, f.9.

18. McCormack, 'Nightmares of History: James Joyce and the Phenomenon of Anglo-Irish Literature', p. 78.

19. Ibid., p.82.

20. A related ambiguity about who shoots whom occurs in *When the Moon Has Set*, where the hero-victim, Columb, is described as resembling his assassin, and is, in more ways than one, his *alter ego*.

21. Edward Stephens, *My Uncle John: Edward Stephens's Life of J.M. Synge*, ed. Andrew Carpenter (London, Oxford University Press, 1974), p. 12.

22. Ibid., pp. 65-6.

3.

RIDERS TO THE SEA:
A Journey Beyond The Literal

OF ALL of Synge's plays, *Riders to the Sea* would appear to be least concerned, explicitly, with language as a dramatic theme. It should, however, be remembered that the title of the play, like that of its companion in time, *In the Shadow of the Glen*, refers us to the Bible, the Book of the Divine Word. Substantial elements of theme and imagery derive, as T.R. Henn and Paul Levitt have illustrated, from the Apocalypse, or Book of Revelation.[1] Revelation might be said to be a teleological prophetic construct. It seeks to reveal the future by naming, or predicting, the form it must take. As the Word of God, it claims the power of a declarative speech act, the ability to bring about the state of affairs to which it refers.[2] Within Revelation the fate of man is inscribed, and sealed, in a book. Synge's play may also be interpreted as a drama of revelation. The play explores the tensions which exist between determinism and freedom, between the dark words and the words of blessing. These tensions are concentrated most powerfully upon and within the person of Maurya, at once their victim and in part their source. The title of the play, *Riders to the Sea*, brings together the connotations of men who ride to the sea by choice, and men who are by necessity consigned to the sea because they are riders or journeymen through life (riders to the sea; grass to the oven; dust to dust). These are themes to which Synge was to return in his only tragic drama, *Deirdre of the Sorrows*. Deirdre's tragic end, drawing into its orbit the fate of the Sons of Usna: 'Dead men, dead men, men who'll die for Deirdre's beauty' (IV, 235), was foretold at her birth, and the

48

action of the play both confirms and questions the prophecy.

Synge's play has been regarded as an archetypal tragedy of a primitive people living and dying with the cyclical stability of a community in perpetual confrontation with nature and untouched by historical change. We would see it, rather, as a drama of a house divided against itself by the pressures of history and time. It explores the conflict between the old gods and the new, between the *Vita Vecchia* of the old way of life, with its task of wresting a living from sea and soil, and the *Vita Nuova* of industrial society. In the old way of life, the pressures of surviving and of maintaining the community are expressed in terms of family rights and bonds, duties and relationships. In face of the irresistible encroachment of a commodity-based society, the tasks of the island people may remain superficially similar, but relationships are changed utterly: they are calculated and stated in terms of price. Maurya stands at the crossroads between the new way and the old. She is the mother who gave birth to the young men who 'must go now quickly' when 'the fair will be a good fair for horses' (III, 9). It is she who knows the human price that can be exacted by the need to make a living, or the urge to face the new life. Maurya presides over her men's funeral rites, and it is she, also, who takes a special pride in providing for them, on the treeless island, a coffin made from bought-in wood, 'and I after giving a big price for the finest white boards you'd find in Connemara'. (III, 9).

The properties on-stage at the opening of the play — nets, oilskins and spinning-wheel — are objects used by the island people to make their daily living, with only the new boards standing anomalously against the wall. The silent actions of Cathleen are acts of making and producing, as she finishes kneading the cake and begins to spin at the wheel. Nora's opening words, 'Where is she?' (III, 5) raise the questions of identity, relationship and place, while Cathleen's staccato enquiry 'What is it you have?' (III, 5) calls attention to the bundle her sister carries — 'a shirt and a plain stocking were got off a drowned man in Donegal' (III, 5). This at present ownerless, unidentified property has come to them through the offices of the young priest, whose words, in spite of his youth, are vested with a peculiar authority by the women. As the cottage door is blown open by a gust of wind, Cathleen anxiously enquires if the priest has used his powerful words to 'stop

Bartley going this day with the horses to the Galway fair' (III, 5). In place of the looked-for proscription, however, the priest has sent a prophetic assurance:

> NORA. 'I won't stop him,' says he, 'but let you not be afraid. Herself does be saying prayers half through the night, and the Almighty God won't leave her destitute,' says he, 'with no son living.' (III, 5)

The repeated verb of attribution, 'says he', reminds us that what the priest offers is a verbal formula. The words claim to guarantee payment in kind for Maurya's costly spiritual investment in the good credit of the Almighty. The glossing of 'destitute', deprived of all worldly wealth, as the equivalent of being left 'with no son living' brings into sharply ironic conjunction the economic and personal dimensions of Maurya's tragic dilemma. What the priest offers here is not a voice which freely calms the wind and stills the sea: it is, in effect, the promissory note of one whose master has already exacted a terrible price from his suppliant. Cathleen and Nora hear another voice challenging the calculating cruel comfort of the priestly prophecy — the voice of the hard, objective reality of the natural world:

> CATHLEEN. Is the sea bad by the white rocks, Nora?
> NORA. Middling bad, God help us. There's a great roaring in the west, and it's worse it'll be getting when the tide's turned to the wind. [*She goes over to the table with the bundle.*] Shall I open it now? (III, 5-7)

When Maurya makes her appearance her first querulous words to Cathleen are a rebuke for extravagantly wasting their hard-won substance, the turf which fuels the precious fire of the domestic hearth.[3] Cathleen's reply leaves open to Bartley the element of chance or choice: they need more turf, she claims, because Bartley will want the cake they are baking '*if* he goes to Connemara' (III,7, my italics). The presence within the play of this element is crucial to its status as tragedy; it is the open door in an otherwise closed system, offering entry to the humanising variable which in turn makes fulfilment of prophecy dependent, within limits, on willed action rather than mere compulsion.[4] In the play, choice and chance create a situation in which the non-ethical concept of sheer movement, of being compelled by the irresistible motion of the objective universe to ride to the sea, provides a context for action, which 'implies the ethical, the human personality'.[5] Once admonition or prescription enters its domain, prophecy itself becomes 'moralized by the negative'.[6] What is denied becomes potentially what is forbidden and what is forbidden 'also has about its edges the positive image' inviting the choice of its opposite.[7]

In the exchange which follows between Maurya and Nora, Maurya attempts to convince herself that she can prevent Bartley's departure. She seeks to lend power to her prophecy by appealing to the voice of the island and the authoritative words of the young priest. Bartley, however, has to calculate the economic cost of waiting against the personal danger of choosing to go. When he enters, emphasis shifts noticeably and emphatically from words to things and from speculation to action. He asks for 'the bit of new rope, Cathleen, was bought in Connemara' (III, 9). As the bread-winner of the family, he introduces the theme of price into the short exchange with his mother and his sisters. His is the first of many references to properties which are also commodities. Like the men of Aran in *The Aran Islands*, Bartley cannot afford to buy a halter; he has to make one from the rope:

> BARTLEY [*beginning to work with the rope*]. I've no halter the way I can ride down on the mare, and I must go now quickly. This is the one boat going for two weeks or beyond it, and the fair will be a good fair for horses, I heard them saying below (III, 9).

Because of their poverty, and their related need to get a good price for what they sell, the remaining son cannot choose with disinterested freedom his time of departure. There is a conflict between his island knowledge of the power of the sea and the powerful market pressures on him to go to the mainland. Sensing this conflict in her son, Maurya tries to resolve it by confronting him with the older and deeper bonds and obligations. The island people have more to consider than what relates only to good fairs for horses. If Michael's body is washed up, they will condemn Bartley for his failure to remain with his mother and sisters to carry out his family duty of making Michael's coffin. Failing to move Bartley visibly with these arguments, Maurya next tries to persuade her son to calculate the price of the horses against the cost, in human terms, of the loss of his life:

> MAURYA. If it was a hundred horses, or a thousand horses you had itself, what is the price of a thousand horses against a son where there is one son only?(III, 9)

Maurya's pleading with Bartley only serves to emphasise the family's dilemma. She wants Bartley as her son; he is her only son living: yet she knows well that he is the one upon whom they depend to get a good price. Her final appeal recognises this cruel contradiction, but it is at the same time a plea for a more humane basis for human relationships. The play's historical tragedy springs from the fact that for the mother, reconciliation is not possible on this side of the grave between the two alienated forms of need, the human and the economic:

> MAURYA. It's hard set we'll be surely the day you're drown'd with the rest. What way will I live and the girls with me, and I an old woman looking for the grave? (III, 11)

The mother's prophetic speech questions the family's ability to survive, economically, when Bartley is drowned. But her words are also a cry of anguish at the human loss they will feel when the last of her sons is gone. Her anticipation of her own death is a reminder, however, that she is asking him to stay in order to take care of the dying. Bartley's *choice* of an alternative to this, limited as this choice is by necessity, is underlined by the deliberate action of changing his clothes: he *'lays down the halter, takes off his old coat, and puts on a newer one of the same flannel'* (III, 11). It is further emphasised by the dynamic note of anticipated activity struck in the exchange between Nora and himself about the hooker. He is taking up the challenge of the future as he purposefully equips himself with purse and tobacco for the journey, promising to return 'in two days, or in three days, or maybe in four days if the wind is bad' (III, 11). Maurya makes one final attempt to hold him back, turning inward to the fire, the focus of the old way of life:

> MAURYA [*turning round to the fire, and putting her shawl over her head*]. Isn't it a hard and cruel man won't hear a word from an old woman, and she holding him from the sea? (III, 11)

Cathleen's rejoinder reminds us of what Kenneth Burke has called the 'sheer emptiness' of words by contrast with the powerful attraction of the 'substance of the things they name'.[8] Like Nora, she realises that Bartley's going is also a turning towards the future:

> CATHLEEN. It's the life of a young man to be going on the sea, and who would listen to an old woman with one thing and she saying it over? (III, 11)

His words of benediction are an invitation to Maurya to consent to this leave-taking, but her anguished cry of despair at being robbed of her last son is her only response:

> MAURYA [*crying out as he is in the door*]. He's gone now, God spare us, and we'll not see him again. He's gone now, and when the black night is falling I'll have no son left me in the world (III, 11).

That Bartley, like 'everyone is left living in the world' (III, 27), has an appointment with death is the one prophecy the fulfilment of which is sure. The staff which Maurya is given by her daughters to support her as she sets out on her pilgrimage to meet her son at the spring well reminds us of this. It is a staff of life and of death. It is the stick which belonged to her dead son, but it is not 'just' a stick; it is 'the stick Michael brought from Connemara' (III, 13): again, a purchased commodity. For the island people such properties are dearly bought. For them, the mainland laws of inheritance are turned on their heads and their lives are the price exacted for possessions:

> MAURYA [*taking a stick* NORA *gives her*]. In the big world the old people do be leaving things after them for their sons and children, but in this place it is the young men do be leaving things behind for them that do be old. [*She goes out slowly.*] (III,13)

When Maurya has gone, the girls turn back to their interrupted preoccupation with the bundle of clothes and the words and commands of the young priest. The bundle is tied with string so perished by the salt sea water that 'there's a black knot on it you wouldn't loosen in a week' (III, 15). As Cathleen cuts the fatal string, we learn that the knife with which she undoes the knot has been bought from a travelling man, a pedlar, who can tell the time it takes 'walking from the rocks beyond' till 'you'd be in Donegal' (III, 15). The action of cutting the string relates the sisters to the Moirae. String and rope link the 'dead' Michael to Bartley, who is about to die to the island way of life. The 'rocks beyond' are the white rocks where Bartley will meet death; Donegal is the place where Michael's body was washed up. Living and dead brothers are thus linked by reference to the traveller's mainland-measured time.[9] The focus of the scene is intensively on objects, particularly on the contents of the bundle. Much of its antithetical richness derives from its being both a parallel and a contrast to the ritual of reading auguries to determine a person's fate. As the two sisters look eagerly at *a bit of a shirt and a stocking* (III, 15), Cathleen speaks to Nora of the difficulty of establishing beyond doubt the relationship between things and words:

> CATHLEEN [*in a low voice*]. The Lord spare us, Nora! Isn't it a queer hard *thing* to *say* if it's his they are surely? (III, 15, my italics)

Words unchecked against objects are not sufficiently precise — but neither do words exist in a one to one relationship to things. Things, if they are to reveal their truth, must be placed in their social context and seen in terms of their customary use. Nora goes to get Michael's shirt 'the way we can put the one flannel on the other' (III, 15). She is seeking to identify Michael by establishing the identity of the material from which the shirts are made. But in this near-subsistence economy, just beginning to be affected by mass production, the use-value of objects is still paramount. Michael's shirt is missing; Bartley had need of it, and so he 'put it on him in the morning, for his own shirt was heavy with the salt in it' (III, 15). The girls are left, therefore, to compare a frugally saved remnant of sleeve with the bit of stuff. Ironically, however, they realise once they do so that the very sameness — the identity — of these two pieces of purchased and machined flannel prevents them from establishing, with certainty, their owner's identity:

> CATHLEEN. It's the same stuff, Nora; but if it is itself aren't there great rolls of it in the shops of Galway, and isn't it many another man may have a shirt of it as well as Michael himself? (III,15)

In order to identify the drowned man, they have to look instead at the hand-knit stocking, 'a plain stocking' it is true, but one into which their relationship with their brother has been worked by the directly recognisable personal labour of their own hands. The language here *identifies the hand-knitted stocking with the man*: the possessive is not used:

NORA [*who has taken up the stocking and counted the stitches, crying out*]. It's Michael, Cathleen, it's Michael; God spare his soul, and what will herself say when she hears this story, and Bartley on the sea?
CATHLEEN [*taking the stocking*]. It's a plain stocking.
NORA. It's the second one of the third pair I knitted, and I put up three score stitches, and I dropped four of them.
CATHLEEN [*counts the stitches*]. It's that number is in it (III, 17).

A compassionate resolve to conceal their knowledge from Maurya while Bartley is away causes Cathleen and Nora to close the bundle and hide it from view. Their act is linked with a pious hope that the mother will have found some relief from sorrow 'after giving her blessing to Bartley' (III, 17). The old woman's wordless keening at last drives Cathleen to challenge her to speak:

CATHLEEN [*a little impatiently*]. God forgive you; isn't it a better thing to raise your voice and tell what you seen, than to be making lamentation for a thing that's done? Did you see Bartley, I'm saying to you? (III, 17)

Maurya claims to have 'seen the fearfullest thing' (III, 19) and Cathleen's immediate and mistaken assumption is that she believes she has *literally* seen Bartley dead. This is the implication of her actions and words when she leaves her spinning-wheel and goes to check for herself the whereabouts of her brother:

CATHLEEN. God forgive you; he's riding the mare now over the green head, and the grey pony behind him (III, 19).

It is this mention of the grey pony which triggers off Maurya's start of renewed terror. It is impossible to do justice to the play if we overlook the apocalyptic resonance of this episode. The grey pony, which is named four times in the course of the brief, tense exchange between Cathleen and her mother, is typologically related to the apocalyptic 'pale horse: and his name that sat on him was Death'.[10] Bartley,

Maurya tells the sisters, 'came along and he riding on the red mare' (III, 19). At that instant, *she saw the dead Michael*. Revelation also tells that 'there went out another horse *that was* red; and *power* was given to him that sat thereon to take peace from the earth, and that they should kill one another'.[11]

Maurya is narrating at this point not a literal encounter, but a *visionary tale*, and like the folk tales in *The Aran Islands*, the vision is a translation into story of what is happening to Bartley as he takes the horses to the fair. That she *is* telling a story is emphasised in various ways. It is suggested by the way in which the girls '*crouch down in front of the old woman at the fire*' (III, 19), becoming an audience; by Nora's use of the folk-formula 'Tell us what it is you seen' (III, 19); by the narrative form of the language and by its repetitive, formulaic, story-telling pattern and style. Its fictional status, which is not to be confused with untruth or lack of reality any more than it can be reduced to literalism, is underlined by the way in which the old woman explicitly links her story with another visionary island tale, of how 'Bride Dara seen the dead man with the child in his arms' (III, 19). When Cathleen mistakes the fictitious, visionary status of her mother's utterance, telling her that she could not have seen Michael, she confirms rather than dispels her mother's vision and it is Maurya herself who defiantly asserts this:

CATHLEEN [*speaking softly*]. You did not, mother; it wasn't Michael you seen, for his body is after being found in the far north, and he's got a clean burial by the grace of God.

MAURYA [*a little defiantly*]. I'm after seeing him this day, and he riding and galloping. Bartley came first on the red mare; and I tried to say 'God speed you,' but something choked the words in my throat. He went by quickly; and 'the blessing of God on you,' says he, and I could say nothing (III, 19).

That Michael may be dead, or that Cathleen has just seen Bartley alive, is not denied by Maurya, but neither is this particularly relevant. Far from invalidating the meaning of her story, these very antinomies establish *its symbolic status* and its imaginative truth.

Although she was saying a prayer as she stood by the spring well, something about Bartley's visionary appearance prevented Maurya from speaking the words 'God speed you' to him. Her emphasis, when she describes the vision of her sons, is upon the speed with which they were travelling away from their island life, and from Maurya's influence or control. Michael was 'riding and galloping' and Bartley, who 'came first on the red mare', 'went by *quickly*'. It would seem that in this moment of vision, Maurya experiences a profound imaginative truth communicated in a form analogous to the metaphoric or symbolic truth of art; a paradoxical perception that the kind of blessing which she was about to offer her son was a dark word hastening his ride to death. For, she continues, explaining why she did not utter her words, 'I looked up then and I crying, at the grey pony, and there was Michael upon it — with fine clothes on him, and new shoes on his feet' (III, 19).[12] Maurya at this moment looks up into the face of death, but also, as, indeed, Revelation prophesies, into the face of a new life. The new clothes are associated with the clothes which the girls have been examining in their own effort to read their brother's story — and thence with the theme of the islanders' struggle to come to terms with this new way of life. Michael is wearing clothes which the islanders could never make for themselves — mainland clothes. Maurya's vision, therefore, indeed prophesies death for the old life of the island. She who had hoped before that the young priest would prevent her son's departure now acknowledges that 'It's little the like of him knows of the sea . . .' (III, 21). What she has confronted is neither more nor less than the imminence and inevitability of Bartley's loss and her own inability to prevent it:

> MAURYA. Bartley will be lost now, and let you call in Eamon and make me a good coffin out of the white boards, for I won't live after them (III, 21).

What is left to Maurya now is neither prophecy nor prohibition, but the responsibility of the story-teller to tell of what has happened and what is happening to the island men, and to face what is to come. Relinquishing prophecy for narration, she begins to establish a place for her menfolk in the stories of the island, stories which bear their own unique witness to the lives and deaths of its people. The language of her elegiac tale is formulaic in its simple solemnity as she continues her solemn naming of those to whom she was daughter, and wife and mother; men who sooner or later were consigned to becoming 'a thing in the half of a red sail, and water dripping out of it . . . and leaving a track to the door' (III, 21). While she speaks, past and present flow into a continuum of now, as the procession that enters on stage takes the form of an exact dramatic enactment of her words. This is indeed an apocalyptic Second Coming. It is not, however, the coming of a resurrected god who has triumphed over death; it is the tragic return of man reduced to the status of a thing: 'Is it Patch, or Michael, or what is it at all?' (III, 21). Cathleen clings hopefully to the possibility of separating the one drowned man from the many, but Maurya is fast moving beyond the need for such a singling out, to a recognition that in this anonymous brotherhood the identity of one man with another is total:

> MAURYA. There does be a power of young men floating round in the sea, and what way would they know if it was Michael they had, or another man like him, for when a man is nine days in the sea, and the wind blowing, it's hard set his own mother would be to say what man was in it (III, 23).

Cathleen may recognise Michael's stocking by the signs of her labour; no such sign of the labour of birth is left to the mother when the sea has exacted its toll and pronounced its last judgement upon unpropertied individuality.

Bartley's death, drowned when 'the grey pony knocked him over into the sea, and he was washed out where there is a great surf on the white rocks' (III, 23), looked at 'literally', is just an accident. In his discussion of this episode Nicholas Grene remarks that 'The grey pony is too literally a horse which Bartley is taking to sell at the fair in Connemara to make it easy to accept it as an analogue of the phantasmal allegorical figure of *Revelation*. The imaginative mode of the two images is totally different'.[13] He continues, however, by arguing later that it is more appropriate to see Michael's appearance in Maurya's vision as analogous with

> the folk concept of the conspiracy of the dead. The dead are thought to return commonly to claim the living — hence the elaborate precautions of St. John's Eve or Hallowe'en to placate the dead souls and prevent them from doing mischief. Michael passes into the service of the 'great majority

of souls', and he comes to force Bartley to join all his other brothers.[14]

Leaving aside the selectivity of such decisions about when horses are literal or non-literal, and the begged question of how a literal horse can have an analogous rider, even if we substitute the folk tale for the Bible, there does not seem to be much to gain, but rather, a great deal to lose, by choosing between these possibilities as if they were exclusive alternatives. Synge knew Frazer's *The Golden Bough*. He had studied comparative mythology as a student of Le Braz, Passy and de Jubainville. He regarded Rabelais and Chaucer as favourite authors and he had read Huysmans, Baudelaire and Wilde. There is ample proof in his notebooks as well as in *The Aran Islands* that he was fascinated by the cultural and sociological cross-currents between myths, traditions, literatures and religions. There is plenty of evidence that his growing awareness of the rich symbolic potential of word, image and myth helped to free his own creative imagination from predestinarian theology and from the related over-zealous application of the doctrine of univocal literalism to language.[15]

For the Aran people, as their stories and anecdotes illustrate, the imaginative mode of the two images (the economic and the religious) was *not* totally different, nor was it for Synge. Their religion, their folk culture, their economy and their life interacted, so that the very story from *The Aran Islands* to which Grene refers can be clearly shown to derive its significance from the plurality of these associations and from the story-teller's power to establish a continuum between religious 'superstitions' and economic phenomena, within the traditional imaginative mode of transfigured realism. Bartley dies by accident; he 'dies' because he chooses to go to trade in the horse for a good price; he dies because he chooses to go, within the limits of choice available to him, on a particular stormy day. He also, perhaps, dies because he feels it necessary to live, to oppose his mother's determined effort to keep him at home as the last son who is needed to bury the dead in a dying order. He dies because Michael is dead and Bartley is, as Grene suggests, claimed by his dead brothers, as well as by his father and his father's father, whose deaths have left *him* as the one who must ride to the sea. He dies because he has been born, because death is both the beginning and the end of life and all men are therefore riders to the sea. It is in this sense, in his ability to bring together such apparently antinomic themes, that the supernatural in Synge is 'oddly matter-of-fact and unmysterious' and the apparently matter-of-fact so resonant with meaning.[16] It is odd, perhaps, when we remember the nature of his religious upbringing, but unmysterious when we trace his journey towards a cognitive aesthetic. *Riders to the Sea* did not emerge from the pen of an unpractised novice who suddenly discovered the poetic mode of symbolic action as an alternative to decadent Continental aestheticism or evangelical literalism: it came from the prepared sensibility of the writer of *The Aran Islands*.

Synge's art is the non-literal and non-assertive art of juxtaposed masterful images: the later Yeats learnt much from his technique. It is an art which 'requires us to suspend commitments to literal reality and to take seriously (though not literally) our poetic or theoretical fictions'.[17] A failure to match with critical imagination the poetic concentration on 'what is patently *not* there in the language, but which emerges in the interplay of juxtaposed associations' leads Malcolm Pittock, also, to the judgement that it is *Riders to the Sea*, and not his reading of it, which fails, because it requires us to accept that Maurya's vision is real and is literally fulfilled.[18] 'It is . . . one thing', writes Pittock, 'for Maurya to see a vision and to believe that vision fulfilled, but quite another for a modern audience, formed in a different cultural pattern, to believe in such superstition with any real seriousness'.[19] But this, precisely, is what Synge does *not* require of us. To react thus is to fall into the trap of reacting to the symbolic in the manner of Mrs Synge. Rather, we need to recognise that the

> interaction of both sets of referents — the two systems or levels, and the literal and pretended — is precisely what makes it impossible to collapse the cognitive import of metaphor to a literal, univisioned, nontensional statement. To *believe* the metaphor literally is to accept an absurdity as truth, to make of metaphor a myth; but to *reduce* metaphor to a literal statement is to destroy what cannot survive except at the intersection of juxtaposed perspectives.[20]

In *Ways of Seeing* John Berger makes a formal point which throws an interesting light on Synge's decision to introduce a visionary and highly stylised episode into the centre of a play in which he was meticulously careful to ensure that all the properties had about them an authentic historical and cultural reality. Referring to Holbein's

painting of the skull in *The Ambassadors* as 'a highly distorted skull . . .
painted in a (literally) quite different optic from everything else in the
picture', he argues that 'if the skull had been painted like the rest, its
metaphysical implication would have disappeared; it would have
become an object like everything else, a mere part of a mere skeleton of
a man who happened to be dead'.[21] Taking this further, Berger later
compares Holbein's solution of his problem with William Blake's
technique:

> As a draughtsman and engraver Blake learnt according to the rules of the
> tradition. But when he came to make paintings, he very seldom used oil
> paint and, although he still relied upon the traditional conventions of
> drawing, he did everything he could to make his figures lose substance, to
> become transparent and indeterminate one from the other, to defy gravity,
> to be present but intangible, to glow without a definable surface, *not to be
> reducible to objects*.
>
> This wish of Blake to transcend the 'substantiality' of oil paint derived
> from a deep insight into the meaning and limitations of the tradition.[22]

Maurya's visionary tale is also a technical solution to a related
challenge. It is no mere part of a simple, primitively superstitious
foretelling of the death of a man who is about to die any more than it is
a flashback to the death of one who has died. The framing of the vision
in the context of a meta-language acts like the different optic in
Holbein's painting, or like Blake's dissolution of crude objectivity.
Synge greatly admired Blake and he had also read and made
substantial notes from Yeats's edition of the poems.[23] Like Blake as
artist and poet, and Holbein as painter, Synge as dramatist had a deep
insight into the meaning of realism and he appreciated the limitations
of restricting realism to the naturalistic mode. He, too, discovered and
developed ways to use the strengths of realism and naturalism and to
transcend their limitations.

It is important to note in Maurya's great funeral oration the
concentration of meta-linguistic references. Her elegiac celebration of
release from the tensions which have sapped her very being is
controlled, grammatically, by the repeated phrase 'I'll have no call',
thus, through negation, translating the necessity from which she is
freed into a compulsion, which has likewise passed away, to answer

words with words. The language of the island as it has been mediated to her in the past has been the language of conflict, the 'two noises' from the east and from the west ' and they hitting one on the other' (III, 25). The voices which she has spent her life religiously trying to appease have cried out in conflict too, for in her words about the 'Holy Water in the dark nights after Samhain' (III, 25) Christian and pagan beliefs, myths and rites collide and mingle as forcibly as surf from east and surf from west crashing on the white rocks where Bartley met his death. Throughout *Riders to the Sea* the tension generated by the co-presence of pagan 'superstition' and Christian 'belief', and the accommodation which the islanders seek to establish between them, can be felt.

In *Riders to the Sea*, however, the young priest remains conspicuous by his absence on the occasion of Bartley's Second Coming. It is not he, but the mother, who assumes the sacerdotal office and performs the last rites for the dead, linking the Christian with the pre-Christian and transcending both as she does so:

> [*To* NORA.] Give me the Holy Water, Nora, there's a small sup still on the dresser. NORA [*gives it to her.* MAURYA *drops Michael's clothes across* BARTLEY's *feet, and sprinkles the Holy Water over him.*] . . . It isn't that I haven't prayed for you, Bartley, to the Almighty God. It isn't that I haven't said prayers in the dark night till you wouldn't know what I'd be saying: but it's a great rest I'll have now, and it's time surely. It's a great rest I'll have now, and great sleeping in the long nights after Samhain, if it's only a bit of wet flour we do have to eat, and maybe a fish that would be stinking. [*She kneels down again, crossing herself, and saying prayers under her breath.*] (III, 25)

Maurya is performing here a eucharistic rite in which her son is and remains dead to the island people. The grace which comes to her now is the graciousness born of the acceptance of death, not the anticipation of resurrection. It comes as a release from the need to pray as a defence against disaster, a need which made her life a form of living death.

What we are presented with in the final moments of the play is an antitype of Easter morning, when the women came and found the tomb empty, and of that general resurrection of the dead which is prophesied in the Apocalypse. In *Riders to the Sea*, however, Maurya does not find an empty tomb, though one, at least, of her sons is missing and only pieces of his clothes remain. In place of the seamless shroud, neatly folded, she takes and unfolds the machine-made flannel and the homespun stocking with its dropped stitches and spreads them beside the body. When she has done so, she sprinkles the last of the Holy Water upon them. For these riders to the sea there is no second washing in the 'pure river of water of life, clear as crystal, proceeding out of the throne of God and of the Lamb'.[24] They have sprung from the waters of Maurya's womb; their cup of life is now emptied. They have returned to the sea and her personal maternal role is all but consummated, as is indicated by her gestures of turning the empty cup mouth downwards on the table, and laying her hands on Bartley's feet: 'They're all together this time, and the end is come' (III, 25-7).

When we turn to the language, we find that it is interacting with the dramatised ritual to create the counterfactual truth which is a characteristic of Synge's drama. The first half of the oration is dominated by the negatives of the twice repeated phrase 'I'll have no call now' (III, 23 and 25). This negative tonality is sustained throughout the first movement of her speech. Semantically, negation has a peculiar appropriateness in the presence of death. But Maurya's double negatives lend to the negation an ironic edge, and at the same time make of them, potentially, the birthplace of a new affirmation. She no longer feels the compelling need to walk abroad praying in 'the long nights after Samhain'. The dark nights of wakefulness are transformed into the long nights for great sleeping — those nights when the Christian church admonishes the faithful to redouble their wakeful prayers for the dead, and the pagan creed held out the hope of snatching them back.

The play does not, however, ask *us* to endorse Maurya's choice, or even to accept it as the best or the only option. We are not even asked to believe that such a choice is possible, any more than to think that her resolve to remain released from the endless saying of prayers will persist. Her words, after all, are followed by a saying of prayers under her breath. It is also important to attend to the timing of the brief exchange between Cathleen and the Old Man, in which the young girl asks 'maybe yourself and Eamon would make a coffin when the sun rises' (III, 25). Cathleen's words continue the anti-resurrection motif in Maurya's speech: the rising of the sun will be a time for *burial* preparations. Rather, her words operate contrapuntally. Cathleen looks through and beyond morbidity to the need to continue the daily round of work while Maurya thinks gratefully of the long nights. The repeated reference to the missing nails in this scene has, perhaps, its religious connotations: for Maurya, forgetting the nails may be part of the process of separation from a crucifying existence. But it reminds us, too, of the dependence of these people upon manufacture in 'the big world', even for their burial.

In *Riders to the Sea* Maurya's passion leads to a perception of the relative nature of all that exists, making it possible for her to enter imaginatively into a new order of things. It is an order in which she is no longer driven by a desperate compulsion to appeal with words to the Word to stand against the voice of change. Synge has taken the apocalyptic Christian myth of collective death and resurrection as it is presented in Revelation and brought it into engagement with the changing way of life and the dynamic religious vision and folk imagination of the island people. The result is a dramatic reworking of both traditions, in which each is dissolved and a new vision is bodied forth. This movement beyond the literal is a journey closer to the enigma of the contradictory nature of reality.

NOTES

1. T.R. Henn, *The Harvest of Tragedy* (London, Methuen, 1956), pp. 197-205; Paul M. Levitt, *A Structural Approach to the Analysis of Drama* (The Hague and Paris, Mouton, 1971), pp. 84-116.

2. Following John R. Searle's classifications, Mary Louise Pratt describes declarations as 'illocutionary acts that bring about the state of affairs they refer to, e.g. blessing, firing, baptizing, bidding, passing sentence'. See Mary Louise Pratt, *Towards a Speech Act Theory of Literary Discourse* (Bloomington and London, Indiana University Press, 1977), p. 81.

3. Compare the stage-business with the turf fire in *When the Moon Has Set*.

4. *Riders to the Sea* has been described by some critics as melodrama rather than tragedy, on the grounds that its characters are victims rather than agents. This, it has been argued, leads to lack of any development or change in the central character, Maurya. See, for example, Robert B. Heilman, *Tragedy and Melodrama: Versions of Experience* (Seattle, University of Washington Press, 1968), pp. 38-40.

5. Kenneth Burke, *Language as Symbolic Action: Essays on Life, Literature and Method* (Berkeley and London, University of California Press, 1966), p.11.

6. Ibid., p. 16.

7. Ibid., p. 10.

8. Ibid., p. 6.

9. In *The Aran Islands* Synge remarks on the islanders' different conception of time from that of the mechanically measured units of the clock. See *Collected Works* Volume II, p. 67, where the old man transforms the mechanical object into a mediating social relationship, through a process of metonymy which is focussed in the word 'face'.

10. Revelation 6.8.

11. Ibid., 6.4.

12. The wearing of shoes by an islander in *The Aran Islands* associates him with the mainland economy and way of life. See *Collected Works* Volume II, pp. 65-6.

13. Nicholas Grene, *Synge: A Critical Study of the Plays* (London and Basingstoke, Macmillan, 1975), p. 53.

THE DRAMA OF J.M. SYNGE

14. Ibid., p. 54.

15. Amongst his jottings on literature in TCD MS 4349, f.24, Synge has copied Erasmus's dictum, 'ubicumque regnat Lutheramismus, ibi literatum est interitus [sic]'.

16. Grene, *Synge: A Critical Study of the Plays*, p. 53.

17. Richard H. Brown, *A Poetic for Sociology: Towards a Logic of Discovery for the Human Sciences* (London, Cambridge University Press, 1977), p. 84.

18. Ibid., p. 88.

19. Malcolm Pittock, '*Riders to the Sea*', in *English Studies* XL1X (1968), p. 448.

20. Brown, *A Poetic for Sociology*, p. 84.

21. John Berger, *Ways of Seeing* (London, BBC and Penguin Books, 1972), p. 91.

22. Ibid., p. 93.

23. Synge's reading of Yeats's edition of Blake is recorded in his notebooks, in TCD MS 4378.

24. Revelation 22.1.

4.
TOWARDS THE ANTITHETICAL VISION:
Syntax And Imagery In *In the Shadow of the Glen*

IN THE Shadow of the Glen, written about the same time as *Riders to the Sea*, explores the dramatic potential of the comic counterpart to Maurya's tragic vision. In this work, the antithetical exploration of biblical and folk themes and images is central to the play's strategy. It launches an attack upon the archetypal *tyrannos* who refuses to change or to die. Daniel Burke, hater of the creative word and guardian of the authoritarian *fiat*, is an incarnation of those defenders of dying truth who, in Bakhtin's words, 'pretend to be absolute, to have an extratemporal importance . . . They do not recognise their own ridiculous faces or the comic nature of their pretensions to eternity and immutability'.[1] In his biography of Synge, Edward Stephens refers to a related intransigence and absolutism in the attitude of the playwright's mother. Her beliefs, he records,

> formed such a closely-knit system that they were not susceptible of modification. The story of the creation, of man's fall in the Garden of Eden and of his subsequent redemption by the atonement formed one consecutive history. Mrs Synge's teaching provided no symbols for the interpretation of undefined spiritual vision. She regarded symbols, such as the sacrificial lamb, as having importance before the Christian revelation, but as having lost their usefulness when the atonement, which they represented, had become an accomplished fact.[2]

For Mrs Synge the atonement was the definitive historical event which

67

brought an end to history. It rendered past biblical symbolism redundant and pre-determined the future. Paradoxically such theological overdetermination translated history into a form of primitive myth — primitive because it was unconscious of its own mythologising activity.

In his journey beyond the literal Synge turned ever more resolutely to the word rather than away from it. Like Gide's Immoraliste, he sought to rediscover 'the "old Adam" whom the Gospels wanted to do away with; whom everything around me, books, teachers, family and even I myself had attempted to suppress'.[3] In *In the Shadow of the Glen* the repressive parental distrust of language and imagination is translated into the persona of the word-hating Daniel Burke. The nay saying morality of the tyrannical old petty landlord/sheepfarmer is confronted and subverted by a powerful appeal to the pastoral Good Shepherd imagery of the Bible. The play derives much of its dramatic strength from the drawing of parallels and establishment of contrasts between the pastoral imagery of Psalm 23 and the New Testament *figura* of the Good Shepherd, and the reality of the daily peasant-pastoral lives of the shepherd farmers of the Wicklow glens. It is within this dual context of biblical myth and local historical and social realism that Synge has placed his dramatisation of the January-May folk tale, a version of which he heard on the Aran Islands from Pat Dirane.

The title of the play unites the particularity of place, the native setting in 'the last cottage at the head of a long glen in County Wicklow' (III, 31) with the universal connotations of the world as the valley of the shadow of death. The local valley becomes synecdochically expanded into a representation of the universe, and the macrocosmic Valley of the Shadow is reduced to the concrete particularity of the Wicklow glen. The intimate historical and autobiographical significance of the play's title for Synge is suggested by two pieces of extraneous evidence from his unpublished writings. His one 'family' essay, 'A Landlord's Garden in County Wicklow', was earlier entitled 'The Garden of the Dead', while a transcript of his fictionalised autobiography, the *Etude Morbide*, had its first title, 'From Twilight to Dawn', changed to 'In the Valley of the Shadow of Death'.[4] In an early handwritten draft of this same work we find the fictional writer — a thinly disguised persona of Synge — resolving to cast off the 'meekness and docility' of the saints, and rejecting, with the aid of Spinoza, any contractual obligation to love God simply on the (dubious) grounds that he may love man.[5] The writer opts instead for 'the highest adoration' which is 'neither the bowing before a ruler nor the running to a father/parent but is rather chiefly as the watching of a storm or battle or evening sun'.[6] The biblical Valley of the Shadow of Death, as Psalm 23 suggests, is also the total context of life, which has to be lived in the shadow of mortality. For the people of the house in Synge's play — Nora Burke is addressed at the outset as the 'lady of the house' (III, 33) — it becomes, when they try to shut themselves away from its influence, both scene and agent of a corrosive stasis and morbidity. For Nora, the pattern of eternal recurrence becomes a nightmare of paralysis from which she finally escapes when she goes out into the valley with the Tramp. For the Tramp and Patch Darcy this same valley is equally full of threats to life, but as the primary world of unromanticised pastoral hardships and hazards, it is the life-giving, life-taking world of process and change. Whereas in *When the Moon Has Set* Columb attempts to negate the antithesis between nature and art, and between nature and man, in *In the Shadow of the Glen* the natural world is allowed its integrity as agent and context of action, as maker and changer of man who makes himself through his struggles to act upon and react towards his environment.

Structurally *In the Shadow of the Glen* is what Paul Levitt defines as a late point of attack play, 'characteristically heavy in exposition'.[7] One of the main themes is the isolation experienced by Nora Burke in a place/situation, become state, where time and life are passing her by. Much of the action is concerned with her mental confrontation or thinking through of her past life, or lack of it, in relation to her present condition and her future hopes and plans. A major challenge to the dramatist is that of making such exposition of the past essentially dramatic. In Kenneth Burke's words 'where the ideas are in action, we have drama; where the agents are in ideation, we have dialectic', and one of the tasks of the dramatist is to avoid the relativism which results from 'the fragmentation of either drama or dialectic'.[8] A substantial contribution to the dramatic tension in *In the Shadow of the Glen* is made by the syntax, which becomes a form of imagery embodying grammatically the conflict of the play, the tension between life and death which is its central preoccupation. We know from Synge's notebooks that when he was working on the text he was also studying with de Jubainville at the Sorbonne the Old Irish verbal system. He enrolled on February 14th 1902 for the philologist's twice-weekly lectures on this topic. The notebooks also reveal that de Jubainville drew attention to the predilection of Gaelic for stative forms. This stative predilection has been carried over into the verbal paradigms of Irish English, which inherits from Irish Gaelic a tendency to project the subject of the English sentence

> in the role of victim, subject to the operation of destiny . . . In the Irish mode the human being is a suffering object dominated by an elemental force; in the English mode the suffering person is subject of the sentence, its central and only concern, not dominated by his condition.[9]

The stative features of the Irish English verbal system find expression in a sentence structure which is characterised by non-finite 'ing' forms linked by coordination with 'and'. This helps to create a mimesis of speech — more particularly of naive or 'peasant' speech. Equally, however, the syndetic linking of non-finite elements may be so organised as to suggest a cumulative build-up of details and impressions which exist in a contiguous, and therefore essentially metonymic, relationship with each other. Syndesis can also communicate a kinaesthetic sense of expansive-inclusive onward movement. When the linking, as so often in *In the Shadow of the Glen*, is between a series of non-finite 'ing' forms, the verb form is not marked for any specific time sequence and it has a static, or stative, shading. The typical pattern of the play's syntax might be described as a series of stair-like modifications, at times incorporating a dialectally calqued cleft sentence in which the word order is therefore more fluid, or dislocated, than in Standard English:[10]

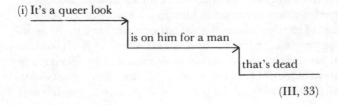

(i) It's a queer look

is on him for a man

that's dead

(III, 33)

(ii)   I,ve a cramp in my back,

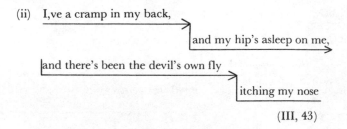

and my hip's asleep on me,

and there's been the devil's own fly

itching my nose

(III, 43)

The formal, forward-moving, right-branching dynamic of the syntax is at times in a state of antithetical tension with the semantic movement of tense back into the past:

(iii)   Then he went into his bed

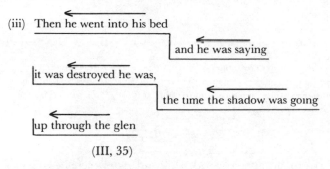

and he was saying

it was destroyed he was,

the time the shadow was going

up through the glen

(III, 35)

These features help to build up an impression of a displaced or alienated time-perspective, of a close contact, yet radical misalignment, between the shut-in routine of the people of the house and the relentless, cosmic rhythms of the natural world. We notice, in (iii) above, that Dan goes in and lies *down* as the shadow was going *up*. Nora's words suggest, without stating it, that the shadow is an agent of destruction, and that Dan is hiding himself away from it in a hopeless effort to escape from its annihilating power. In almost all of the longer speeches of the play up to Scene 4, when the tempo changes, one can trace a subtle combination of past, present and future references in verb forms which are marked for tense, modified by time or place adjuncts, and interwoven with stative, non-finite progressive forms.[11] A representative example occurs in the Tramp's reply, in Scene 1, to Nora's provocative challenge that anyone from outside the house could not 'know the lonesome way I was with no house near me at all' (III, 37):

71

I knew rightly.
(*simple past*)

And I was thinking,
(*past + progressive*)

and I coming in through
(*non-finite progressive*)

the door,

that it's many a lone woman
(*simple present*)

would be afeared of the like of me
(*modal, future / conditional / stative association*)

in the dark night,
(*time-place conflation*)

in a place
(*place adjunct*)

wouldn't be as lonesome
(*modal, future / condit. / stative*)

as this place
(*place adjunct*) (III, 37)

Coming in from the outside world of hill and glen, where he is face to face with the constant threat of mortality, the man of the roads is far more capable than the master of the house of appreciating a lonesome woman's secret hopes and fears. The Tramp's diagnosis of Nora's situation suggests a condition of potential activity frozen in a state of conditional inactivity, of contact *not* made with the realities of time and place. The impression of lonely fear and fragile hope, shut in from yet reaching towards life, is reinforced by the visual imagery. Nora's place, or state, is a shadowy, limbo-like world of the not-living, not-dead — a place 'where there aren't two living souls would see the little light you have shining from the glass' (III, 37). In this case, a 'real' object, the light, associated with Nora by contiguity, becomes a metonymic container, or concrete simulacrum, for her own imprisoned life, and a symbol also of her unfulfilled sexual desires. The sense that for Nora past, present and future are eternally present and possibly unredeemable — because they are shut away from action in her

72

moribund existence with Daniel Burke, her 'not-dead' spouse —
becomes explicit in Scene 3, when she considers the prospect of
marrying Michael Dara. As she reviews her past, the diurnal and
seasonal cycles and the related cycle of human life seem to threaten
and involve her, yet simultaneously to be passing her by. Her
meditation moves from purpose, her intention of marrying Michael in
order to secure herself against the insecurity of age, through passion,
her recollection of the suffering passivity of her existence with Dan, to
perception, her insight into the common subjection of all that exists to
process, change and death. The speech begins with a reference to
Nora's present situation, foregrounding place.

> NORA [*slowly, giving him his tea*]. It's in a lonesome place you do have to be
> talking with someone . . . in the evening of the day (III, 49).

Her 'talking' and 'looking' 'in the evening of the day' have strong
biblical connotations of life itself drawing to a close. She is divided
between her urge to defend herself against the insecurity of living and
her awareness that in order to live more fully she must make demands
upon life which were not met by her existence with Daniel Burke:

> if it's a power of men I'm after knowing they were fine men, for I was a
> hard child to please, and a hard girl to please [*she looks at him a little sternly*],
> and it's a hard woman I am to please this day, Michael Dara, and it's no
> lie, I'm telling you (III, 49).

The steady, strong movement through life and time is halted
abruptly by Michael's pointed question:

> MICHAEL [*looking over to see that* THE TRAMP *is asleep and then, pointing to
> the dead man*]. Was it a hard woman to please you were when you took
> himself for your man? (III, 49)

Nora's reply to this mocking challenge, itself phrased as a question,
suspends time once more in paralysed conditionality. For her, this
marks a second moment of choice, a crucial moment of self-
confrontation:

> What way would I live and I an old woman if I didn't marry a man with a
> bit of a farm, and cows on it, and sheep on the back hills? (III, 49)

Her first impulse is once again to defend herself against the threat of growing old, but the aching conditionality of her query — its absence of explicit reference to past or future — forces into consciousness her deep-seated realisation that to marry Michael Dara would be to repeat the viciously synchronic cycle of not-being which characterises her relationship with Daniel Burke: she is proposing to marry Michael on identical terms and for the same fearful reasons.

The question which Nora poses, 'What way would I live?', is central to the play. Its corollary must be the extent to which either Daniel Burke or Michael Dara might be said to *be* living men, men who can offer life. For Michael, about to count out the stocking of money left by Dan, life is equated with possessions and cash. His counting of Dan's money emphasises that for him Nora, too, is a commodity: his proposal of marriage invites her to sell herself once more. As she watches the young man counting the gold, her dreary existence passes before her as a static (grammatically stative) procession. She sees herself deprived of agency, become merely an observer of the passing years. Her lament rises, in a cumulative crescendo of non-finite verb forms, until she sees herself as a fixed and tormented point at the centre of a moving, whirling cosmos, trapped in the nightmare of her own stasis. What life can there be, she asks,

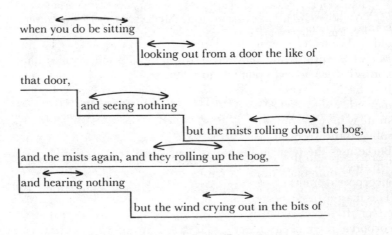

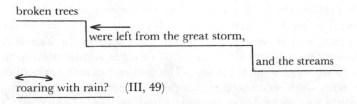

broken trees were left from the great storm, and the streams roaring with rain?   (III, 49)

Nora's 'seeing nothing', 'hearing nothing', 'Isn't it a great while I am', 'Isn't it a long while I am', (III, 49, *passim*) build up into a negative threnody for the barren negation of her life. As her keening continues, she sees herself divorced from activity, eternally 'sitting here in the winter, and the summer, and the fine spring, with the young growing behind me and the old passing' (III, 49). Her cosmic pity and terror are given a local habitation and a name as she remembers *young* Mary Brien 'with two children, and another coming on her in three months or four' (III, 51) and *old* Peggy Cavanagh, 'with no teeth in her mouth, and no sense, and no more hair than you'd see on a bit of a hill and they after burning the furze from it' (III, 51). Outside and inside environment, macrocosm and microcosm, are pressed into contiguity as she envisages the universe itself caught up in a relentless and necessary process of birth and decay, but leaving her morbidly isolated from generation or action.[12]

As Nora's vision becomes simultaneously most individual and most compassionately universal: 'You'll be getting old, and I'll be getting old . . . We'll all be getting old, but it's a queer thing surely' (III, 51-3, *passim*), the process of decay through which the language is leading us *is acted out antithetically for the audience.* Daniel Burke rises, unnoticed at first by Nora, Michael Dara or the Tramp, as the very figure of morbidity with '*his white hair . . . sticking out round his head*' (III, 51). The strategy here is essentially metadramatic: the action both realises and subverts the words. It is also metonymic in the sense in which Kenneth Burke uses the term in his essay 'Four Master Tropes'. 'The basic "strategy" in metonymy', writes Burke, 'is this: to convey some incorporeal or intangible state in terms of the corporeal or tangible'.[13] This master trope, according to Burke, is materialistic in its semantic effect. It reverses the time-bound, historically conditioned loss of corporeal reference from metaphor. Mortality as an abstract general state lamented by Nora materialises in Dan's resurrection. The drama

75

of his rising from the dead — yet not literal rising because he is feigning or playing at death — derives from a playing out of the story of the resurrection as if it were true. The episode confirms the histrionic power of the myth, but it simultaneously subverts any literal-minded temptation to regard the act as fact. The continuities and distinctions between this form of symbolic realism and Mrs Synge's mythologising of history are nicely exploited by the dramatic strategy. The old man's resurrection may appear to bear witness to immortality, but the dramatic context makes him a terminological reduction, a metonymic *figura* of death-in-life.

If *In the Shadow of the Glen* belongs to the type of literature which is organised primarily along metonymic lines, we would expect the tropic patterns to tend towards simile rather than metaphor. The verbal images in *In the Shadow of the Glen* do in fact incline markedly towards this tropic pattern. They also fulfil David Lodge's expectation that such similes should draw their basis for comparison from the contextual semantic field — in this case from the microcosmic world of the shepherds and sheepfarming of the Wicklow glen.[14] In the play, the following complete or conventionally constructed similes occur:

(i)   He [Dan] made a great lep, and let a great cry out of him, and stiffened himself out *the like of* a dead sheep (III, 35).

(ii)   The sheep were lying under the ditch and every one of them coughing, and choking, *like* an old man (III, 39).

(iii)   it's more *like* a pack of old goats than sheep they were (III, 47).

(iv)   the white hair sticking out round you *like* an old bush where sheep do be leaping a gap (III, 51).

(v)   your head'll be *the like of* a bush where sheep do be leaping a gap (III, 55).

(vi)   till the end will come, and they find her stretched *like* a dead sheep with the frost on her (III, 55).

It will be noticed at once that all of these similes contain references to sheep. In (i) and (vi) Nora and Dan respectively compare each other when dead to a dead sheep, but whereas Nora believes Dan to be literally dead, he is maliciously anticipating her end. Examples (iv) and (v) similarly echo each other, with Nora referring to Dan's old age, and Dan anticipating hers. The imagetic analogue this time is a bush, but also 'a bush where sheep do be leaping a gap'. In (ii) there is an important reversal of the roles of tenor and vehicle, when the Tramp compares the (literal) sheep to an (imagetic) old man, while in (iii), the inefficient herd, Michael Dara, follows a good biblical precedent by comparing his scattering, wilful mountain ewes to goats. In the Bible, the pastoral imagery is a vehicle for describing relationships between people and the deity — in the New Testament, between the redeemed and the Redeemer. The gospels, too, reverse the tenor and vehicle of the image of Christ as shepherd and man as sheep when the Redeemer is figuratively represented as the sacrificial lamb, offered up for the people.

The biblical connotations of the sheep/goats simile which precedes Michael's confession of lack of expertise with his flock call to mind the gospel reference to the Good Shepherd who will separate the sheep from the goats. Michael's inability to handle his sheep also places him, by analogy, with the hireling whose flock scatters because he 'careth not for the sheep'.[15] Likewise we are prepared by syntactic and collocational patterns to recognise in Patch Darcy certain qualities which he shares with the Good Shepherd: 'There was never a lamb from his own ewes he wouldn't know before it was marked' (III, 47).

Associations between Patch Darcy, the absent antagonist to Daniel Burke, and the Good Shepherd are also established consistently in the text. The Tramp's account of Patch's last hours suggests that, like the scriptural Good Shepherd, Patch stayed with his sheep through the great storm, talking to them out of the thick mist. Darcy — 'that was a great man, young fellow, a great man' (III, 47) — is compared implicitly *but not identified metaphorically with* the Son of Man. The implied, but this time antithetical, comparison continues with the account of his death: 'and the third day they found Darcy . . . and I wasn't afeared any more' (III, 39).

It is important to recognise that the dramatic strategy consistently refuses to *identify* Patch Darcy with the Good Shepherd. Patch courageously, even heroically, stayed by his sheep but he could not protect them from the hardships of nature or from mortality — they were 'coughing, and choking, like an old man' (III, 39). There are no claims that he can offer them life everlasting. Although he is a legendary figure who lives on in the 'great stories' (III, 39) of the people of the glen, and although he is praised as a 'great man', Patch was found when he had been 'eaten with crows' (III, 37). Also, the Tramp's fear of Patch ends when he finds that the great man is dead, not risen like Dan Burke or like Christ.

Our obvious 'risen man' in the play, then, is not Darcy, but Dan. This role, too, is, however, antithetically treated, once again discouraging any too easy type-to-type identification. Dan is playing at death and resurrection: he is a fraudulent corpse. But he is also little better than a fraud when he claims to be a living man. As Nora tells the Tramp, 'Maybe cold would be no sign of death with the like of him, for he was always cold' (III, 35). It is he himself who asks the splendidly ironic and ambivalent question, 'How would I be dead, and I as dry as a baked bone?' (III, 43). Nevertheless it *is* the non-dead old man who enacts the resurrection in the play and does it twice, for good measure. It is he who is dressed in a queer white robe, who carries a stick or staff and whose hair sticks out like an old bush round his head — a reminder of the crown of thorns. These parallels between Daniel Burke and Christ encourage us to recognise retrospectively the allusions, in Nora's description of her spouse's feigned expiry, to the account, in Luke's Gospel, of the death of Jesus: he 'was saying it was destroyed he was, the time the shadow was going up through the glen' (III, 35). Luke recounts how, as Christ's agony reached its climax, 'there was a darkness over all the earth until the ninth hour'. [16] On the hour, 'the sun was darkened . . . And when Jesus had cried with a loud voice . . . he gave up the ghost'. [17] Dan chooses the moment for his *salto mortale* with an evangelically impeccable sense of pathetic fallacy: 'when the sun set on the bog beyond he made a great lep, and let a great cry out of him, and stiffened himself out the like of the dead sheep' (III, 35).

In establishing and sustaining the tension between type and antitype in the play's quest for the true Good Shepherd hero, the real Son of Man, Synge subtly develops the theme of the sexual deprivations and longings in Nora's existence. The significance of 'he was always cold, every day since I knew him — and every night, stranger —' (III, 35) is obvious. It is underlined by her description of herself as a lone woman, by the Tramp's remarks about the little light and by the double meaning of the references to her intercourse with Patch Darcy and the 'power of men' she is 'after knowing' (III, 49). By contrast Dan is by his own confession moribund, sterile and impotent, 'as dry as a baked bone' (III, 43) with 'a great drouth on me' (III, 57).

Michael Dara and Dan clearly are both inadequate partners for Nora: neither measures up to the criteria established in the play for a man. As a shepherd, Michael is something of a fraud himself. Nora describes him as 'a kind of a farmer has come up from the sea' (III, 41).[18] He compares unfavourably with the Tramp, being too 'afeard of the dead' (III, 45) to look at Dan. Like his ancient rival he displays a marked propensity for criticising and complaining. He shares his mentor's drouth and his thirst. The fate of his unfortunate ewes: 'they were running off into one man's bit of oats, and another man's bit of hay, and tumbling into the red bogs till it's more like a pack of old goats than sheep they were' (III, 47) betrays his comparable sexual inadequacies — as well as his equally literal-minded indifference to the self-revelatory powers of language. Apart from his frustrated pursuit of sheep, lambs and ewes, Michael's other interest is money. He is the hireling shepherd. Instead of leading his sheep, he chases them about.

For Michael, the fact that Dan has left 'a good sum' (III, 49) should compensate Nora for having taken the old lecher as her man and it is certainly more than ample to buy off his suspicions about her other relationships. His counting aloud of the gold is carefully orchestrated with Nora's lament for her own barrenness as she thinks of Mary Brien, 'with two children, and another coming on her in three months or four' (III, 51), effectively making the point that for him price is more important than progeny. His presumptuous conviction that Nora will marry him is prefaced by references to money: 'Twenty pound for the lot, Nora Burke . . . and then you'll marry me' (III, 51). If Michael becomes their master, Nora and the sheep will share the same fate: both will be considered in terms of maximum return for minimum investment. This anticipated repetition of her eked-out existence with Dan becomes Nora's own waking nightmare when she begins to see the inevitable consequences of allowing Michael to take Dan's place:

> NORA. In a little while, I'm telling you, you'll be sitting up in your bed — the way himself was sitting — with a shake in your face, and your teeth falling, and the white hair sticking out round you like an old bush where sheep do be leaping a gap (III, 51).

As if conjured up by Nora's words, Dan rises to incarnate her worst fears, and to complete the identification between himself and the young pretender to his bed.

At the moment of his second resurrection, Nora remembers Dan with a 'rough word in his mouth, and his chin the way it would take the bark from the edge of an oak board you'd have building a door' (III, 53). With the link between Dan and oak boards and door established, yet another biblical line of metonymic association emerges. Deictic references to the cottage door abound in Dan's speeches in Scene 4: 'You'll walk out now from that door' (III, 53). 'Let you walk out through that door, I'm telling you' (III, 55). 'Let her walk out of that door, and let you go along with her stranger' (III, 55). 'Go out of that door, I'm telling you, and do your blathering below in the glen' (III, 57).

If we turn to the New Testament sources of the Good Shepherd story, the full significance of these emphatic references is revealed, and we are also returned, with renewed understanding, to Nora's lament 'what good is a bit of a farm . . . when you do be sitting, looking out from a door the like of that door' (III, 49). The dramatic strategy once again draws its symbolic strength from the Bible and at the same time stands the sacred text on its head. In John, Chapter 10, we find the following pastoral verses:

> Then said Jesus unto them again, Verily, verily, I say unto you, I am the door of the sheep. All that ever came before me are thieves and robbers . . . I am the door: by me if any man enter in, he shall be saved, and shall go in and out, and find pasture.[19]

In Synge's dramatised version there can be little doubt that Dan newly risen from the dead, '*in queer white clothes*' (III, 53) with his hair standing out round his head, like a furze bush, and a stick in his hand, standing by the door and referring pointedly and repeatedly to it, is an analogue, and at the same time a complete opposite, of the Good Shepherd: he is the door, but a door that shuts and imprisons rather than allowing the sheep to go in and out. Unlike the Good Shepherd, Dan can neither tolerate any living voice nor offer any life-giving benediction. The highest, and only, praise he offers in the play is conferred upon Michael Dara for his verbal parsimony, for being 'a quiet man' (III, 59). As always, his own words speak eloquently against him. His spiteful rejection of Nora's kindly pity clinches the antithetical analogy:

> DAN. It's proud and happy you'd be if I was getting my death the day I was shut of yourself. [*Pointing to the door.*] (III, 55)

The scriptural theme continues as Michael, the hireling, tries to scuttle out through the door, abandoning Nora to her fate. Counter of the cash, he is the thief that cometh not, but for to kill and to destroy. Dan, the fraudulent pastor, drives Nora away, refusing to shelter or feed her: 'let you not be passing this way if it's hungry you are, or wanting a bed' (III, 55).

Where does the Tramp fit into this biblical-pastoral scheme? The title 'stranger' conferred on him by Nora should equate him scripturally with the hireling. Yet although the Tramp is not a shepherd, he speaks knowledgeably of sheep, can judge a bad shepherd when he sees one, and admires Patch Darcy's pastoral skills. Perhaps the most significant feature of his agentive role is the way in which he is linked with the absent Patch. Like Nora, he knew Darcy and he shares her admiration for him as a man. Like Darcy, he is a man who spends his time intimately connected with the earth, walking on his two feet, passing up and passing down. Very early in the drama, in what we might call one of the play's unobtrusive similes, he compares himself with Patch. He'd 'maybe have . . . been eaten with crows *the like* of Patch Darcy' (III, 37). Patch's name supplies yet another line of association between the two men: while watching over Dan, the Tramp sits patching his coat with the sharp needle which Nora has taken from her breast. This patched coat is a nice contrast with Dan's queer, white, seamless garment, which is, in effect, a shroud. But the implication that the Tramp has assumed Patch Darcy's mantle is not left solely to sartorial details. The words which collocate most particularly with him in play are the semi-synonymous items 'talk', 'blather' and 'voice', which link him with Darcy's 'living voice' (III, 39). It is because of his talk that Dan detests him, and that Nora finally chooses to go with him:

> NORA. You've a *fine bit of talk*, stranger and it's with yourself I'll go (III, 57, my italics).

It does a grave injustice to the complexity and strength of Synge's vision to see the Tramp's offer as an invitation to a form of romantic escapism. Neither he nor Nora despises what the house at least potentially might have to offer. The Tramp appreciates the shelter from 'the rain falling', the 'light', and 'sup of new milk and a quiet decent corner where a man could sleep' (III, 33, *passim*). He looks to the house for tidiness and order, and commends the 'fine spirits, and good tobacco, and the best of pipes' (III, 37). The invitation to Nora is offered only after he has interceded unsuccessfully *twice* on her behalf, once with Dan, and once with Michael Dara:

> TRAMP [*pointing to* MICHAEL]. Maybe himself would take her.
> NORA. What would he do with me now?
> TRAMP. Give you the half of a dry bed, and good food in your mouth (III, 55).

Only when Michael fails her utterly does the Tramp turn to Nora, with the words which echo her initial kindly greeting:

> We'll be going now, lady of the house — the rain is falling but the air is kind, and *maybe* it'll be a grand morning by the grace of God (III, 55, my italics).

Nor are the harshly autonomous realities of the natural world comfortably stylised or aestheticised in the Tramp's invitation. Although a fine bit of talk may help man — and woman too — to come to terms with mortality, it does not afford protection against the hardships of life and the inevitability of death. Throughout the Tramp's final speeches, negative and affirmative elements coexist in a state of dramatic antithesis. The negative forms in the Tramp's oration serve a severe functional purpose, and the Irish English cleft sentence pattern foregrounds the negation. The hard realities of existence and the shadow of mortality are present in the very syntactical choices, as Nora wryly appreciates when she replies, 'I'm thinking it's myself will be wheezing that time with lying down under the heavens when the night is cold' (III, 57). What *is* offered is a release from the obsessive paralysis of inactivity, from 'sitting up on a wet ditch . . . making yourself old with looking on each day and it passing you by' (III, 57), an escape from the morbidity of those whose 'talk', like Dan's, is 'of getting old . . . and losing the hair off you, and the light of your eyes'(III, 57).

The pastoral themes in *In the Shadow of the Glen* are developed in such a way that they establish a bridge between the literal and the figurative, the local and the biblical context, without sacrificing the integrity of each to the other. Just as easy identification between types is prevented, so too the differentiation between characters is not simply, or simplistically, conceived. The epithet 'queer' is the lexical link which binds all of the characters together into a common brotherhood akin to that which Maurya invokes in *Riders to the Sea*. Dan is 'queer'; Michael Dara talks of Patch Darcy going 'queer in the head'; the Tramp speaks of 'queer' looks and 'queer' talk. At the moment of Dan's second 'resurrection', Nora's expression of wondering pity gathers us all into the processes of mortality, echoing as she does so the words of the Aran girl who remarked to Synge, 'Priests is queer people, and I don't know who isn't' (II, 114):

> NORA. It's a pitiful thing to be getting old, but it's a queer thing surely . . .
> God forgive me, Michael Dara, we'll all be getting old, but it's a queer
> thing surely (III, 51-3).

Nora's sense of the irony of human life is 'true irony, humble irony . . . based upon a sense of fundamental kinship with the enemy, as one *needs* him, is indebted to him, is not merely outside him as an observer but contains him *within*, being consubstantial with him'.[20] But Dan rejects her gracious offer and she leaves him with a final warning that in so doing he has chosen a living death, a 'black life', and will soon exchange his game for the reality: 'it's not long, I'm telling you, till you'll be lying again under that sheet, and you dead surely' (III, 57). Shutting the door on Nora and the Tramp, and pulling his erstwhile rival into his drouth-ridden haven, the impotent Daniel Burke offers Michael Dara, with characteristic parsimony, a 'little taste' (III, 57) of his whiskey. Like two characters in a Beckett play, the old man and the young, the closed oak door and the blasted sapling, drink a pledge to each other. Language takes its final revenge when the mercenary Michael, the man of few words, offers to nay-saying Dan, the risen corpse, the pious prayer

God reward you, Daniel Burke, and may you have a long life and a quiet life, and good health with it (III, 59).

Drinking a toast with the water of life to longevity, silence and stasis, they turn the word for the last time against themselves, effectively pledging each other's annihilation.

NOTES

1. Mikhail Bakhtin, *Rabelais and His World*, translated by Hélène Iswolsky (Cambridge Massachusetts and London, Massachusetts Institute of Technology, 1968), pp. 212-13.

2. Edward Stephens, *My Uncle John: Edward Stephens's Life of J M Synge*, ed. Andrew Carpenter (London, Oxford University Press, 1974), p. 36.

3. André Gide, *L'Immoraliste* (Paris 1929), p. 61. The English quotation given here is from Frederic Jameson, *The Prison-House of Language; A Critical Account of Structuralism and Russian Formalism* (Princeton and London, Princeton University Press, 1972), p. 177.

4. TCD MS 4350, f. 87.

5. Ibid., f. 59.

6. Ibid., f. 59.

7. Paul M. Levitt, *A Structural Approach to the Analysis of Drama* (The Hague and Paris, Mouton, 1971), p. 26.

8. Kenneth Burke, *A Grammar of Motives* (New York, Prentice-Hall, Inc., 1945), p. 512.

9. P.L. Henry, *Language, Culture and the Nation* (Dublin, Comharchumann Chois Fharraige, 1974), p. 10.

10. I am indebted to Dr Loreto Todd of the Department of English, University of Leeds, for this description of the pattern of Synge's syntax, and for suggesting the method of representing it which is adopted here.

11. The references to 'scene' follow Synge's practice of adopting the classical French definition of 'a portion of the total play in which the stage is occupied by an unchanging group of players'. See Alan S. Downer (ed.), *The Art of the Play: An Anthology of Nine Plays* (New York, Holt, 1955), p. 170.

12. Nora's paralysis has an affinity with Eveline's in Joyce's short story of that name, in *Dubliners*.

13. Burke, *A Grammar of Motives*, p. 506.

14. David Lodge, *The Modes of Modern Writing: Metaphor, Metonymy, and the Typology of Modern Literature* (London, Edward Arnold, 1977), p. 113.

15. The Gospel According to St John, 10.13.

16. The Gospel According to St Luke, 23.44.
17. Ibid., 23. 45-6.
18. Michael is, in this sense, a dead, or drowned, man, as well as an alien.
19. The Gospel According to St John, 10.3.
20. Burke, *A Grammar of Motives*, p. 514.

5.
THE PLAY OF LIFE:
The Tinker's Wedding Revisited

ALTHOUGH THE Rabelaisian note is part of the tonality of *In the Shadow of the Glen*, the dominant mood, as the title suggests, is elegiac. In *The Tinker's Wedding* the mood is one of gay festivity as Synge takes up and develops the wedding-with-blows motif which plays a major part in the popular Carnival tradition. The play is a Mayday folly; into its earlier drafts were incorporated elements of the folk drama of The Green Man, a popular version of the Gawain story. The main reason why it was not staged by the Irish National or Abbey Theatre during his life-time was almost certainly because, in Synge's own words, it was thought 'too immoral and anticlerical' (IV, xiv).

One of the rare critical assessments of the play to offer an adequate approach to its formal and thematic properties takes its title from Synge's judgement: it is Denis Donoghue's short but suggestive essay 'Too Immoral for Dublin', in which he argues that while he does not wish to 'exaggerate the merits of the play', its unjustifed dismissal by critics is caused by a failure to appreciate the nature of its comedy.[1] 'In this play', writes Donoghue, 'Synge has contrived his comic effects from the sheer interplay of attitudes on certain questions of morality and social living'.[2] The comedy 'depends on the mock-conflict between certain attitudes in the tinkers themselves and all those other conventions which are covered by the word "orthodoxy"'.[3] The key to the drama lies in the word 'mock-conflict': both tinkers and priest, as this analysis hopes to show, are as much influenced by each other's 'orthodoxies' as by their own. The whole spirit of the drama is that of a

87

playful challenge to conventional judgements and behaviour. The designs which the work has upon us as audience have to be met, Synge suggested, with an attitude of mind which is 'rich and genial and humorous', in which we are prepared to laugh and be laughed at 'without malice', while acknowledging the seriousness of our need for 'the nourishment, not very easy to define, on which our imaginations live' (IV, 3).

The Tinker's Wedding undoubtedly differs in some obvious respects from the rest of Synge's plays. It is the only one with a two-act structure, if we exclude the two-act version of *When the Moon Has Set*; the 'alternative society' is represented not by peasants or tramps but by tinkers; and it alone risks bringing on-stage the character of a priest in a setting contemporaneous with Synge's audience. It is also the most consistently funny of the comedies, sustaining throughout the mood of a festive game. The tinker's wedding itself — there are two ceremonies in the play, a wedding and an anti-wedding — is a version of the traditional *nopces à mitaines*. Far from the violence being gratuitous, it has roots in the carnivalesque folk ritual. In the carnival idiom we find

> a characteristic logic, the peculiar logic of the 'inside out' (*à l'envers*), of the 'turnabout', of a continual shifting from top to bottom, from front to rear, of numerous parodies and travesties, humiliations, profanations, comic crownings and uncrownings.[4]

Part of the logic of reversal involves a linguistic shift from language which is censored and hierarchic to the freedom of the banquet world which 'had the power of liberating the word from the shackles of piousness and fear of God'.[5] Having made this claim, one must, however, enter a caveat against any easy identification of the tinkers with anarchy, freedom or an Edenic life which 'possibly antedates the Fall of Man', and of the priest with conventional morality and law.[6] The dramatic action, including the play's notoriously 'illogical' resolution, defies any such yea or nay interpretation.

The two-act structure of *The Tinker's Wedding* presents us with a plot in which the relationship between tinker and priest is essentially dialectical rather than exclusively antagonistic. Synge based the action upon an anecdote which he recounts in the Wicklow notebooks about a tinker couple who made a bargain with a priest to marry them for half a sovereign plus a tin can, but who told him on their return that they couldn't give the can because 'the ass gave it a kick this morning the way it isn't fit for you at all' (IV, 229). The teller of this brief tale adopts the expected social attitude towards the tinkers, regarding them as schemers and liars, while no attempt is made to pass any judgement on the priest. With this slight episode as the starting point, Synge develops a plot in which tinkers and priest, usually regarded as being at opposite ends of the social spectrum, are brought together by the apparently irrational, motiveless desire of Sarah Casey to legalise and solemnise her longstanding relationship with Michael Byrne.

The action through which the plot moves is from an initial situation of uneasy tension through a relationship of temporary compromise when the bargain is struck between tinkers and priest to a hasty parting of the ways. They do not, however, part company without considerable mutual disturbances and readjustments taking place, which reveal the tensions which unite as well as divide them. Throughout the play, Synge works continuously to make us aware of the bonds between the two groups. As in so many of his plays, he disturbs conventional expectations and encourages us to look for the interdependent forces of coherence and incoherence beneath the social surface.

The Tinker's Wedding takes up and in a sense inverts the dramatic movement of *In the Shadow of the Glen*. Here also there are four present characters: Sarah Casey, a young tinker, her man, another Michael, his widowed mother, Mary, and the Parish Priest, who assumes, with important differences, Daniel Burke's implicit sacerdotal role. In place of Patch Darcy, the play's absent hero, is Jaunting Jim, a man with 'a grand eye for a fine horse, and a grand eye for a woman' (IV, 11).[7] In *The Tinker's Wedding* Sarah Casey is a woman of the roads, but the 'sort of tent' (IV, 7) the tinkers have set up on a particular May evening is dangerously '*near a village*' (IV, 5) and next a '*chapel-gate*' (IV, 7), and Sarah, in the opening lines of the play, expresses a strange desire to 'see his reverence this place, Michael Byrne, and he passing backward to his house to-night' (IV, 7). The young woman has felt what to her tinker man and his mother seems a retrogressive springtime madness — a backward and perverse urge to have Michael make her securely, by law, religion and social convention, his sworn bride at the altar. Sarah plagues Michael to make her a ring that is 'having [his] hands destroyed' (IV, 7) and that cuts her own finger 'with the edges sharp' (IV, 9). She wants to be bound to Michael by the same law and sacrament as the grand ladies from the city of Dublin.

Unlike Michael Dara of *In the Shadow of the Glen* or the priest-ridden Shawn Keogh of *The Playboy of the Western World*, Sarah's man is bitterly opposed to his woman's pious intentions. 'What will you gain', he asks angrily 'dragging me to the priest this night?' (IV, 7). Yet the three characters have much in common, their greed — Michael Byrne, like Michael Dara, is always concerned about gain — their verbal parsimony, and a concomitant poverty of imagination which prevents all of them from understanding their women's needs on anything higher than a bread-and-butter level. Michael Byrne cannot see why Sarah should want anything more than the physical comfort she has and he is shocked rather than moved by her poetry talk. He recalls how he once made her 'quiet and easy' with 'a great clout in the lug' (IV, 9), and he mocks at her delight in Jaunting Jim's poetic name for her, 'The Beauty of Ballinacree' (IV, 11).

It seems clear that Michael's inability to respond to Sarah's energetic, if idealising, poetic vision of herself as a Spring goddess when 'you'll be waking up in the dark night and thinking you see me coming with the sun on me, and I driving a high cart with Jaunting Jim going behind' (IV, 11) is at least partly the cause of her connubial dissatisfaction. His chief reason for conceding to her wishes about the wedding is his fear that by losing Sarah he will be losing a very saleable commodity:

MICHAEL [*gloomily*]. If I didn't marry her she'd be walking off to Jaunting Jim maybe at the fall of night; and it's well yourself knows there isn't the like of her for getting money and selling songs to the men (IV, 35).

Sarah hopes to transform her existence with Michael by taking him before the priest, who is 'a big boast of a man with a long step on him and a trumpeting voice' (IV, 13). This vigorous description of his reverence's person goes beyond the bounds of admiration for the religious powers of his office alone. As well as the strange poetic attraction which she feels towards the spoken word of the priest — Michael is a man of few words — she seems excited by the virile physical presence of the man. We have here an interesting contrast to the emaciated holy father of *The Well of the Saints* with 'your worn feet, and your welted knees, and your fasting, holy ways' (III, 149).

The theme of the priest's double life is suggested by certain tropic patterns in the play and by a Rabelaisian use of props. It is hinted at early on in Michael's reference to certain very unpriestly nocturnal pursuits:

> MICHAEL. It's often his reverence does be in there playing cards, or drinking a sup, or singing songs, until the dawn of day (IV, 13),

and it is further developed by the language and the stage business when Sarah orders Michael to 'make a great blaze now' (IV, 13) with the fire, so that when he arrives the holy man can look upon her face. Already in the opening scene a more than passing affinity has been established between clergyman and tinkers, which must surely disturb the audience's ability to decide how to respond to each group just as effectively as does the admiring appointment of a self-confessed murderer to the post of pot-boy and defender of lone women in *The Playboy of the Western World*. Far from there being 'no lasting commerce possible between the two modes of existence', the bonds which unite them are subtle and strong.[8] As soon as they meet, we are asked to reverse any orthodox expectations about their relationship to each other: it is his reverence who bargains for money and holds out against marriage, while Sarah pleads for the sacramental setting to rights of her unblessed liaison, virtuously offering him a hard-earned half-sovereign bearing upon its face the imprint of that paragon of marital propriety, Queen Victoria:

> SARAH [*pleadingly, taking money from her pocket*]. Wouldn't you have a little mercy on us, your reverence? [*Holding out money.*] Wouldn't you marry us for a half a sovereign, and it a nice shiny one with a view on it of the living king's mamma? (IV, 15)

The obvious incarnation of opposition to the rules and regulations which the holy father officially represents is old Mary Byrne, who has no time — at least until violence threatens — for going to the chapel, and who knows full well that paying gold to his reverence would scarcely 'make a woman stop when she's a mind to go' (IV, 35). Mary's emblem is the beer jug and her anthem the law-defying anti-clerical song 'The Night before Larry was Stretched'. She makes her entrance carrying a jug of porter and singing her song at the very moment when the priest, having coveted the can which Michael is making, agrees to marry the couple if it is thrown in as part of the price. Yet even Mary is not simply the anarchic *antagonist* of the priest. She has in common with him a love of the bottle, or the jug, and if she regards the official sacraments of the church as 'all in my eye,/By the clergy first invented' (IV, 17), she is not without her own rites and rituals to help her pass the time when she is 'sitting lonesome on a fine night, hearing the dogs barking, and the bats squeaking, and you saying over, it's a short while only till you die' (IV, 27). She resolves before night passes to celebrate a bacchanalian communion with his reverence and she shrewdly recognises a related irreligious urge in him:

> MARY [*sees the priest, and holds out jug towards him*]. God save your reverence. I'm after bringing down a smart drop; and let you drink it up now, for it's a middling drouthy man you are at all times, God forgive you, and this night is cruel dry (IV, 17).

Vivian Mercier in his essay on the play suggests that Synge may have meant us 'to understand that the Priest is drunk in Act I and sober in Act II' and he raises the question of whether, if this is so 'he might have dared to be more explicit in drafts than in the published version'.[9] Taking up this suggestion, and examining the drafts, we find the speculation richly confirmed.[10] In one draft, Michael refers to the priest as 'talking to himself above on the road' while Nora — the name first given to Sarah Casey — describes him as 'a big boast of a man *with drink taken*'.[11]

Again, in the exchange between Mary Byrne and the priest, his reverence is more pointed in his criticism of the bishop, as well as confessing to springtime urges in himself:

> PRIEST. It's hard life I'm telling you, a hard life surely on a fine spring, and there's the Lord Bishop coming up in the morning and he an old bitter man would have you destroyed if he seen a thing at all — — (*he sighs again*) — —[12]

In the draft version of Act II, Nora/Sarah refers to the priest as 'only humbugging us . . . the time he'd drink taken' and she mocks at him by asking scornfully 'Wouldn't any fool talk you round the time you're after drinking your glass?'[13]

Earlier drafts certainly substantiate Mercier's speculations about Synge's intentions. But drama is, of course, more than words upon the page. In the final version of the play, Synge's controlled handling of the potentially dangerous theme of the close, non-hierarchic, human relationship between priest and tinkers, partly directed, no doubt, by his awareness of the social constraints within which he was working, lends to the final version a pervasive comic irony, in which words, gestures, tropic patterns and properties all act in collusion to create an effect which is essentially subversive of any attempt to divorce them from each other. The initial encounter between Mary and the priest is worth examining in detail, to show how a pattern is created which subtly suggests that the celibate man of the cloth shares with the widowed Mary a drouth which needs more than a jug of porter for its satisfaction. The empathy which is established between them also prepares the way for Mary's final plea on his behalf when Sarah and Michael suggest that they run him in a boghole to keep him from talking.

As Mary enters and presses her services upon the priest, carrying the jug of porter in both hands, like a chalice, she advances towards him singing her 'hymn' over the fire. This is the fire which Michael has fanned into a great blaze so that Sarah's physical charms may be illuminated and it is also the one in which he has forged wedding-ring and gallon can. The tinkers' fire is the bonfire of the carnival tradition, symbol alike of death and of birth. Mary Casey is the great representative, in the play, of this dual principle of death and birth which characterises folk literature and folk rituals. It is old Mary who offers to charm away the fears of the dark with her 'story would be fit to tell a woman . . . in the spring-time of the year' (IV, 25). Mary's story has 'great queens in it, making themselves matches from the start to the end, and they with shiny silks on them the length of the day, and white shifts for the night' (IV, 23). It is she who delights, finally, even in the imprecations called down on the tinkers by the priest. When she calls upon him here to sit with her by the fire and 'drink a sup' (IV, 17), she is transforming the flames that devour from a funeral pyre to a 'gay kitchen hearth'.[14] The priest's words of warning against Mary's advances, 'Let you not be falling to the flames. Keep off, I'm saying' (IV, 17), speak from the world of prohibition and fear which is his official dwelling-place. But they are also only a half-hearted attempt to ward off the temptation which he feels, as a man, to abandon himself to the carnival spirit.

The old woman continues her tone of bantering sympathy by starting to sing a 'bad wicked song' (IV, 19) about lying in a ditch and beating a tenpenny can, holding the porter-jug aloft as she does so. The song about the beating of the can takes up the *nopces à mitaines* theme. It looks back to Michael's forging of the gallon can and the tin ring and forward to the ritual beating of the priest when the tinkers tie him in the sack which held the purloined vessel. 'The wedding drum', writes Bakhtin, 'had an erotic connotation. To beat this drum meant to perform the sexual act; the "drummer" . . . was the lover'.[15] Mary breaks off from her singing not out of deference to the priest's innocence or the sanctity of his office, but rather because 'it's bad enough he is, I'm thinking, without ourselves making him worse' (IV, 19). Her words here appear to give the lie to Mercier's suggestion that the tinkers 'seem never to have eaten of the Tree of Knowledge, for they have no sense of sin'.[16] At this point Mary is lifted aloft, chalice and all, at her own request, by Sarah and laid down in the ditch. From this position she continues her secular celebration of the Last Supper, her own *missa de potatoribus*:

> MARY [*to the* PRIEST]. Let you drink it up, holy father. Let you drink it up, I'm saying, and not be letting on you wouldn't do the like of it, and you with a stack of pint bottles above, reaching the sky (IV, 19).

The mention of the sky-high stack of priestly pints finally brings about his reverence's capitulation. Carrying the play's process of comic role-reversal full circle, the old woman pronounces her blessing on their secular communion. This ceremony is, we would argue, *the* tinker's wedding — and Mary is both celebrant and bride. The physical contact of the pat on the leg startles the priest back into an orthodox reassertion of his institutional moral role:

94

PRIEST [*interrupting her*]. What is it I want with your songs when it'd be better for the like of you, that'll soon die, to be down on your two knees saying prayers to the Almighty God? (IV, 21)

Mary neatly turns the tables by reminding his reverence that the saying of prayers belongs more properly to his office than to hers, for 'I've heard tell a power of times it's that you're for' (IV, 21). She is not averse, either, to the priest's peculiar poetic attractions. Mary has a great regard for, and curiosity about, the power of words, but when she urges him to perform for her, with a magnificently subversive assumption of equal authority she offers him benediction and communion as a reward:

MARY [*catching hold of him*]. Stop till you say a prayer, your reverence; stop till you say a little prayer, I'm telling you, and I'll give you my blessing and the last sup from the jug (IV, 21).

When Sarah tries to capitalise on this shockingly unorthodox behaviour by persuading his reverence to marry her as an insurance against growing into 'an old, flagrant heathen, would destroy the world' (IV, 21), Mary comically continues the process of subversion by presenting the worthy effort at orthodoxy as sure evidence of the degeneracy of the younger generation and their lack of moral standards, even going so far as to accuse Sarah of flirting with the priest. Left alone, the old woman is shaken by the fear of death:

MARY [*standing up slowly*]. It's gone they are, and I with my feet that weak under me you'd knock me down with a rush, and my head with a noise in it the like of what you'd hear in a stream and it running between two rocks and rain falling (IV, 25).

In her solitude, unlanguaged Nature appears to her frightening and dehumanising, just as it does to the solitary Nora Burke, left with the silent Dan. The story-teller's art, like language itself, is a social art, and deprived of listeners, Mary has little use for her fine tales and small consolation from them either. Like Nora, she knows what it is to feel the shadow of death, 'sitting lonesome on a fine night hearing the dogs barking, and the bats squeaking, and you saying over, it's a short while only till you die' (IV, 27). The old tinker's commitment, however, is to

95

this life. She refuses to deceive herself with the belief that her stories can offer her an escape from the reality of age and death. Scorning 'a little stroke on your head' (IV, 27) she filches the tin from the sack and exchanges it for the empty porter bottles. On her way to barter it for a good drop she goes out defiantly singing the secular anthem with which she first greeted the priest.

By the end of the first act, Synge has succeeded in establishing an unorthodox but profoundly human relationship between the old tinker woman and the priest. As the second act opens, Sarah's wedding preparations are going on apace, with the emphasis on her ambition to have herself and Michael look and behave like any of the priest's orthodox, baptised and shriven couples from the village. When the old woman wakens, the action begins to revolve again around the gallon can, or the substitute porter bottles, wrapped in the sack. Sarah's angry reaction to Mary's proposal that she should 'sell the can to the parson's daughter below, a harmless poor creature would fill your hand with shillings for a brace of lies' (IV, 31) prepares the way for the violence which is to characterise this act: Sarah is in deadly earnest about her determination to be made decent. If, however, there is a weakness in the play, it occurs at this point. Frightened and angered by Sarah's violence, Mary retorts by threatening to blacken her reputation with all and sundry by 'telling old and young you're a weathered heathen savage, Sarah Casey, the one did put down a head of the parson's cabbage to boil in the pot with your clothes, and quenched the flaming candles on the throne of God the time your shadow fell within the pillars of the chapel door' (IV, 33). As old and young tinkers quarrel, the priest enters and Sarah, in pursuit of Mary, '*springs round nearly into* [his] *arms*' (IV, 33). He is described as '*half-terrified at the language he has heard*' (IV, 33) and he is moved by his fear to renege on his promise to wed the tinker couple.

It is difficult to accept that a change from inebriation to sobriety would make the priest of Act I quite so easily shocked simply by any of the words which he has overheard here. Granted that he may be superstitious, or even uneasy about administering the sacrament to people so obviously removed from the theological state of grace, his reaction nevertheless seems excessive. It is interesting, therefore, to return to our examination of earlier versions of the play, to see if Synge at any time contemplated a stronger alternative motivation for his change of heart — and we do, indeed, find that this is the case. In an unpublished draft, Mary threatens to reveal Sarah's gaming at enticing 'downy boys' and 'aged fellows' to give her money by promising to meet them in the hills.[17] Such a reputation would, of course, have far more serious implications for the priest if he were known to have had dealings with Sarah than the possibly tamer, if more comic, crime of the stewed clothes and the cabbage, or even the sudden quenching of the candles. The cooking together of clothes and cabbage, nevertheless, is an act of culinary unorthodoxy which is related tropically to the Widow Quin's lamb stew in *The Playboy of the Western World*, in which the Lord Bishop felt the elements of a Christian. Both recipes, in turn, have their origins in carnivalesque folk parodies of the Lord's supper, and both have sexual connotations. In one such ceremony, for example, Rabelais's Kissarse celebrates the earth's coq à l'âne fecundity in a speech praising the Oceanic Sea which is 'pregnant with a potful of cabbage'.[18]

A concealed vestige of the hinted involvement of his reverence in the shadier side of such *commercium hominum* remains in the published version of Synge's play, in the priest's uneasy reaction to Sarah's threat to report him to the bishop: 'I'm thinking it's a risky thing getting mixed in any matters with the like of you' (IV, 33). It also emerges in a later threat from Sarah about the revenge the tinkers will take if he reports them to the peelers:

> SARAH. If you do, you'll be getting all the tinkers from Wicklow and Wexford, and the County Meath, to put up block tin in the place of glass to shield your windows *where you do be looking out and blinking at the girls* (IV, 45, my italics).

The priest's determination to possess Sarah's can as well as her gold also lends weight to the suggestion that priest and tinker share a knowledge of each other which makes the holy father's recantation, followed by his second capitulation to Sarah's insistence that he marry her, all too *appropriately* sudden.

His reverence's instructions to Sarah and Michael to 'come up to the chapel when you see me looking from the door' (IV, 35) provide the occasion for Mary to realise what plans are afoot and to confront the couple with what she sees as the folly of orthodox marriage rites. Twice Sarah insists that the sacred rites will confer respectability on her — only to have Mary remind her that the social status which she envies may cause more problems than it solves:

> MARY [*soothingly*]. It's as good a right you have surely, Sarah Casey, but what good will it do? Is it putting that ring on your finger will keep you from getting an aged woman and losing the fine face you have, or be easing your pains, when it's the grand ladies do be married in silk dresses, with rings of gold, that do pass any woman with their share of torment in the hour of birth? (IV, 37)

'The end of festive freedom', notes Bakhtin, 'is clearly heralded by the ringing of the morning church bells'.[19] As Mary reaches the chapel-gate, the priest comes out in his surplice, obviously impatient at the length of time he is being forced to spend praying. The change in the holy father's costume at this point marks his resumption of an official role now that the sober morning has dawned. In assuming his robes of office, he divests himself of his nocturnal masculinity: surplice and cassock are 'female' garments. The gaming between the two sides is rapidly drawing to a close. The time of hard reckoning is signalled by the priest's demand to see the colour of the tinkers' gold and to take the can in his hands. He is in no mood now for Sarah's fine words. In his greedy determination to view and to handle the can he scornfully dismisses her attempts to praise it as a work of art:

> PRIEST [*taking the bundle*]. Give it here into my hand, Sarah Casey. What is it any person would think of a tinker making a can? (IV, 41)

Sarah's fulsome praise of the can and of her husband's tinkering skills compounds the comedy of the anti-climax. As the three empty porter bottles fall limply from the sack the responses of tinker and priest are again a reversal of expectations: it is the tinker who offers a supernatural explanation of the dramatic event and the priest whose reaction is mercenary:

> PRIEST [*opens the bundle; the three empty bottles fall out*].
> SARAH. Glory to the saints of joy!

PRIEST. Did every any man see the like of that? To think you'd be putting deceit on me and telling lies to me, and I going to marry you for a little sum wouldn't marry a child.

SARAH [*crestfallen and astonished*]. It's the divil did it, your reverence, and I wouldn't tell you a lie. [*Raising her hands.*] May the Lord Almighty strike me dead if the divil isn't after hooshing the tin can from the bag. (IV, 41)

No amount of persuasion or prayer from either woman consoles the priest for the loss of the coveted tin can. Sarah offers to 'be saying fine prayers for you, morning and night, if it'd be raining itself, and it'd be in two black pools I'd be setting my knees', and Mary unavailingly begs him to wed Sarah for the best of religious reasons. 'Marry her, your reverence, for the love of God' (IV, 41). But the old woman's uncharacteristic conversion to pious orthodoxy intimates to Sarah the real and very unspiritual cause of the hooshing of the vessel out of the sack. Faced with the grim threat of real violence, Mary appeals directly to the representative of religion to defend her:

MARY [*hiding behind the* PRIEST]. Keep her off, your reverence, keep her off for the love of the Almighty God. What at all would the Lord Bishop say if he found me here lying with my head broken across, or the two of yous maybe digging a bloody grave for me at the door of the church? (IV, 43)

As the priest imperiously waves Sarah off, she suddenly sees in his defence of Mary and his church an unholy alliance which gives her the opportunity to turn the tables on him for his previous greedy bargaining:

SARAH. I'll not go a step till I have her head broke, or till I'm wed with himself. If you want to get shut of us, let you marry us now, for I'm thinking the ten shillings in gold is a good price for the like of you, and you near burst with the fat (IV, 43).

As poor tinkers and rich priest confront each other, they do so not on the grounds of ignorance of each other's ways, but out of a knowledge which has about it more than a suggestion of past collusion:

PRIEST. Gather up your gold now, and begone from my sight, for if ever I set an eye on you again you'll hear me telling the peelers who it was stole the black ass belonging to Philly O'Cullen, and whose hay it is the grey ass does be eating. (IV, 43-5)

The priest's threat to invoke against the tinkers the formal power of the law is too much. Mary quickly claps her hand over his mouth and calls on the others to 'knock him down on the road' (IV, 45). Gagging him with the sack which formerly held the can and the porter bottles, the tinkers hastily gather their few possessions and prepare for the flight. Mary's behaviour towards the priest in this episode may seem to the modern mind to be an irrational and illogical combination of gratuitous violence and unmotivated praise. If, however, we relate the play back to its source in the ritual of the *nopces à mitaines*, the throwing down of the gauntlet to authority appears in a very different light — and one which has close associations with the Puck Fair celebrations in Kerry, which Synge observed on one of his visits to that county. In the folk tradition, 'threshing is as ambivalent as abuse changed into praise'; it is directed against 'the representatives of the old law, of the rights of a world that is dying and receding'.[20] The blows themselves have 'a broadened, symbolic, ambivalent meaning; they at once kill and regenerate, put an end to the old life and start the new'.[21] The old tinker's approach to the bound and gagged priest is characterised by precisely this kind of ambivalence. Mary seeks to confer upon the whole episode the status of a necessary game in which she tells him that the tinkers are 'sick and sorry . . . to tease you' (IV, 47). Her resentment is not directed against his person — to her, he is 'a good boy . . . now, your reverence' (IV, 47) — but against his attempt to use his *office* to 'rob poor sinners of their scraps of gold' (IV, 47). After all, had he taken pity on their poverty, none of the trouble would have arisen about a price for the wedding. She widens her protest to include a general criticism of the irrelevance of the official and officious rites and rituals of orthodoxy to their way of life. The apparently stable society towards which the young Sarah Casey felt attracted is seen, from Mary's perspective, as rigid, unable to take account of process and change. It is represented *in absentia* by the geriatric bishop 'and he an old man, would have you destroyed if he seen a thing at all' (IV, 19).

True to the spirit of the folk festival, however, Synge's dramatic vision is antipathetic towards bare negation. The dialectical action of the play recognises that the old world is inseparable from the new. When Michael and Sarah threaten to pursue their vengeance single-mindedly, Mary restrains them by recalling that they have that very night celebrated a festive communion with his reverence — and she still retains her fascination with the power of his words. She persuades them to release him from the sack so that she may hear him 'swear a mighty oath he wouldn't harm us' (IV, 47). His reverence obligingly swears — but in a disappointingly faint voice. As he does so, Sarah performs an anti-ritual of non-marriage, placing the tin ring on his finger to bind him to his promise. Lest the audience should make the mistake of believing that either Sarah's vow, or the priest's oath not to harm them, or, indeed, any other such word, can be binding on actions 'until the end of time' (IV, 49), the ceremony reminds us of Mary's warning about the inability of rings of gold themselves to maintain, *in saecula saeculorum*, the status quo. Synge does not, however, concede total victory to either side. To do so would be to sell short the greatest strength of the play's volcanic energy — its insistence on the creative nature of the comic-ironic interplay between the two sides. As if revived by Michael's celebratory praise of drink, his reverence stands up and prepares to fulfil the old tinker poet's longstanding ambition to 'hear a scholar, the like of you, speaking Latin to the saints above' (IV, 21). The prayer she does hear is no saintly benediction. The holy father calls down 'the fire of heaven from the hand of the Almighty God' (IV, 49). Yet even this curse has by no means a purely negative effect. It is set in the context of that 'true ambivalent . . . laughter' which 'does not deny seriousness but purifies and completes it'.[22] Mary's last words to the priest, 'there's an old villain' (IV, 49), are one admiring poet's complimentary tribute to another in celebration of the Movements of May. As the tinkers all call out together 'Run, run. Run for your lives' (IV, 49) the man of the church may be left 'master of the situation'. But he is master of an empty stage, for life has taken itself elsewhere, to continue its festivities on the Green of Clash.

Far from *The Tinker's Wedding* being a tasteless or crude anomaly in Synge's dramatic development, it relates to his other plays in the way in which Molière's farces relate to 'his more "thoughtful" plays like *Le Misanthrope* and *Le Tartuffe*'.[23] The play belongs firmly in the mainstream of the growth of Synge's strategy and style from the combined sources of folk culture and the European comic tradition to which his preface directs our attention. Its comic geniality is a testament to the ability to delight in the emotions of the people, without ever forgetting that 'the emotions generated in the Irish situation were a two-edged weapon'.[24]

The dramatisation of antinomic relationships in *In the Shadow of the Glen* and *The Tinker's Wedding* prepares the ground for the emergence, in *The Well of the Saints*, of Synge's 'new typical couple'.[25] The Tramp in *In the Shadow of the Glen* and Mary Casey in *The Tinker's Wedding* are renowned for their great talk. Like the artist, they threaten the socially endorsed verbally constructed orthodoxies. They are, therefore, a threat to any society which seeks to derive its sense of reality from the myth of its permanence. In *The Well of the Saints* Synge turns his dramatic attention very explicitly to ritual and language, still within the context of weddings. He chooses as his protagonists a couple whose lack of sight makes them doubly dependent for identity on linguistic mediation. A blind person, like a word, is, in Tony Tanner's phrase, 'almost literally a presence and an absence combined'.[26]

NOTES

1. Denis Donoghue, ' "Too Immoral for Dublin": Synge's *The Tinker's Wedding*', *Irish Writing* 30 (1955), p. 56.

2. Ibid., p. 61.

3. Ibid., p. 61.

4. Mikhail Bakhtin, *Rabelais and His World*, translated by Hélène Iswolsky (Cambridge Massachusetts and London, Massachusetts Institute of Technology, 1968), p. 11.

5. Ibid., p. 288.

6. Vivian Mercier, 'The Tinker's Wedding', in S.B. Bushrui (ed.), *Sunshine and the Moon's Delight: a Centenary Tribute to John Millington Synge 1871-1909* (Gerrards Cross, Bucks. and Beirut, Colin Smythe and the American University of Beirut, 1972), p. 82. Nicholas Grene takes a similar line when he claims that 'the tinker's life which he imagines, free and unfettered by convention, is very obviously an ideal for Synge — too obviously, we may feel'. See Nicholas Grene, *Synge: A Critical Study of the Plays* (London and Basingstoke, Macmillan, 1975), p. 107.

7. Jaunting Jim is the name given to The Tramp in early drafts of *In the Shadow of the Glen*.

8. Donna Gerstenberger, *John Millington Synge*: Twayne's English Authors Series, 12 (New York, Twayne Publishers, 1964), p. 64.

9. Mercier, 'The Tinker's Wedding', in S. B. Bushrui (ed.), *Sunshine and the Moon's Delight*, p. 78.

10. There is one one-act typescript of the play in the Trinity Collection of Synge Manuscripts, and three complete two-act versions. See TCD MSS 4336-7.

11. TCD MSS 4336-7, f. 25, first two-act version.

12. Ibid., f. 26.

13. Ibid., f. 26.

14. Bakhtin, *Rabelais and His World*, p. 210

15. Ibid., p. 204.

16. Mercier, 'The Tinker's Wedding' in S.B. Bushrui (ed.) *Sunshine and the Moon's Delight*, p. 82.

17. TCD MSS 4336-7, f. 124, 'You're a known divil. I'm saying, for raising money off of downy boys and aged fellows letting on you'd

meet them on the hill tops and not going near to them at all' (third
two-act version).

18. Quoted in Bakhtin, *Rabelais and His World*, p. 425.

19. Ibid., p. 259.

20. Ibid., p. 205.

21. Ibid., p. 205.

22. Ibid., pp. 122-3.

23. Douglas Duncan, 'Synge and Jonson (with a parenthesis on
Ronsard)', in S.B. Bushrui, (ed.), *Sunshine and the Moon's Delight*, p. 208.

24. Jack Mitchell, 'The Role of Emotion in the Theatre of Sean
O'Casey', *Irland: Gesellschaft und Kultur*, 2 (Halle, 1979), p. 126.

25. 'The complicated forces which produce literature tend or
usually tend to express themselves in antinomies just as the forces of
humanity at every new period produce a new typical couple'. TCD
MS 4393, f. 30.

26. Tony Tanner, *Adultery in the Novel: Contract and Transgression*
(Baltimore and London, Johns Hopkins Press, 1979), p. 15.

6.
WORD AND VISION:
Language As Symbolic Action In
The Well of the Saints

IN *Language as Symbolic Action* Kenneth Burke examines the sense in which the word itself 'can be considered a kind of act'.[1] He argues that the word 'becomes a different act by reason of its placement in a different scene'; its function as sign must be assessed in relation to verbal and non-verbal, or situational contexts.[2] Evidence of Synge's theoretical interest in the subject-object relationship and in the nature and function of language and of art may be found in his notebook for the year 1894-5, which predates his first visit to Aran and records his readings from Leslie Stephen, Darwin, Herbert Spencer, Marx, Nietzsche, Spinoza, Comte and Hegel. His notes from Spencer's writings indicate a preoccupation with aesthetic products and games as substitute activities and with the role of representation and re-representation in relation to consciousness and perception. Synge records that 'some aesthetic feelings are merely perfected modes of sensation, others such as the delight in contemplating a noble action or fictitious character are re-representative in an extreme degree'.[3] 'Transfigured Realism', he writes, 'simply asserts objective existence as separate from and independent of subjective existence. But it asserts neither that any one mode of this existence is in reality that which it seems, nor that the connexions among its modes are objectively what they seem'.[4]

The interplay between subjective and objective existence, and the complex nature of the connections between the modes, are explored and dramatised in *The Well of the Saints*. Appropriately, therefore, the

105

play is characterised by the density and frequency of explicit reference to language as language and by a preoccupation with the interactions between language, consciousness and perception. Drama is the ideal medium in which to explore such relationships. Essentially, it sets up a situation in which a process, a person or an object exists as itself, yet does not so exist, since process is fictional plot, person is *dramatis persona* and objects are props. Once we enter into the convention of play, every element takes on an ambivalence of identity in which it *plays at* being what its outward form suggests it conventionally, or usually, is. Thus, every detail of scene, costume, gesture, property, as well as the words themselves, become, in the theatre, semiotic material. Drama therefore challenges any literalising tendency to take the names and concepts of things as *aeternae veritates*, while it also questions the nominalist assumption that we cannot know more than the names.

During the first and last acts of *The Well of the Saints*, the two main protagonists, Martin and Mary Doul, are, as their name suggests, blind — or dark. They are therefore acutely dependent for their vision of objective and subjective 'reality' upon the mediating role of the word as it is interpreted to them by the 'seeing' people of the village. Paradoxically, the blind couple earn their living by selling lights to these villagers, lights which they make by extracting the pith from rushes. The word 'pith' has a polysemantic character which is activated when Mary urges Martin to hide their light-making activities from the people:

> MARTIN DOUL [*listening*]. There's someone coming on the road.
> MARY DOUL. Let you put the pith away out of their sight, or they'll be
>   picking it out with the spying eyes they have, and saying it's rich we are,
>   and not sparing us a thing at all (III, 75).

The semantic ambiguity of the word 'pith' in this context brings into play the creative movement of language between the objective and the subjective, calling our attention also to the relationships established by the word between object and image. The word 'pith' denotes the spongy centre of the rushes, the raw material of the lights made by the blind couple. But through a historical process of abstraction which is part of the symbolic, image-making activities of the community of language users, 'pith' has also come to mean the substance, or substantial quality of words, their force, vigour or energy. Additionally, it means, figuratively, the essential or vital part of anything, its spirit, essence or substance.[5] All of these meanings, and more importantly, the problematical nature of the creative interplay between them, are considered in this play about the activity of 'symbol-using (symbol-making, symbol-misusing)' man.[6]

The choice of blind protagonists foregrounds from the outset of *The Well of the Saints* the possible divergence between word and referent. The dependence of Martin and Mary upon words for orientation, or placement in scene, is implied by the opening question:

MARY DOUL. What place are we now, Martin Doul?
MARTIN DOUL. Passing the gap (III, 71).

A gap is, in one sense, a vacancy, a non-place between two places or situations. With the acute synesthetic perception of the blind, Martin describes place in terms of movement, but movement past emptiness. The word 'passing' also means both 'travelling past' and 'missing' the gap. It is worth recalling here that the highly stylised nature of the Abbey acting would have heightened these tensions between word and action and between meaning and meaning. In Synge's time, the actors assumed a gesture and then held it, remaining immobile while they spoke, thus giving to movement a quality of stasis. That there *is* a perceptual gap between appearance and language becomes explicit when Martin refers to Mary plaiting her 'yellow hair' (III, 71). Martin's and Mary's senses may, perhaps, be acute enough to enable them to know the place they are in, the time of day and the seasons of the year, but they *appear* to us not to know either themselves or each other. Martin is suspicious of words as objective indicators of reality. He has also discovered the power of talk to provide a distraction from unpleasant or contradictory perceptions. Mary's 'queer cracked voice' (III, 71) offends and disturbs him, so he shuts it out with his talk about her yellow hair. Mary, too, acknowledges that there may be a possible discrepancy between hearing and seeing. A life that's 'a bad life for the voice', she argues, may be the best life 'for keeping a white, beautiful skin — the like of my skin — on your neck and on your brows' (III, 71). Instead of beauty being intrinsic to the person — and our eyes suggest

107

to us that neither Martin nor Mary is conventionally beautiful —
beauty and splendour are made to appear fugitive possessions, perhaps
only skin, or word, deep:

> MARY DOUL. I've heard tell . . . there isn't anything at all like a fine skin
> for putting splendour on a woman.
> MARTIN DOUL [*teasingly, but with good-humour*]. I do be thinking odd
> times we don't know rightly what way you have your splendour, or
> asking myself, maybe, if you have it at all (III, 71).

To reassure but also to silence Martin, Mary marshals the evidence
and power of words, but she uses them, one might say, solipsistically, to
testify *against* words:

> MARY DOUL. Let you not be making the like of that talk when you've
> heard . . . a power . . . saying fine things of my face, and you know rightly
> it was 'the beautiful dark woman', they did call me in Ballinatone (III,
> 71-3).

The couple are, in fact, engaged in a strenuous metalinguistic effort to
hold their fears of not being 'fine looking' (III, 73) in abeyance, and to
stylise their dreams of perfection into permanence. Mary's words
locate the source of the blind couple's apparent illusions about
themselves firmly in the discourse of the community. She seems unable
— or perhaps unwilling — to notice the commonsense, referential
discrepancy between her belief in her 'yellow hair' and 'white
beautiful skin' and the epithet 'dark' which 'they' use to describe her in
Ballinatone. But the semantic ambiguities go deeper than the level of
possible divergence between word and referent. 'Dark' means 'blind'
(Ir. G. 'dall') *and* 'dark-haired or -skinned', but the word also has
certain biblical connotations: with the Song of Solomon, 'I *am* black,
but comely', and with the Pauline image of seeing through a glass
darkly.[7] Already, then, actions and words have begun to activate a
semiotic process of dream-like displacement which is directed *towards
the audience.* How far do our conventional referential norms measure up
to the situation? How far are we, as well as Martin and Mary, products
or victims of these norms, or of deviations from them? Are the
protagonists, perhaps, manipulators of words, using language to avoid
rather than to achieve self-recognition?

The verbal web of truth and lies becomes more tangled as the couple argue about what they have heard tell. Mary introduces the meta-dramic theme of *playing at* looking by suggesting that 'the young and silly do be always making game of them that's dark, and they'd think it a fine thing if they had us deceived, the way we wouldn't know we were so fine-looking at all' (III, 73). In one sense, being blind, neither Martin nor Mary *can* look; they are excluded by their disability from the community of the sighted. But since everything that the sighted people see is permeated by language, what they see and mediate to the blind couple are also signs which emerge 'only in the process of social interaction'.[8] Sharing words with the community, Martin and Mary share in the mediated, reflecting and refracting world of signs. To see one's self to be 'fine-looking' requires the mirror-like regard of others, and the image depends at least partly on the mirror. Martin is impatient with the mere mediated image. He longs for a time-and-language-cancelling insight, to enable them to 'know surely we were the finest man, and the finest woman, of the seven counties of the east' (III, 73), a vision which would free them from having to 'heed a thing they'd say' (III, 73).

Mary's response to Martin's attack on the villagers warns against any simplistic equation of sight with certain knowledge and ultimate truth, yet she, too, identifies herself through and with the stories of her own perfection told by the seeing people in the community. The irony remains that she only has as evidence for her beauty the images mediated to her by the villagers' talk. This, she suspects, may well be lies:

MARY DOUL. Ah, there's a power of villainy walking the world, Martin Doul, among them that do be gadding around, with their gaping eyes, and their sweet words, and they with no sense in them at all (III, 75).

Even as she speaks, her words turn against the couple. They are hopelessly trapped in the circularity of linguistic constructs. The very openness of the villagers' gaping eyes may well declare itself as a form of semantic emptiness — a blindness not much different from their own sightless condition. Starting with verbal evidence for each other's fine looks, they have now arrived at a point where they condemn as empty lies the sweet words of the people. Their identification of seeing

109

with sightlessness is neatly completed when Mary tells Martin 'You'd be as bad as the rest of them if you had your sight' (III, 75).

When Timmy the smith announces that he's 'after walking up in great haste from hearing great wonders in the fair' (III, 77), it seems as if the couple are about to be offered a way out of their word-dependent dilemma — but the wonder is a wonder *heard*, and therefore itself a verbal construct. The word 'wonder' is also treacherously polysemantic. It may signify (i) something out of the normal range of expectation or experience; (ii) the emotion provoked by such an event; or (iii) v. the mental activity of being curious to know the truth: but used ironically, it refers, in the dialect, (iv) to something which one suspects of being an *untruth*; or (v) v. to the process of doubting whether something is true. In keeping with his doubting mood, Martin is at first contemptuous of what he dismisses as mere talk:

> MARTIN [*rather contemptuously*]. You're always hearing queer wonderful things, and the lot of them nothing at all. (III, 77)

Timmy counters the criticism by promising that the word will become deed 'here at the crossing of the roads' (III, 77). This is to be the perfect wonder, bigger 'than was ever done on the Green of Clash, or the width of Leinster itself' (III, 77). As yet, however, they only have Timmy's word for the power of the water — and Timmy has the word of his informants:

> TIMMY. Did ever you hear tell of the place across a bit of the sea . . .
> MARY DOUL. I've heard people have walked round from the west and they speaking of that.
> TIMMY [*impressively*]. There's a green ferny well, I'm told, behind of that place (III, 79).

The first impulse of Martin and Mary when they hear of miracles is to break from the obsessive self-referentiality of language by getting physical hold of the wonder as if it were a thing:

> MARY DOUL. Maybe we could send a young lad to bring us the water. I could wash a naggin bottle in the morning, and I'm thinking Patch Ruadh would go for it, if we gave him a good drink and the bit of money we have hid in the thatch (III, 79).

The wonder, however, is not 'just' water, a purely natural object. It needs to be activated by special words, and it has the disturbing limitation, for anyone hoping to achieve perfect secular vision, of having its power destroyed by any worldly thought, word or deed. The couple, it appears, cannot escape their dependence on language. Martin's frustrated anger explodes in his reply to Timmy's insistence that he accept the story as proof of the deed:

> MARTIN DOUL. Can't you open the big slobbering mouth you have and say what way it'll be done, and not be making blather till the fall of night (III, 81).

The gross physicality of the insult seems to embody an exasperated determination to force a distinction between a literal saying of the truth and the fiction of making blather. It is a vain attempt to make Timmy spit the wonder out as object rather than sign. When the blind couple hear the tale for the second time, the longed-for vision does indeed seem almost tangible, but Martin's optimistic words as he sets out to grasp it return us subversively to the play's opening preoccupation with placement in scene:

> MARTIN DOUL [*feeling for his stick*]. What place is he, Timmy? I'll be walking to him now (III, 81).

Martin's credulity seems to have been won by the promise that the true light of knowledge will be brought by 'a fine holy man, . . . a saint of the Almighty God' (III, 81). But how illuminating is the vision of this Saint? Timmy declares that the holy father's prayers and fasting have made him 'as thin as one of the empty rushes you have there on your knee' (III, 81). Doubt is quickly cast upon his sense by the ease with which he has parted from the water because of what 'the lads told him' (III, 83). Martin and Mary have found their sightless way round the world, but the visionary Saint fears to 'carry them things through the briars, and steep, slippy-feeling rocks he'll be climbing above' (III, 83). When the holy man does exercise his seeing power it leads him to a superficial judgement — by appearances — which even blind Mary finds laughable:

> MOLLY BYRNE. . . . so he looked round then, and gave the water, and his

big cloak, and his bell to the two of us, for young girls, says he, are the cleanest holy people you'd see walking the world. [MARY DOUL *goes near seat.*]

MARY DOUL [*sits down, laughing to herself*]. Well, the saint's a simple fellow, and it's no lie (III, 83).

There are, then, similarities between the blind couple and the unseeing Saint. The process of identification between himself and Martin is dramatised by the ritual dressing of the blind man in the holy father's cloak and bell. Such a change of identity is by no means unattractive to Martin. Dressed in the priest's clothes, he becomes his like; he begins to look as he looks, to see as he sees. The role-playing begins to create the character. It stirs up in Martin a desire for a spiritual alternative to his worldly dream, and he seems prepared to substitute for secular beatitude the attractions of 'the beauty of the saints' (III, 85). As Mary listens to Martin's 'bell-ringing with the saints of God' (III, 87), however, it begins to dawn on the couple that there may be some deep antagonism between the 'little silvery voice' (III, 85) of the prayer-bell and their wedding vows:

MARY DOUL. How would he be bell-ringing with the saints of God and he wedded with myself?

MARTIN DOUL. It's the truth she's saying, and if bell-ringing is a fine life, yet I'm thinking, maybe, it's better I am wedded with the beautiful dark woman of Ballinatone (III, 87).

The Saint's opening address to the couple continues to cast doubt on the nature and value of his way of seeing. The promise that they will be able to see 'the holy priests itself praying to the Lord' (III, 89) offers little in the way of visionary advancement — prayer, after all, is more appropriately heard than seen — and the water he carries comes from a depressingly deathly source:

SAINT. It's on a bare, starving rock that there's the grave of the four beauties of God, the way it's little wonder, I'm thinking, if it's with bare starving people the water should be used (III, 89).

As he envelopes himself in his cloak, shutting himself off from worldly contamination, his words close in reductively on the two. The hoped-for great wonder becomes little and Martin and Mary are reduced to 'a thing':

> SAINT. So it's to the like of yourselves I do be going, who are wrinkled and poor, a thing rich men would hardly look at at all (III, 89).

The holy father's distaste for any language other than his own quickly becomes apparent. Preparing to cure the pair, he orders the people to be quiet and admonishes them to direct their silent thoughts against what he sees as abuses of language, 'against false prophets and heathens, and the words of women and smiths, and all knowledge that would soil the soul or the body of a man' (III, 91).

When the holy father takes Martin, separately, up into the church, the comments of the villagers express their own ambivalent feelings about this mediator with the deity. Timmy praises the 'fine, beautiful voice' (III, 91) of the miracle-worker, but he is less sure of the effects of 'the fasting' (III, 91) on his manhood. This discrepancy between voice and virility leads Molly Byrne to regret that the villagers have to depend at all upon such alien linguistic powers. For her, the Saint does not belong in 'this place' (III, 91) and they would not have him at all 'if a man knew the way to be saying prayers' (III, 91). Before long the people begin to quarrel, to accuse each other and to make invidious comparisons between themselves and the blind couple. Once again the dispute concentrates on the gap between words and reality, with Mat Simon stoutly arguing the case for their own powers of lying against the truth of the Saint's way of seeing:

> MAT SIMON. That's the truth now, Molly, and it's more joy dark Martin got from the lies we told of that hag is kneeling by the path, than your own man will get from you, day or night, and he living at your side (III, 93).

A Latin chant — words which the people cannot understand — announces the return of the 'cured' Martin. Already his restored sight takes the form of divided vision. His newly opened eyes move restlessly between the world of the Saint and the world of natural objects:

> MARTIN DOUL [ecstatically]. Oh glory be to God, I see now surely . . . I see the walls of the church, and the green bits of ferns in them, and yourself, holy father, and the great width of the sky (III, 93).

113

Although he may be able to see, it is painfully obvious as he looks for his wife that sight has not brought him sure knowledge; rather, it seems to the onlooking villagers that what sense he had before has deserted him. Passing by Mary Doul as she scrambles towards him, he draws away from her in disdain and turns instead to Molly Byrne. Mocking him cruelly for his delusion, the villagers turn his visionary efforts into a ritual game of blind man's buff, spinning the sighted neophyte from one to the other. As they call on him to find his dream in the real world, he is made to lower his bid for perfection:

> MARTIN DOUL [*with misgiving, to another girl*]. Is it yourself it is ? You're not so fine-looking, but I'm thinking you'd do, with the grand nose you have, and your nice hands and your feet (III, 93).

It is, nevertheless, in his determination to find satisfaction in this world rather than in words or dreams alone that Martin's hope for redemption, or secular transfiguration, lies. His very willingness to accept less complete alternatives to his visionary Mary is a testimony to a capacity for accepting imperfection and change.

Martin's fall from dream to reality seems complete when Mary, likewise 'cured', emerges from the church. Ironically, he first recognises her not by sight but by hearing:

> MARTIN DOUL [*wheeling round*]. It's her voice surely . . . [*They stare at each other blankly.*] (III, 97).

At once the crowd taunt them, relentlessly urging the couple to exercise their desiderated ability to match appearance with words:

> MOLLY BYRNE [*to* MARTIN DOUL]. Go up now and take her under the chin and be speaking the way you spoke to myself . . .
> MARTIN DOUL [*in a low voice, with intensity*]. If I speak now, I'll speak hard to the two of you . . .
> MOLLY BYRNE [*to* MARY DOUL]. You're not saying a word, Mary. What is it you think of himself, with the fat legs on him, and the little neck like a ram? (III, 97)

Martin's lavish praise of God when he saw Molly collapses, at the sight of Mary, into its opposite. The couple proclaim their divorce from one another in a flyting crescendo of abuse. Threatening to turn their bitter words into violent deeds, they accuse each other of deceit. It is a deceit for which neither of them is solely responsible, yet in which each of them shares, for they share the language whose powers of playing lies made possible what the miracle re-presents to them *as* lies:

> MARY DOUL [*interrupting him*] . . . It's the devil cured you this day, I'm saying, and drove you crazy with lies.
> MARTIN DOUL. Isn't it yourself is after playing lies on me, ten years, in the day, and in the night, but what is that to you now the Lord God has given eyes to me, the way I see you an old, wizendy hag, was never fit to rear a child to me itself (III, 99).

The return of the Saint is heralded, as usual, by an order for silence. His ludicrously inadequate assessment of the situation highlights once more the myopic shallowness of his own vison. 'Are their minds troubled with joy', he asks, 'or is their sight uncertain the way it does often be the day a person is restored?' (III, 99). The baptismal drama has seduced Martin and Mary into a new game of knowing each other, which his celibate imagination cannot comprehend. Again separating husband from wife, he prays for his version of enlightenment to come upon them:

> SAINT [*coming between them*]. May the Lord who has given you sight send a little sense into your heads, the way it won't be on your two selves you'll be looking — on two pitiful sinners of the earth — but on the splendour of the Spirit of God, you'll see an odd time shining out through the big hills, and steep streams falling to the sea. For if it's on the like of that you do be thinking, you'll not be minding the faces of men, but you'll be saying prayers and great praises, till you'll be living the way the great saints do be living, with little but old sacks, and skin covering their bones (III, 101).

The blind couple set out on their journey towards truth with absolute notions of the great wonders they should be. Now, the longed-for transcendent wonder is reduced by the moralising power of the priest to a life-denying exhortation to asceticism. Their desire for a vision of beauty is to be satisfied by odd glimpses of the Spirit of God. 'Odd' means both 'intermittent' and 'strange' or 'distorted' — a dark seeing indeed. In addition, the once-blind couple are admonished to accept an existence in which emulation of the saints is to detach them from each other, make them indifferent to their fellow men and reduce them to a level of physical degradation and decay below anything they have as yet reached. Small wonder that Martin's talk gives way to a wordless dismay, a silence which pleases the life-despising monk:

> SAINT [*to* TIMMY]. Leave him go now, you're seeing he's quiet again. [TIMMY *frees* MARTIN DOUL.] And let you [SAINT *turns to* MARY DOUL] not be raising your voice (III, 101).

If the Saint had his way, he would like to spread a similar silence over the whole village — or more ambitiously, over the whole country:

> SAINT. Let the lot of you, who have seen the power of the Lord, be thinking on it in the dark night, and be saying to yourselves it's great pity, and love he has, for the poor, starving people of Ireland (III, 101).

Having wrought his terrible miracle he intends to take refuge from the contamination of the world, and the deluge of its pollution, high above the waters. He is 'going to sleep this night' (III, 101), in the bare, starving rocky 'bed of the Holy Kevin' (III, 101), Ireland's arch-misogynist, who earned his reputation for heroic celibacy by throwing down into the waters of the monastic lake at Glendalough the misguided woman who tempted him to look upon the beauty of her face.

With the opening of Act II the context shifts from the ruptured introspection of the first movement to a world of activity, specifically, of labour at the forge. The emphasis now falls upon Martin's and Mary's experience of the hardships of the environment in which they find themselves forced to work. The setting and properties — the forge, the broken wheels, the boarded well — mark the couple's entry into the hard world of objectivity. Awakened into the community of the sighted, one might expect their separation from the life of the villagers to be drawing to an end. But they find themselves now doubly alienated. Martin has had to sell himself to Timmy the smith in return for 'food, and a corner to sleep, and money with it' (III, 103). He complains of 'working hard, and destroying myself, the length of the day' (III, 103). Timmy is a hard task-master with a reputation for meanness, who angrily rebukes his new hand for 'idling, and blathering' (III, 107) whenever he attempts to rest or talk.

The sacramental cure of the blind couple has led to an almost total estrangement between man and wife. Although the sighted pair have nothing now to say to each other, their newly acquired vision does not spare the villagers. When blind, the two saw only through the lies of the people. Now it appears that the villagers have never really seen themselves. The couple's penetrating eyes and ready tongues have turned all eyes inward, 'setting every person in this place, and up beyond to Rathvanna, talking of nothing, and thinking of nothing, but the way they do be looking in the face' (III, 111). They, in their turn, have become a self-referential mirror to the community.

Martin Doul has by no means accepted the Saint's vision of what he should see as the only vision of life. He holds fast to his hopes of finding in this world the realisation of his dream of beauty, and in spite of his suffering, he still finds it possible to bless 'the saints, and the holy water, and the power of the Lord Almighty' (III, 111) *when he sees Molly Byrne in the flesh*. This kind of seeing is certainly not what the Saint intended.

Martin's encounter with Molly Byrne in this act is central to the play's exploration of the seemingly exclusive opposites of light and dark, vision and blindness, dream and reality. As he confronts her, the torment of having his sight is repaid by the pleasure of 'looking on a grand, white, handsome girl, the like of you' (III, 111). Yet this compensatory ability to 'see' Molly's visionary beauty is rooted in his former blindness rather than his new insight. As he woos Molly, he is already growing dark again. When she taunts him about the 'grand day' (III, 113) of his life when his sight was restored, he compares this 'bad, *black* day' (III, 113) to a deprivation of vision, a time when insight was taken from him:

> when I was roused up and found I was the like of the little children do be listening to the stories of an old woman, and do be dreaming after in the dark night that it's in grand houses of gold they are, with speckled horses to ride, and do be waking again, in a short while, and they destroyed with

the cold, and the thatch dripping maybe, and the starved ass braying in the yard (III, 113).

He is powerfully attracted towards this child-like world of story, dream and myth, and would gladly exchange present sight for his previous blind vision:

> For it's a fine sound your voice has that time, and it's better I am, I'm thinking, lying down, the way a blind man does by lying, than to be sitting here in the grey light, taking hard words of Timmy the smith (III, 113-15).

As he tries to entice Molly away, Martin does so with promises of light: but the light is unseen light, of which he has 'heard tell' (III, 115). He promises her a life 'in the lands beyond' — a life of fictional activity, 'a fine life passing abroad through them towns of the south, and we telling stories, maybe, or singing songs at the fairs' (III, 115). Martin's talk at this point is indeed 'queer talk' (III, 115), moving in restless paradoxes between lies and truth, dream and reality, seeing and imagining, blindness and sight. His incantatory words begin to cast over Molly a powerful spell. His blind vision both secularises and aestheticises the double vision of the Saint, as he sees mortality in the old woman rotting for the grave and claims to find in Molly a Persephone to his Hades — a dazzling conveyor and destroyer of light to his dark vision:

> MARTIN DOUL. It'd be a fine thing if a man would be seeing, and losing his sight, the way he'd have your two eyes facing him, and he going the roads, and shining above him, and he looking in the sky, and springing up from the earth, the time he'd lower his head, in place of the muck that seeing men do meet all roads spread on the world (III, 117).

His invitation unmasks the limitations and dangers of these exclusive alternatives. On the one side is the dream of an escape to an illusory Land of Youth, on the other, acceptance of the Saint's vision of this world as a place where we rot and rot. Yet are these worlds polar opposites? Or are they not, rather, related? There are strong suggestions, carried by the negatives, that the world to which Martin calls Molly away is a non-world: the language challenges the substantiality of the woman and the promised land. The words move with a probing negating discontent around the alternative vision:

> MARTIN DOUL. Put down your can now, and come along with myself, for I'm seeing you this day, seeing you, maybe, the way no man has seen you in the world. [*He takes her by the arm and tries to pull her away softly to the right.*] Let you come on now, I'm saying, to the lands of Iveragh and the Reeks of Cork, where you won't set down the width of your two feet and not be crushing fine flowers, and making sweet smells in the air . . . (III, 117).

The scent of mortality hangs about this regressive appeal to 'come along now, let you come on the little path through the trees' (III, 117): the drift towards annihilation declares itself in the negatives. The sylvan imagery looks back to Columb's call to Sister Eileen in *When the Moon Has Set*, to become 'a beautiful note in the chant of the forest of leaves', and forward to the retreat of Deirdre and the Sons of Usna to the woods of Alban in Synge's last play. Katharine Worth rightly remarks that 'Synge's strange language is at its least life-like here: the queer, bony structure, the intricately linked phrases, the alien word order . . . almost defy us to take it as the ordinary speech of common men'.[9] Yet we are no more justified in attributing to Synge the intention of offering this vision as *his* alternative to reality than we would be in attributing to Shakespeare a belief that the forest of Arden was an alternative to the England of Elizabeth. Nor is this the kind of vision which Martin and Mary achieve in the end: indeed, both stylistically and in terms of content the two visionary epiphanies are quite distinct. Leaving with Martin on the terms which he offers here would indeed mean for Molly, or for Mary, a loss of sense. He is tempting her towards a world which is merely a verbal construct, and one which tries to escape the change and flux of life. In some respects, therefore, her crying out to Timmy the smith must be seen as an opting for life:

> MOLLY BYRNE [*crying out towards forge*]. Timmy . . . Timmy the smith . . . [TIMMY *comes out of forge, and* MARTIN DOUL *lets her go.* MOLLY BYRNE, *excited and breathless, pointing to* MARTIN DOUL.] Did ever you hear that them that loses their sight loses their sense along with it, Timmy the smith? (III, 119).

Her tragedy is that the only alternative which she can see is the life of the forge.

Temporarily deluded by the belief that he can by words alone make the like of a fleshly Molly to dwell eternally with him, Martin is trying to perform his own aestheticising version of the Saint's religious miracle — as Molly's scornful comment makes quite clear:

> MOLLY BYRNE [*as before*]. He's a bigger fool than that, Timmy. Look on him now, and tell me if that isn't a grand fellow to think he's only to open his mouth to have a fine woman, the like of me, running along by his heels (III, 119).

The result of Martin's incantatory effort is quickly shown to be, in dramatic terms, *exactly the same as it was when the Saint pronounced his Latin prayer*. The woman who appears to Martin is not the like of Molly Byrne; she is, in fact, Mary Doul. Mary's appearance dissolves Martin's dream, and the gap between fine words and reality seems even wider. The climax of his passion is signalled by his fear that 'a storm of thunder is coming, or the last end of the world' (III, 119). But in his suffering and humiliation Martin reaches towards Mary — not towards Molly — and to her he appeals for confirmation of his identity. As he does so, he staggers and trips over the very real stumbling-block of Molly's tin can:

> [*He reaches* MARY DOUL, *and seizes her with both his hands – with a frantic cry.*] Is it the darkness of thunder is coming, Mary Doul? Do you see me clearly with your eyes? (III, 119)

The confirmation of his identity which Mary offers is a wordlessly concrete reminder of the Saint's miracle turned curse. She strikes him a cruel blow across the face with an empty sack.

If, however, Molly Byrne believes that unlike Mary Doul, she can remain forever a fine woman, or, as she flatteringly describes herself, 'a well-reared civil girl' (III, 123), then she is just as deluded, Mary reminds her, as Martin:

> MARY DOUL [*defiantly*]. When the skin shrinks on your chin, Molly Byrne, there won't be the like of you for a shrunk hag in the four quarters of Ireland (III, 121).

120

Mary's decomposing words — 'shrunk', 'wrinkled young', 'turning...
like . . . thin grass', 'turning a thing' — powerfully remind us of our
common mortality and of the shared mortality of man and nature.
They are also the ultimate apotheosis in the play of the Saint's vision of
life on earth as a living death, a vision which Martin and Mary have to
confront rather than avoid if they are to free themselves from a
situation in which, whatever way they look, they see nothing but
annihilation. Martin has failed in his bid to find heaven on earth, but
he stubbornly continues to refuse the Saint's heaven as a substitute. If
he cannot have Molly on earth, he will see herself and Timmy not in
Paradise, but in Hades. He defiantly pictures Timmy and Molly 'on a
high bed, and they screeching in hell' (III, 123). If his tragi-comic
quest has to end in an Inferno, of one thing at least he is sure: he will
exclude the heavenly Father from his kingdom:

> MARTIN DOUL. It'll be a grand thing that time to look on the two of
> them; and they twisting and roaring out, and twisting and roaring again,
> one day and the next day, and each day always and ever. It's not blind I'll
> be that time, and it won't be hell to me I'm thinking, but the like of
> Heaven itself, and it's fine care I'll be taking the Lord Almighty doesn't
> know (III, 123).

Martin has begun to assert his autonomy in the face of the worst that
the Saint can do to him. Out of the negation of the negatives of his fate
he has begun to construct an alternative not-blind vision. 'Not-blind' is
neither seeing the way the Saint would have them see, nor enduring
the blindness of solipsistic dependence on nothing but words responding
to words.

The opening of Act III emphasises the way in which the Saint's
miracle has separated Mary and Martin from each other. The setting
is the *same as in the first Act* (III, 125) but the gap in the centre is filled
with briars, blocking the way that the couple used to take — and Mary
is alone. She has, however, *a few rushes with her* and *it is an early spring
day* (III, 125). The fear of being alone is Mary's greatest fear. She
grieves over the sense of alienation she will feel, with the people
'passing me by, pointing their fingers, maybe, and asking what place is
himself' (III, 125). Without Martin she will be a lone woman with no
'quiet or decency' (III, 125). She is preoccupied with the related need

to 'get my living working alone' (III, 125). The rush lights remind us again of the important fact that Martin and Mary are workers who earn their few halfpence on the road. Mary's speech acknowledges the indifference of nature to her condition, and recognises fully the objectivity of the environment. The winds are cold, and she will grow older. Each of them in turn sees feelingly that external Nature is a condition with laws of cause and effect independent of human will. They can no longer delude themselves into thinking that the words of people or of priest can make them forever 'the finest man, and the finest woman, of the seven counties of the east' (III, 73). Recognition of the reality of process and change, is, however, neither pathetic fallacy nor resigned determinism; it becomes instead the basis for a new form of action which releases them from their role as victims in a failed aesthetic game. 'What', asked Brecht, 'is beauty? It is beautiful to resolve difficulties. So beauty is an act'.[10] It is precisely when Mary begins to recognise her subjection to the objectivity of change, by feeling her hair 'and it twisting from my brow' (III, 125) that she begins to find a new and active way to relate her subjective longing for beauty to her objective self. This way, because it both accepts and transforms necessity, is the antithesis of escapism or despair.

The theme of lonesomeness, of loss of reciprocity, is taken up by Martin. The separate entry of the couple, unseeing and unseen, emphasises their lack of each other. Without a fellow human being to engage in meaningful utterance, Martin's powers of orientation fail. Perception becomes fearful, and far from offering him consolation or escape, the unlanguaged sounds of nature leave him 'destroyed with terror and dread' (III, 127). His words acknowledge that the natural process of growing old and dying cannot be verbalised out of existence. The sounds around him all declare their involvement in movement and change; from this he cannot escape. His rediscovery of Mary begins when he takes a 'dying oath' on the changing sun and moon that a 'thing was breathing on the stones' (III, 127). He has started to reach towards an engagement with mutability as the ground of being. He discovers Mary as he begins to move in response to movement. Feeling for his stick he '*touches her hand as he is groping about and cries out*. "There's a thing with a cold living hand on it setting up at my side" ' (III, 127). The fearful experience of life as life-in-dying and dying-in-life, which is not the same as the Saint's dying to live or living to die, is the stone wall of reality against which he has to stumble before he can find a new way of passing the gap. His initial reaction to this dawning conscious-ness of objectivity is a resolve that if he escapes from this terrible non-place, he will adopt the Saint's way of life in earnest: 'I'll be saying prayers morning and night, and not straining my ear after young girls, or doing any bad thing till I die —' (III, 127). But through the very vehemence of his negation, Martin gives voice to the true nature of his yearning: the objects of his desire, as Mary quickly recognises, *are* the young girls and the bad things, and not the kind of godliness exemplified by the Saint.

If by 'telling lies to the Almighty God' is meant, as Mary's interpretation of Martin's prayer suggests, rejecting the exhortations of the Saint to life-denying asceticism, then such lying is a powerful, carnivalesque gift which, as users of language, we cannot afford to neglect. Lying — the ability to use language to project an alternative to the official, or authorised, version of the word and the world — can, of course, be turned either towards evasion of reality or towards an engagement with it. As the two blind protagonists continue their journey towards a new perception of self in other, and of self both in and apart from nature, a sense of dynamically developing engagement with life begins to emerge, meeting and subverting the guilt-ridden saintly vision, or representation, of age and death. This new vision reaches out to the world around them, which is rejuvenated by the natural cycle of spring:

> MARTIN DOUL [*coming towards her, wiping sweat from his face*]. Well, sight's a queer thing for upsetting a man . . . But if it's shaken I am for a short while, I'll soon *be coming to myself* (III, 127, my italics).
> MARY DOUL. You'll be grand then, and it's no lie (III, 127).

The dialectal use of the progressive form of the verb in Martin's speech, 'BE+coming', insists on the discovery of identity as an on-going, compositional-decompositional process. It is not a passive looking; it is a journey and an activity.

Inspired by Martin's insult, which hurls at her, for the last time, the image she saw of herself when the 'light' of the Saint's miracle was in her eyes, Mary begins to surmount the difficulties of no longer being able to accept the tales of 'the liars . . . below' (III, 129). Progressively she constructs an irrefutable lie — irrefutable because of its acceptance of conditionality — about her splendid beauty-that-is-to-become. In a gradual crescendo of self-assurance, her words change a verbal image into a symbolic activity. Claiming to have 'seen a thing in them pools put joy and blessing in my heart' (III, 129), she measures the vision in the pool against the pitiful show of the little drop of water in the Saint's can. At first she seems to Martin to be 'the maddest female woman is walking the counties of the east' (III, 129) but when she challenges him to prove that her words *are* lies, he begins to respond to the new way of seeing. Tentatively he concedes to Mary the possibility of the rejuvenation — a remaking, but not a denial, of their past:

> MARTIN DOUL. If it's not lies you're telling, would you have me think you're not a wrinkled poor woman is looking like three scores, maybe, or two scores and a half? (III, 129)

The couple are working out, through reciprocity, a mode of access to the past which makes it available for the construction of a positive present-and-future. Once again the subtle use of dialectal negatives distinguishes between not-lies and truth: not-lies is neither escapist illusion nor univocal literalism. The words reject the either-or, yea-nay dichotomy, and Mary responds to their encouragement by developing a new and confident articulation of past and present which is a constructive making of self:

> MARY DOUL. I would not, Martin [*She leans forward earnestly.*] For when I seen myself in them pools, I seen my hair would be grey, or white maybe in a short while, and I seen with it that I'd a face would be a great wonder when it'll have soft white hair falling around it, the way when I'm an old woman there won't be the like of me surely in the seven counties of the east (III, 129).

Mary's words testify to her refusal to accept as fixed and final the condition of being a pitiful show. She does not deny the process of growing old — indeed, it is this process, this negation, which allows her to become herself. Nor is her vision more than provisional: we notice again that, as in *In the Shadow of the Glen*, the language of transformation organises itself around a central absence: 'there *won't* be the like of me *surely*. But it also organises the absence into becoming. Mary juxtaposes the dynamic active image created for and by her in the pools to the stylised, but limiting, moralising vision brought about by the drop of water in the Saint's can. By welcoming the snows of time, she claims her provisional place in the pantheon of beautiful women — and the stories about these women contribute to her hope:

> MARY DOUL [*triumphantly*]. . . . I'm telling you a beautiful white-haired woman is a grand thing to see, for I'm told when Kitty Bawn was selling poteen below, the young men itself would never tire to be looking in her face (III, 129).

This new mode of perception accepts the autonomous and active role of Nature but insists that men, and women too, 'create nature by bringing it within the control of human society and commerce'.[11] Kitty Bawn offers the men not well-water or words only, but poteen, the potent, secular distillation of the water of life.

Mary's audacious imaginative leap across the gap blocked by the thorny miracle of the Saint inspires Martin to hope for himself, but he turns at first for a sign of salvation — Martin is the great seeker of signs — to the vestigial traces of moralised saintly sight:

> MARTIN DOUL[*taking off his hat and feeling his head, speaking with hesitation*]. Did you think to look, Mary Doul, would there be a whiteness the like of that coming upon me? (III, 129)

Inevitably he is disappointed. Recalled to her baptismal vision, Mary taunts him with a picture of his animal ugliness:

> MARY DOUL. I can't help your looks, Martin Doul. It wasn't myself made you with your rat's eyes, and your big ears, and your griseldy chin (III, 131).

The operative words here are 'It wasn't myself made you'. By implication, the blame for the particular making which Martin fears as final rests with his own acceptance of the vision of the holy father: but the remedy also lies with him, with his ability to recognise that he shares with all the world's phenomena their condition of unfinished metamorphosis. As Mary challenges him to say 'anything but lies' (III,

131) he bursts forth into a joyful hymn of praise to his own future distinction:

> MARTIN DOUL [*bursting with excitement*]. I've this to say, Mary Doul. I'll be letting my beard grow in a short while — a beautiful, long, white, silken, streamy beard, you wouldn't see the like of in the eastern world . . . and a beard's a thing you'll never have, so you may be holding your tongue (III, 131).

Mary's response acknowledges their reconciliation, but the controlling irony which is characteristic of Synge's anti-utopian vision recognises also the *et in Arcadia* presence which is both witness to and ground of their secular transfiguration:

> MARY DOUL [*laughing cheerfully*]. Well, we're a great pair, surely, and it's great times we'll have yet, maybe, and great talking before we die (III, 131).

Martin and Mary no longer seek a way to the holy city of the Saint. They choose, rather, to revel in 'things growing up, and budding from the earth' (III, 131). Their joyous hymn to life celebrates the fertility of the natural world: 'The lambs is bleating, surely, and there's cocks and laying hens making a fine stir a mile off on the face of the hill' (III, 133). Yet for self-conscious man, integration into nature can never be complete without loss of consciousness of self, and in time, this integration must come. The note of mortality, therefore, the acknowledgement of death, echoes in their springtime epithalamium as the couple listen to 'the lambs of Grianan, though it's near drowned their crying is with the full river making noises in the glen' (III, 133). Their words anticipate Timmy's elegiac valediction as the pair set out on their own last journey.

Martin's and Mary's new awareness has not yet been tried out: it remains action at the symbolic/linguistic level. But their confidence in their ability to tell lies which will deceive 'a priest itself' (III, 131) is soon to be put to the test. The '*faint sound of a bell*' (III, 133) cuts across the secular paean of lambs and cocks and hens. The couple's sense of rejuvenation is underlined by Martin's comic identification of the noise as that of 'the old saint, I'm thinking' (III, 133), but the celibate's new summons quickly begins to undermine the fragile worldly faith of husband and wife.[12] As they try to run off, Martin fears that the erstwhile miracle may have weakened their powers of perception:

> MARTIN DOUL. I'm afraid after the time we were with our sight we'll not find our way to it at all (III, 133).

Their way is blocked by the withered thorn-tree pulled into the gap — a rootless tree of death. Martin is full of apprehension about his ability to cope with the returning threat of sainted insight. As he begins to doubt, Mary, too dreads having to look on life once more through the eyes of the Saint:

> MARY DOUL [*nearly in tears*]. It's a poor thing, God help us, and what good'll our grey hairs be itself, if we have our sight, the way we'll see them falling each day, and turning dirty in the rain? (III, 135)

The shadow of the past has fallen across them again, so that even the cleansing rain-water is a threat. Shrinking from the priest's words, they bid each other to be silent.

When Timmy, dressed in his wedding garments, discovers the couple lying in their bed of thorns beside the church, he is determined to make them share in the nuptial feast. Once more he sends for the Saint. 'Those I cure a second time', warns the holy father, 'go on seeing till the hour of death' (III, 139). For the blind couple, the moment of active choice has arrived. This time, they know from experience how the vision of the Saint makes them look. Defiantly Martin resists the efforts to force them once more to their knees in childish submission:

> MARTIN DOUL [*more troubled*]. We're not asking our sight, holy father, and let you be walking on and leaving us in our peace at the crossing roads, for it's best we are this way, and we're not asking to see (III, 139).

His request is tolerant and modest. They are prepared to let the priest go his own way, only asking in return that they be allowed to choose theirs. But Martin's and Mary's road is a crossing of the way of the Saint which he cannot tolerate. He rebukes Martin for refusing 'to be looking on the earth, and the image of the Lord is thrown upon men' (III, 139). Finding this passive looking a poor exchange for their own active way of seeing, Martin begins his point-by-point rejection of this view of the world, in words which simultaneously evoke and reject the image of the crucified Christ, and with it, the Saint's version of Christian eschatology:

> MARTIN DOUL [*raising his voice, by degrees*]. That's great sights, holy father... What was it I seen my first day, but your own bleeding feet and they cut with the stones, and my last day, but the villainy of herself that you're wedding, God forgive you, with Timmy the smith. That was great sights, maybe... (III, 141).

In place of the Saint's order to look for the thorny 'as if' gold of the furze-bushes, where the holy men have built churches, Martin offers the blind couple's words of commitment to a fertile world awaiting the creative labour of man:

> MARTIN DOUL [*fiercely*]. Isn't it finer sights ourselves had a while since and we sitting dark smelling the sweet beautiful smells do be rising in the warm nights and hearing the swift flying things racing in the air [SAINT *draws back from him*], till we'd be looking up in our own minds into a grand sky, and seeing lakes, and broadening rivers, and hills are waiting for the spade and plough (III, 141).

In contrast to the priest's aesthetics of reflection, Martin's words create a vision of activity in which man has a role to play in changing reality.

Like the villagers in *The Playboy of the Western World*, the people cannot tolerate very much of this reality. They call on the Saint to break up the unholy alliance and at least to claim Mary for the old man in the skies:

> PEOPLE. That's it, cure Mary Doul your reverence (III, 143).

Mary tries to resist them but her faith begins to waver under the insistence that if the pair refuse to see as the Saint sees, then neither shall they eat. As she gives way hesitantly, the scene is set for a re-enactment of the first encounter with the priest. Moving forward, the holy father struggles to '*take* MARTIN DOUL's *hand away from* MARY DOUL' (III, 145). As he does so, Martin defiantly asserts his conjugal claims. Condemning the Saint for his interfering officiousness, he challenges his divisive acts and words:

> MARTIN DOUL [*pushes him away roughly, and stands with his left hand on* MARY DOUL's *shoulder*]. Keep off yourself, holy father, and let you not be taking my rest from me in the darkness of my wife . . . What call have the like of you to be coming in where you're not wanted at all, and making a great mess with the holy water you have and the length of your prayers? [*Defiantly.*] Go on, I'm saying, and leave us this place on the road (III, 145).

The Saint's veneer of meekness and love cracks and in its place he calls on the brute force of the villagers. Confronted by collective violence, Martin clings to Mary, rebuking the crowd for their own spiritual blindness:

> MARTIN DOUL [*throwing himself down on the ground clinging to* MARY DOUL]. I'll not come, I'm saying, and let you take his holy water to cure the blackness of your souls today (III, 145).

Marriage for the Saint is sacrosanct only according to his version of the word, and he orders the villagers to pull the couple apart. This time, however, Martin finds salvation in a superbly comic subversion of submission to the word. Calling out a loud recantation of his heathen apostasy, he proclaims his readiness to accept from the Saint 'anything that you will' (III, 147). Praising the 'great joy' (III, 147) Mary will have looking on the Saint's face, and praying for the singular vision which will enable him to 'see when it's lies she's telling' (III, 147), he kneels meekly. The Saint eagerly seizes the chance of making the deviant couple as normal and conformist as everybody else who says 'Yea' to his 'Yea' and 'Nay' to his 'Nay'. He moves towards the blind pair to sprinkle them again 'with the power of the water from the grave of the four beauties of God' (III, 147). But the power of lying can be enacted by a dirty deed as well as by a gallous word. Silently and suddenly Martin strikes the murderous coup-de-grace. Hitting the can of water from the Saint's hands, he sends it rocketing across the stage. His triumph reaches its climax when he reminds the Saint that there is more vision and power in the dark sense of a blind man than is dreamed of in the ascetic 'fasting, holy ways have left you with a big head on you and a thin pitiful arm' (III, 149). The Saint's vision is all in the mind and nothing in the labour of the deed.

The blind couple have finally found their way through the thorny gap of vacancy. But their double-edged vision is an intolerable threat to the single-eyed. The villagers angrily order the couple to 'go on from this place' (III, 149). As he gropes towards his stone with Mary Doul, Martin makes a final appeal for tolerance and understanding. Like Mary in *The Tinker's Wedding*, he offers a modest defence of the right not to despair of earthly beauty simply because it is imperfect and transitory:

> MARTIN DOUL. We're going surely, for if it's a right some of you have to be working and sweating the like of Timmy the smith, and a right some of you have to be fasting and praying and talking holy talk the like of yourself, I'm thinking it's a good right ourselves have to be sitting blind, hearing a soft wind turning round the little leaves of the spring and feeling the sun, and we not tormenting our souls with the sight of the grey days, and the holy men, and the dirty feet is trampling the world (III, 149).

Even this degree of commitment to life is too much for the sainted people. Martin's blessing of the earth might bring down on them a terrible word from the heavens of God. Priest and villagers together drive the blind couple out, but as they do so, the people's words unwittingly suggest that a transfer of power has taken place from the heavenly Father to the earthly couple:

> PEOPLE [*all together*]. Go on now, Martin Doul. Go on from this place. Let you not be bringing great storms or droughts on us maybe from the power of the Lord. [*Some of them throw things at him*] (III, 149).

As Martin and Mary prepare to leave, they go as honest makers and purveyors of light to anyone willing to give them halfpence on the road. They go, not to the woods, but to seek in the 'towns of the south . . . people will have kind voices maybe, and we won't know their bad looks or their villainy at all' (III, 149). Like Nora and the Tramp in *In the Shadow of the Glen*, they are under no illusions about the way they have chosen, 'walking with a slough of wet on the one side and a slough of wet on the other, and you going a stony path with a north wind blowing behind' (III, 151). But their creative engagement with the provisional and the incomplete offers an objectively grounded resolution of the essentially solipsistic dilemma which confronted them at the outset of their journey towards self-knowledge.

Martin's and Mary's new way of seeing and doing is a social engagement with living in which language offers its users the possibilities and responsibilities of choice. Going forth, the blind couple take each other's hands; if they are drowned, then in that final immersion 'the two of them will be drowned together' (III, 151). Ironically, it is the Saint, as he prepares to call the whole village up into the church to put his blessing on them all, who speaks the final tribute to the couple's transfiguration. 'They', he tells Timmy the smith disapprovingly, 'have chosen their lot' (III, 151). As Molly and Timmy prepare to submit themselves to the holy father's rites and rituals, we, the audience, have more than a passing notion of which couple have chosen the better part. And as the curtain falls on the procession to the church, we must surely hear once again the echo of Mary Doul's voice calling out her triumphant warning:

The Lord protect us from the Saints of God! (III, 133)

NOTES

1. Kenneth Burke, *Language as Symbolic Action: Essays on Life, Literature and Method* (Berkeley and London, University of California Press, 1966), p. 359.

2. Ibid., p. 359.

3. TCD MS 4379, f. 84.

4. Ibid., f. 85.

5. Oxford English Dictionary.

6. In his essay, 'Definition of Man', Kenneth Burke 'decided that a final codicil was still needed, thus making in all:

Man is the symbol using (symbol-making, symbol-misusing) animal inventor of the negative (or moralized by the negative) separated from his natural condition by instruments of his own making goaded by the spirit of hierarchy (or moved by the sense of order) and rotten with perfection.'

Burke, *Language as Symbolic Action*, p.16.

7. The Song of Solomon 1.5.

8. V.N. Volosinov, *Marxism and the Philosophy of Language*, translated by Ladislav Matejka and I.R. Titunik (New York and London, Seminar Press, 1973), p.11.

9. Katharine Worth, *The Irish Drama of Europe from Yeats to Beckett*, (London, Athlone Press, 1978), p. 131.

10. Bertolt Brecht, *Werke*, 20, p. 154. Quoted in Dieter Richter, 'History and Dialectics in the Materialist Theory of Literature', translated by Vicki Hill and Charles Spencer, in *New German Critique*, 6 (1965), p. 40.

11. Elliot Krieger, *A Marxist Study of Shakespeare's Comedies* (London and Basingstoke, Macmillan, 1979), p. 59.

12. Bakhtin notes that 'the image of a small tinkling bell' appears in carnivals 'in the mythical images . . . of "Erl-King's retinue" '. See *Rabelais and his World*, translated by Hélène Iswolsky (Cambridge Massachusetts and London, Massachusetts Institute of Technology, 1968), p. 214.

7.
METADRAMA IN *THE PLAYBOY OF THE WESTERN WORLD*

IN *THE Well of the Saints*, language becomes for the central characters a mode of symbolic action which enables them to come to terms with, and to transcend, the verbal games of the villagers and the dogmatic authoritarianism of the Saint. Synge's last completed work, *The Playboy of the Western World*, might justifiably be described as the apotheosis of the metadramatic itself.[1] Many critics have remarked how the exuberance of the language in this play strains towards a kind of self-conscious parody, calling attention to its poetic status and also to a certain histrionic extravagance. Others have seen in Christy Mahon a character who is made into a hero by the dramatic role which he is called upon to enact. Only Thomas Whitaker, however, in his essay 'On playing with *The Playboy*', seems to appreciate the importance of play as a major dramatic theme.[2] The work explores the complex interactions between play, world and word, which Pegeen simplifies, with tragic consequences for herself, into a division between gallous story and dirty deed. One way of looking at the structure of the work is to see it as a series of progressively intensifying incursions into the doubly dramatic world of self-referential play. Periodic carefully orchestrated excursions into the mimetic reflection of the 'real' world take place in a series of comic debunking episodes, until, in the scene in which Christy bites Shawn's leg and Pegeen burns Christy's leg with a sod of turf, we arrive at a turning-point in the hero's role *as* playboy, and in the play's questioning of the nature of drama and its relationship to the world of the audience.

133

The opening lines of *The Playboy of the Western World* strike a metadramatic note, introducing us to a list of costumes and props, some of them having a remarkably ancient and honourable theatrical genealogy, to be used on a festive occasion. Pegeen is speaking and writing an order for

> Six yards of stuff for to make a yellow gown. A pair of lace boots with lengthy heels on them and brassy eyes. A hat is suited for a wedding-day. A fine tooth comb. To be sent with three barrels of porter in Jimmy Farrell's creel cart on the evening of the coming Fair (IV, 57).

Momentarily here, language and action exactly coincide. They are to be separated almost immediately. Pegeen, scornful of Shawn Keogh's indecent haste to abandon the need to move abroad in the darkness and to assume instead what he sees as the comfortable state, or stasis, of matrimony, calls into question her intention of ever becoming his bride.

> PEGEEN [*with rather scornful good humour*]. You're making mighty certain, Shaneen, that I'll wed you now (IV, 59).

Shawn Keogh is obviously not the character envisaged by Pegeen Mike in her search for a hero for her drama; indeed, she tells her would-be husband, the whole village is sadly bereft of anyone suitable for such a role. But as well as a heroine looking for a hero, we also have the makings, at the outset, of an audience in pursuit of a spectacle. We quickly learn that an absent character, 'himself', soon to materialise as Pegeen's father, is above at the crossroads making plans to attend Kate Cassidy's wake. The dual references to wakes and weddings establish two of the important ritual or game-like parameters within which the action of the play takes place. They also set the context or scene within which we first hear news of the playboy, Christy Mahon.

The pervasive mood of the opening movement, however, is not uniformly, or even predominantly, comic. The atmosphere, rather, is one of uneasy, ill-defined fear. Pegeen fears 'the long nights' and 'these twelve hours of dark'; Michael James dreads the thought of 'crossing backward through the Stooks of the Dead Women'; Shawn is frightened of everything from 'the cows breathing, and sighing in the stillness of the air' to 'Father Reilly and . . . the Holy Father and the

Cardinals of Rome' (IV, 57–63 *passim*). An actor-audience without a hero, they are fearful of lifting the curtain to discover only 'a long night and with great darkness' (IV, 61). These characters are unable to supply Pegeen even with 'a penny pot-boy to stand along with me and give me courage in the doing of my work' (IV, 65). When called upon to protect his bride-to-be, Shawn runs away in fear of Father Reilly and the Holy Father in Rome, leaving only the empty 'coat of a Christian man' (IV, 65). The dismantling of Shawn when he refuses to stay with Pegeen is the first of a series of episodes which revolve around the metadramatic stage business of changing costumes. It prepares for the elaborate and sustained playboy association between Shawn and Christy Mahon. Later in the drama, yet another coat, Shawn's wedding-coat, will be donned by Christy as he goes forth to claim Pegeen as his bride. Far from being simple antagonists, Shawn and Christy, anti-hero and hero, are related to each other: they are not two characters but one.[3] Similar homological relationships are also established between Pegeen, the Widow Quin and the Widow Casey, between Michael James and Old Mahon, and between Christy and his father. Because such shifting psychic complexities are an indispensable part of the comic strategy, anticipating Brecht's dramaturgy of 'the new human type', we shall examine in some detail certain of the ways in which they are constructed and maintained throughout the play.[4]

The general fears that Pegeen may really need a protector begin to focus on rumours, started by Shawn himself and repeated by Michael James, of the presence of 'a kind of fellow above in the furzy ditch, groaning wicked like a maddening dog' (IV, 61); 'a queer fellow above going mad or getting his death, maybe, in the gripe of the ditch' (IV, 65); and finally, 'The queer dying fellow's beyond looking over the ditch' (IV, 67). The apparition of this spectre — the death and resurrection motif is important — is enough to make Shawn run back into the room for fear that 'he'll be having my life and I going home in the darkness of the night' (IV, 67). When the nameless fellow materialises, he comes forth more like a trembling incarnation of fear itself than as fit cause of the general trepidation. He also bears a remarkable resemblance in appearance and conversation, or the lack of it, to Shawn Keogh:

[*For a perceptible moment they watch the door with curiosity. Someone coughs*

outside. Then CHRISTY MAHON, *a slight young man, comes in, very tired and
frightened and dirty.*]
CHRISTY [*in a small voice*]. God save all here! (IV, 67)

This shadow of Shawn seems very unpromising material indeed for
the villagers to work up into either villain or hero. They treat their
character at first as a kind of neutral mirror upon which to project their
own fears — fears of landlords and bailiffs, of press-gangs and police, of
punishment for forgery, lynching and lust. Confronted with the good
fortune of a potential, if reluctant, chief actor, or scapegoat, they try to
get their drama under way by seeking to cast this nameless individual
in a variety of conventional roles. Each of them in turn catechises him
in an effort to make him name the deed he has done. Even language,
however, seems to be beyond Christy's capabilities and so they begin to
treat him like a schoolboy needing to be taught the meaning and use of
words. His inability to match word with deed elicits the following
markedly metalinguistic exchange:

MICHAEL. It should be larceny, I'm thinking?
CHRISTY [*dolefully*]. I had it in my mind it was a different word and a
  bigger.
PEGEEN. There's a queer lad! Were you never slapped in school, young
  fellow, that you don't know the name of your deed?
CHRISTY [*bashfully*]. I'm slow at learning, a middling scholar only.
MICHAEL. If you're a dunce itself, you'd have a right to know that
  larceny's robbing and stealing. Is it for the like of that you're wanting?
  (IV, 69)

Christy's difficulties with language, his self-deprecating remarks
about his scholarship, will be echoed almost word for word by his rival,
in Act II, when Shawn describes himself as 'a poor scholar with
middling faculties to coin a lie' (IV, 115).

The prompting of his interrogator begins to make Christy respond.
They are an eager audience, anxious to involve him in some kind of
plot. Finally, Pegeen challenges him with being a mere sayer of words,
not a doer of deeds:

PEGEEN [*coming from counter*]. He's done nothing, so. [*To* CHRISTY.] If
  you didn't commit murder . . . there isn't anything would be worth your
  troubling for to run from now. You did nothing at all (IV, 71).

136

Appropriately, it is her mock threat to murder him — containing in itself an element of play — which spurs Christy into naming his act:

> CHRISTY [*twisting round on her with a sharp cry of horror*]. Don't strike me . . . I killed my poor father, Tuesday was a week, for doing the like of that (IV, 73).

This comparison between Pegeen's projected deed and Christy's putative crime is the first of several parallels which are drawn throughout the play between himself, Pegeen, the Widow Quin and various other characters, based on their shared potential for murder. As question and answer follow each other in quick succession, the parricidal drama is rehearsed by the questioners and played out by Christy. *The motive and the cue for passion?* 'He was a dirty man, God forgive him' (IV, 73). *The weapon?* 'I just riz the loy' (IV, 73). *The deed?* 'And let fall the edge of it on the ridge of his skull' (IV, 73). *The scene?* 'Oh, a distant place, master of the house, a windy corner of high distant hills' (IV, 75).

The first rehearsal of his deed wins for the player the approval of the actor-audience — his first round of applause. But the alacrity with which the men then leave Christy to protect Pegeen, hurrying off from the reported drama of Old Mahon's murder to the dionysiac celebrations of a real wake, suggests that to them, the play has been a diverting drama of convenience. The game has been played to the gallery on their terms and they have duly applauded the hero whom they have created. When they depart for the wake, Pegeen is left not with a hero, but with two cowards. Her father-slaying pot-boy is just as fearful as Shawn of father figures, the law and women. Their shared lack of maturity is underlined when Pegeen refers to them disparagingly as 'lad' and 'young fellow' (IV, 79).

Once he is left alone with Pegeen, Christy collapses into a Shawn-like exhibition of weary self-deprecation. The occasional flashes of pride which he manages are sparked off by Pegeen equating him unexpectedly with 'the great powers and potentates of France and Spain' (IV, 79). His own account of himself is of a 'quiet simple poor fellow' whose closest approach to fame was that he 'near got six months for going with a dung-fork and stabbing a fish' (IV, 83). Far from being a father-slaying hero, or a useful father-substitute, Christy

137

appears more like a changeling child in danger of being 'stolen off and kidnabbed while himself's abroad' (IV, 89).

If Shawn Keogh and Christy Mahon are uncomfortably alike, when the Widow Quin and Christy first meet, deeper than surface relationships are quickly established also between these two unlikely confrères. The Widow has a reputation for homicide — she 'hit himself with a worn pick', a deed which Pegeen regards as 'a sneaky kind of murder' (IV, 89). But their apparent complicity in crime is not the only implied association between the young lad and the older woman. In this first encounter Synge carefully prepares the ground for the scene in Act II when, urged on by the Widow, Christy re-enacts for the second time the murder of his father. The later scene, in Act II, leads to the first mock-wedding in the play, between the hero and the older woman, a wedding which rowdily celebrates their shared reputation for slaying. Already in Act I the Widow is emerging as possible rival to Pegeen for Christy's hand. Moved by jealous realisation of this, Pegeen recounts, for Christy's edification, the wildly comic yet weirdly serious black mass tale of the stew made by the Widow Quin for the bishop of Connaught, from a black ram which she suckled at her breast. This atavistic story activates a series of sinister tropic links between the playboy and the Widow which revolve around images and rites associating Christy Mahon with Christ as the sacrificial sheep or lamb.

For the greater part of the angry exchange between Pegeen Mike and the Widow Quin in Act I as to which of them should possess him, Christy, who has risen from near death, sits with his blistered feet, at supper, holding his cup and cake. If he believes he has slain his da, the Widow has destroyed her man, buried her children and cooked her foster-ram in a stew. She takes a perverse delight in having been formed by the Lord God 'to be living lone', that is, without a man, but she claims that there isn't her 'match in Mayo for thatching or mowing or shearing a sheep' (IV, 89). Pegeen warns Christy of the notoriety won by the androgynous Widow for 'shaving the foxy skipper from France for a threepenny bit and a sop of grass tobacco would wring the liver from a mountain goat' (IV, 89). If we link this with the warning to Christy that he will find her 'leaky thatch is growing more pasture for her buck goat then her square of fields, and she without a tramp itself to keep order in her place at all' (IV, 89), we begin to appreciate that it was not for nothing that Synge described several scenes in *The Playboy of the Western World* as Rabelaisian. The rewards given the Widow for shaving the skipper begin to appear more as trophies carried off in a sexual game than as mere payment for services rendered to a hirsute mariner.

Our suspicions that there is nothing simple about the Widow's relationship to Christy are intensified when we learn, in Act II, that he murdered his da, or so he believes, because he was being forced by his father to wed another widow, the Widow Casey, a woman remarkably like the Widow Quin, 'of noted misbehaviour with the old and young' (IV, 101). Just as Pegeen tells of the Widow Quin's malpractices, so Christy accuses the Widow Casey of witch-like behaviour 'and she a hag this day with a tongue on her has the crows and seabirds scattered, the way they wouldn't cast a shadow on her garden with the dread of her curse' (IV, 103). It is well known in Christy's parish, he tells us — recalling the Widow Quin's fostering and cooking activities — that the same Widow Casey 'did suckle me for six weeks when I came into the world' (IV, 103). Nor is this the only comic hint of complicated incestuous goings-on in the maze of shifting relationships. We hear from Christy himself that Old Mahon had his own designs on the Widow Casey, 'and he without a thought the whole while but now he'd have her but to live in and her gold to drink' (IV, 103). The pattern of forced marriage with a surrogate mother threatens to repeat itself for Christy when the Widow Quin offers in Act II to make it possible for Shawn Keogh, at a price, to wed Pegeen. She will remove the obstacle to their union by marrying Christy herself. To complicate matters still further — or perhaps to underline our point — there is clear evidence from the drafts of *The Playboy* that Synge toyed with the possibility of marrying either the Widow Quin or Pegeen Mike off in the end to Christy's da.

The tropic pattern deriving from sheep imagery runs like a *leitmotif* through all of these sequences, forging further psychic links between the characters. To enable him to marry his first cousin, Shawn awaits a dispensation on a sheepskin parchment from the Holy Father. Part of the bride-price demanded by the Widow for ensuring that the wedding between relations can go ahead is to be Shawn's mountainy ram, the wedding-ring which he intended for Pegeen and the loan of his own bridegroom's suit, the way she can 'have Christy decent on the wedding day' (IV, 117). At the precise moment that this dubious and dangerous bargain is being driven, our playboy hero is busy attiring himself in Shawneen's hat, breeches and new coat 'is woven from the blackest shearings for three miles round' (IV, 115). Having dressed himself in the coat of black shearings, Christy *becomes* as randy as any mountainy ram. Swaggeringly he declares his intentions of 'going abroad on the hillside for to seek Pegeen' (IV, 119), who, coincidentally, if we care to see these sequences as coincidence rather than as a series of ironic correspondences, has gone in pursuit of *her* 'mountainy sheep' (IV, 113).[5]

Our hero, then, is living dangerously. The tropic allusions repeatedly associated with the formidable Widow Quin conspire to suggest a powerful and dangerous sexuality. The stakes for which she plays her part in the playboy game are substantial. It is she who puts Christy 'down in the sports below for racing, lepping, pitching, and the Lord knows what' (IV, 99), and who first, and twice, confers on him, albeit ironically, the title of the playboy of the western world. The price she wants for her contrivings, from both Shawn and Christy, is high. Effectively, it is no less than total possession. To her 'a ewe's a small thing'; from Shawn she demands 'the red cow you have and the mountainy ram, and the right of way across your rye path, and a load of dung at Michaelmas, and turbary upon the western hill' (IV, 117). In the almost identical bargaining scene with Christy she asks for 'a right of way I want, and a mountainy ram, and a load of dung at Michaelmas' (IV, 131). The tropic, often metonymic, correspondences here between people and properties leave little doubt about the fate awaiting her suitors if they accept the Widow Quin's terms. Both Christy and Shawn, or shall we say Christy-Shawn, are too much in the son for their comfort: domination by the father is by no means the only threat to their independence or identity. Indeed, Pegeen also often treats both Shawn and Christy with an imperiousness which equals that of the older woman: the Widow Quin herself prophetically warns Christy of the 'right torment will await you here if you go romancing with her like' (IV, 91).

The central characters in *The Playboy of the Western World* restlessly merge and melt into each other. This theme of multiple role-playing is also embodied in the broad structure of the play. Each of the three acts presents us with a parallel pattern: Christy is cast in the role of hero (or potential hero) in a play within the play. He is then called upon to try out his status in relation to those who have encouraged his assumption of heroism. He meets with Pegeen in a love-scene, and he is placed in a situation in which he must measure his new status against his past. In Acts II and III, this past materialises to confront him in the person of his father. Christy's happy realisation at the end of the first act that the killing of his da — or his enactment of it for his audience — has 'two fine women fighting for the likes of me' (IV, 93) marks the first stage in his role-playing. Neither we nor Christy can yet be sure, however, of what self is likely to develop as our hero slowly hides himself away, like an infant returning to the womb, under Pegeen's quilt. In what he hopefully sees as his triumphant end is merely his dramatic beginning.

> CHRISTY. Well it's a clean bed and soft with it, and it's great luck and company I've won me in the end of time (IV, 93).

He will be called upon to resume his play-acting at the crowing of the cock.

When the curtain goes up on Act II, it reveals a setting identical to that of the opening of the play. Christy is naming and enumerating a list of properties and holding a girl's boot, which he is cleaning. Like Pegeen in Act I, he is imaginatively projecting himself into the role of the married state:

> CHRISTY [*to himself, counting jugs on dresser*]. Half a hundred beyond. Ten there. A score that's above. Eighty jugs. Six cups and a broken one. Two plates. A power of glasses. Bottles, a school-master'd be hard set to count, and enough in them, I'm thinking, to drunken all the wealth and wisdom of the County Clare. [*He puts down the boot carefully.*] (IV, 95)

Holding the mirror up to check his identity, he compares his reflection with the face he saw in the past, in 'the divil's own mirror we had beyond, would twist a squint across an angel's brow' (IV, 95) and he speculates optimistically about his future good looks. His actor-like musings are interrupted by the advent of yet another audience in search of a drama. Caught waiting in the wings, with his 'long neck naked of the world' (IV, 95), Christy repeats Shawn's defrocked disappearance in Act I. When the stranger girls come seeking their hero, 'there's nobody in it' (IV, 95). The painfully constructed heroic identity has vanished and the disappointed stage audience is left thinking 'Shawn Keogh was making game of us and there's no such man in it at all' (IV, 95). These words again introduce explicitly the theme of making game, while the juxtaposition of the reference to Shawn Keogh with the reference to the non-existent, or no-man, Christy, continues the process of identification between the two. The scenes which follow maintain the close structural parallels to the opening scenes of Act I, with a marked intensification of the metadrama. Honor, Nellie, Sara and Susan have come in search of *their* hero, bearing gifts, but Christy has risen and vanished and only the covers are left. Continuing the theme of dressing up, the girls try to evoke the presence of their hero by feeling, smelling, peering at and trying on Christy's boots:

> SUSAN [*smelling it*]. That's bog water I'm thinking, but it's his own they are surely, for I never seen the like of them for whity mud, and red mud, and turf on them, and the fine sands of the sea. That man's been walking, I'm telling you. [*She goes down right, putting on one of his boots.*] (IV, 97)

By putting herself — literally — in these boots Sara hopes to assimilate something of their wearer's heroic identity.

The ritual of gift offerings which takes place when Christy finally emerges and shows himself forth to the women as 'the man killed his father' (IV, 97), has been seen by several critics as a parody of the bringing of gifts to Christ by the Magi — but the gifts also have an Easter connotation which both evokes and subverts the resurrection motif. The newly risen hero is offered 'duck's eggs', 'a little cut of a cake', recalling his earlier appearance with cup and cake at supper, and 'a little laying pullet — boiled and all she is — was crushed at the fall of night by the curate's car' (IV, 99). As Sara urges Christy to lay his hand on the sacrificial bird — 'Is your right hand too sacred for to use at all?' (IV, 99) — she notices that he is a very strange fellow indeed — nothing less, perhaps, than the very reverse of his face value:

> [*She slips round behind him*]. It's a glass he has. Well I never seen to this day,

a man with a looking-glass held to his back. Them that kills their fathers is a vain lot surely (IV, 99).

Christy's acceptance of the gifts (he piles them, patten-like, on the glass) is followed by the ritualised pantomime of his showing forth to the Widow Quin:

GIRLS [*giggling*]. That's the man killed his father.
WIDOW QUIN [*coming to them*]. I know well it's the man; and I'm after putting him down in the sports below for racing, lepping, pitching, and the Lord knows what (IV, 99).

He is called upon now to assume a whole succession of personae or masks and as the mock-eucharistic ritual proceeds, his role as hero-victim is elaborated. The cannibalistic connotations in the Widow's ambiguous admonition to the congregation, 'you'd have a right to have him fresh and nourished in place of nursing a feast' (IV, 101), are emphasised when she lifts him up bodily and places him on a bench. The hero is once again being fattened for a role-playing feast:

WIDOW QUIN. Come here to me [*she puts him on bench beside her while the* GIRLS *make tea and get his breakfast*], and let you tell us your story before Pegeen will come (IV, 101).

That Christy is beginning to learn his part as 'a fine, gamey, treacherous lad' (IV, 101) shows in the histrionic panache with which he responds to his second catechesis. He entertains his audience this time with a much more theatrical reconstruction of the murder of his da, including graphic descriptions of characters and a direct rendering of dialogue. Encouraged by the applause, he waxes eloquent not just of word but of gesture, until, with a climactic upsurge of dramatic confidence, he achieves the breakthrough into a mimesis of action itself. Using the chicken-bone remnant of the communion-feast as a prop, he reproduces the earth-shattering parricidal blow with the loy:

SUSAN. That's a grand story.
HONOR. He tells it lovely.
CHRISTY [*flattered and confident, waving bone*]. He gave a drive with the

scythe, and I gave a lep to the east. Then I turned around with my back to the north, and I hit a blow on the ridge of his skull, laid him stretched out, and he split to the knob of his gullet. [*He raises the chicken bone to his Adam's apple.*] (IV, 103)

This performance warrants recognition of Christy as a New Adam — with a spouse whose reputation matches his own:

> SUSAN. I'm thinking the Lord God sent him this road to make a second husband to the Widow Quin, and she with a great yearning to be wedded though all dread her here. Lift him on her knee, Sara Tansey (IV, 103-5).

But as he is lifted like a baby onto the Widow's knee and she mockingly calls out 'Don't tease him' (IV, 105), we once again ask how far they see him as man or as child, as hero or as victim. Do they take their playboy seriously, or is he their fool merely — an entertaining sport? The mock-sacramental feast is rounded off by the first of the play's two mock-weddings as Sarah's imagination takes flight into a parodic litany in praise of heroes:

> SARA [*going over to dresser and counter very quickly, and getting two glasses and porter*]. You're heroes surely, and let you drink a supeen with your arms linked like the outlandish lovers in the sailor's song. [*She links their arms and gives them the glasses.*] There now. Drink a health to the wonders of the western world, the pirates, preachers, poteen-makers, with the jobbing jockies, parching peelers, and the juries fill their stomachs selling judgements of the English law. [*Brandishing the bottle.*] (IV, 105)

The mock-nuptials between Christy and the Widow Quin are interrupted by the sudden return of Pegeen. She quickly deprives him of his audience and ordering him to put away scenery and props, methodically strips him of his heroic role:

> PEGEEN [*imperiously*]. Fling out that rubbish and put them cups away. [CHRISTY *tidies away in great haste.*] Shove in the bench by the wall. [*He does so.*] And hang that glass on the nail. What disturbed it at all? (IV, 105)

The effect of his play-acting does not wear off as quickly on this second occasion. Threatening to repeat the act of murder — and not just with a chicken-bone — Christy *'takes up a loy and goes towards her with feigned assurance'* (IV, 107). Scornfully reducing his deed to a mere story, however, Pegeen treats him to an account of what the real consequence of his claimed deed may be. He is made to see himself not in the mirror of heroic drama, but reflected in the pages of the 'papers the post-boy does have in his bag' (IV, 107)· Pegeen menaces him with:

> a story filled half a page of the hanging of a man. Ah, that should be a fearful end, young fellow, and it worst of all for a man destroyed his da, for the like of him would get small mercies, and when it's dead he is, they'd put him in a narrow grave, with cheap sacking wrapping him round, and pour down quicklime on his head, the way you'd see a woman pouring any frish-frash from a cup (IV, 107).

Her newspaper melodrama recalls Christy sitting quiet with his cup and ominously foreshadows her own treacherous treatment of her hero at the end.

Christy's playing at being a hero seems only to have led him to a Lucifer-like fall, from which he will have to start to build his identity all over again. Cut off from the acclaim and acceptance of the people, he becomes acutely aware of the need for an audience. 'What would any be but odd men', he asks Pegeen, 'and they living lonesome in the world?' (IV, 111). Christy's poetry-talk in this scene draws its inspiration from a growing realisation of his need to love and to be loved: only through relationship can identity be established. His speeches have a lyrical-elegiac quality devoid for the moment of the boastful delight in heroic exaggeration which characterised his second enactment of the murder. His mood when Pegeen seems to cease 'making game' of him is one of *'fearful joy'* (IV, 113). When, however, it is succeeded by the enraptured hope that all his struggles are over, and the belief that he has almost reached the final goal of a happy ever after life with Pegeen, Shawn Keogh and the Widow Quin burst rudely in upon them both:

> SHAWN [*to* PEGEEN]. I was passing below and I seen your mountainy sheep eating cabbages in Jimmy's field. Run up or they'll be bursting surely (IV, 113).

Pegeen runs to the rescue of the sheep — foreshadowing, perhaps, her ultimate pursuit of conventional morality and her own retreat from rich pastures. As she does so, the Widow closes the door and *'sits down with an amused smile'* to watch the next act in the villagers' play: 'Shaneen has long speeches for to tell you now' (IV, 113) — and he has brought along costumes and props.

The playing out of the play within the play takes up where it was broken off by Pegeen's intrusion. On this occasion it is Shawn who is the bearer of gifts, while Christy reverses roles by catechising his rival as the latter tries to persuade him to disappear for ever from the scene with 'the half of a ticket to the Western States' (IV, 113). As Christy, urged on by the Widow Quin, dresses himself in Shawn's clothes, thus becoming his like, Shawn desperately wishes that he could clothe himself in Christy's reputation for action:

> SHAWN. Oh, Widow Quin, what'll I be doing now? I'd inform again him, but he'd burst from Kilmainham and he'd be sure and certain to destroy me. If I wasn't so God-fearing, I'd near have courage to come behind him and run a pike into his side. Oh, it's a hard case to be an orphan and not to have your father that you're used to, and you'd easy kill and make yourself a hero in the sight of all. [*Coming up to her.*] Oh, Widow Quin, will you find me some contrivance when I've promised you a ewe? (IV, 117)

The playboy's second downfall from envied hero to trembling victim is comically sudden. Swaggering out in his rival's black sheep's coat to claim Pegeen, he comes face to face instead with the eschatological nightmare — 'the walking spirit of my murdered da', 'that ghost of hell' (IV, 119). Shawn-like once more, he scuttles away to hide behind the door.

With the materialisation of Old Mahon, we are offered a further reconstruction of Christy's persona, as the formula of question and answer once more elicits an account of the murder. This time the character who emerges is 'an ugly young streeler with a murderous gob on him', 'a lier on walls, a talker of folly, a man you'd see stretched the half of the day in the brown ferns with his belly to the sun', a shirker of work who'd 'be fooling over little birds he had — finches and felts — or making mugs at his own self in the bit of a glass we had hung on the wall' (IV, 119-23, *passim*). There can be little doubt that aspects of Christy's persona are reflected — and refracted — in his father's description of him; but we are scarcely willing, by now, to take these words at face value. If Old Mahon condemns his son for lazy dreaming, narcissism and even effeminacy — 'he was taken with contortions till I had to send him in the ass cart to the females' nurse' (IV, 123) — we have more than a suspicion that such vices might well be seen, from another perspective, as virtues. In any case, the Widow Quin's words of wonder:

> WIDOW QUIN [*clasping her hands*] Well, I never till this day heard tell of a man the like of that (IV, 123),

remind us that his father's image of Christy is one more verbal construct. If Christy is 'the looney of Mahon's' (IV, 123), perhaps he has become so because that is a part which Old Mahon wishes him to play — or perhaps, like Lear's fool or Brecht's Gayly Gay, he sometimes wears motley by consent.

By the end of the play's second act, the quest for the hero has by no means succeeded in establishing for him once and for all a definitive identity. Rather, we might say, as Walter Benjamin said of the writer for epic theatre, that Synge's attitude towards his plot is 'like that of a ballet teacher to his pupil. His first aim is to loosen her joints to the very limits of the possible'.[6] The final act intensifies and then goes beyond the theme of role-playing, reminding us as it does so that where action is concerned, 'it can happen this way, but it can also happen quite a different way'.[7] If we examine the drafts of this act, we notice the unusual number of possible endings which Synge considered before settling for the unconventional resolution of Christy's exit with his father 'like a gallant captain with his heathen slave' (IV, 173). The conclusions which he drafted and rejected take up and play with the theme of a complicated nexus of possible relationships between Christy and the other leading characters:

(1) Pegeen might marry Shawn (Christy's double and her cousin — because of which relationship of consanguinity she needs a papal dispensation, sought through Father Reilly)

(2) She might marry Christy's father, thus becoming his mother, by law,

and going out with Christy presumably as her legitimised son

(3) The Widow Quin might take Christy into her care: as son? or husband? or both? or neither?

(4) The Widow might marry Christy's father — thus becoming his mother, or

(5) perhaps most curious of all, Christy might marry the Widow Quin upon the refusal of Pegeen's father to wed her, i.e. Christy might marry the rejected lover of the father of his erstwhile bride, thus becoming, in a sense, surrogate father to Pegeen.[8]

We appear to have here still further evidence of characters who are the subjects of psychic decomposition, that kind of 'atavistic strain' which 'tends to break down the duality of Self and World, and hence to blur and make more fluid the contours of individual identity'.[9] This might seem to be at odds with the usual critical contention that the play ends with a triumphant assertion of Christy's uniqueness and individuality. It would only be so, however, if we were to regard individuality as the polar opposite of collective identity. A society in quest of a hero might be said to be a people in search of a focus for their collective, and historical, identity, while a character in search of an audience is in some sense seeking the social identity which helps to establish and reflect his individual personality.

The third act begins, like Acts I and II, with a variation on the theme of hunt the hero. Philly's and Jimmy's conversation brings into comic conjunction once again the topics of weddings and wakes. Their debate raises the question of the possible outcomes of play-acting, gaming, and story-telling, for Christy:

JIMMY. He's right luck, I'm telling you!
PHILLY. If he has he'll be rightly hobbled yet, and he not able to say ten words without making a brag of the way he killed his father and the great blow he hit with the loy (IV, 133).

In the last act there takes place the double, and double-edged, apotheosis of hero and play. We shall argue that we have in this act not one, but two endings. The comic mock-conventional finale of the play within the play, of the playing with Christy as hero, occurs when Michael James assumes the role of officiator at the mock wedding of Christy and Pegeen, a ceremony in which father and priest converge in the one actor, and the institutional religiosity of Shawn Keogh and Father Reilly is contemptuously rejected as a breeder of 'puny weeds' (IV, 157). This conclusion conforms closely to the traditional pattern outlined by Northrop Frye. Shawn is cast out as *pharmaikos* or scapegoat, carrying away with him all of Christy's weaknesses and society's fears, and the hero, having come through his ordeals, wins his bride and gains the blessing of the father, who looks forward to the new society and the rearing up of 'lengthy families for the nurture of the earth' (IV, 157).[10] The second or actual ending of the drama goes beyond the traditional heroic anagnorisis, surmounting its own theme of play-acting as it pushes towards a defiantly unusual peripety. The heroine, in the end, turns upon and tragically loses her hero; the hero finds his identity through a process of being rejected by and rejecting his beloved; and instead of going out with his bride, the hero-son leaves with the father or *tyrannos* not finally converted and likely to remain so, but firmly held in subjection as his offspring's slave.

Synge has prepared from the beginning of the play for both 'mock' and 'real' ending by the fact that Christy's killing of his father has always been an unverified story — a verbally constructed and collectively formulated symbolic act — and his discontinuous and antinomic progress to heroism a socially induced and condoned game. Both story and deed have undergone repeated re-tellings and re-enactments, all of which, like the characters themselves, are multi-dimensional, partial and fluid, and often contradictory. We can scarcely anticipate, therefore, any simple resolution into a literal statement determining once and for all whether or not Christy 'really' slew his father. That Christy's story, or his dramatically constructed deed, occupies a fictional domain between and distinct from 'history' and 'lies' is emphasised by the *Hamlet*-like exchange between Philly and Jimmy about the bones of the mighty dead. Jimmy's certain proof that there exist in Dublin skulls of old Danes drowned in the flood, an appropriate comic combination of history and biblical myth, is the reported 'fact' that somebody told him so:

> JIMMY [*pugnaciously*]. Didn't a lad see them and he after coming from harvesting in the Liverpool boat? 'They have them there,' says he, 'making a show of the great people there was one time walking the world. White skulls and black skulls and yellow skulls, and some with full teeth and some haven't only but one.' (IV, 133-5)

Philly's reciprocating reminiscences of how he played games with the bones of a dead hero are made flesh as Mahon rises from the dead and challenges any story to match his own personal history:

> MAHON [*getting up*]. . . . Lay your eyes on that skull, and tell me where and when there was another the like of it, is splintered only from the blow of a loy.
> PHILLY. Glory be to God! And who hit you at all?
> MAHON [*triumphantly*]. It was my own son hit me. Would you believe that?
> (IV, 135)

The timing of Mahon's appearance is splendidly theatrical. One time-perspective operates along a synchronic axis, linking word with action for the audience in the theatre, while another more diachronic organisation of separated events presents itself to the audience on the stage. We, in the theatre, have already seen Old Mahon as he '*passes the window slowly*', his appearance contributing a carefully synchronised mimetic irony to Jimmy's wager that Christy's father 'should be rotten by now' (IV, 133). We also watch as, unknown to Jimmy and Philly, 'OLD MAHON *comes in and sits down near the door listening*' at the precise moment when Jimmy refers to the possibility that if the two halves of his skull *were* flung up by a man digging spuds in a field, then 'they'd say it was an old Dane, maybe, was drowned in the flood' (IV, 133). Like Hamlet's father, this ghost also walks in time. By his materialisation for us at this precise point, and his unobserved presence as the pair tell their heroic tales, there is a sense in which Old Mahon becomes identified with the mighty dead — but also acts as an alienating comic-ironic control upon the stories.

If seeing, as opposed to saying, is believing, the time for the play's definitive epiphany would seem to approach as the stage audience prepare to watch Christy at the sports. But if the stage audience are allowed to see Christy's heroic deed, Synge turns the dramatic irony this time squarely *on the audience in the theatre*. For us, Christy's apotheosis as playboy occurs off stage and is mediated to us through the words and reactions of the stage spectators, who are also responding in their turn to the audience on the strand. At the very, and only, moment when the identification of all with Christy as champion and hero appears complete, total and unanimous, with an irony which anticipates Brecht's practice of theatrical alienation, Synge leaves his 'real' audience utterly dependent on words, thus discouraging us from identifying with the general acclamation:

> WIDOW QUIN. There was a lep! [*Catching hold of* MAHON *in her excitement.*] He's fallen! He's mounted again! Faith, he's passing them all! . . .
> JIMMY. He's neck and neck!
> MAHON. Good boy to him! Flames, but he's in! [*Great cheering, in which all join.*]
> MAHON [*with hesitation*]. What's that? They're raising him up. They're coming this way. [*With a roar of rage and astonishment.*] It's Christy! by the stars of God! I'd know his way of spitting and he astride the moon (IV, 141).

Mahon's recognition of Christy, or is it his spitting image, breaks the unanimity of praise. It is rapidly followed by the Widow Quin's vehement denial of the father's assertion that what he sees *is* the Christy he claims to know:

> WIDOW QUIN [*shaking him, vehemently*]. That's not your son. That's a man is going to make a marriage with the daughter of this house, a place with fine trade, with a licence, and with poteen too (IV, 141-3).

There is, of course, a very important sense in which the Widow is right: the Christy who has won the race, triumphing in the face of the knowledge that his father is not dead but risen, is not the person Mahon has described to the people.

As Mahon leaves, pursued by Jimmy and Philly in the expectation of as good an entertainment from the father as they've had from the son, voices off-stage call out in loud applause at Christy's victory. The hero appears, dressed for the playboy part and accompanied by his actor-audience who shower upon him new names and new titles:

> VOICES. There you are! Good jumper! Grand lepper! Darlint boy! He's the racer! Bear him on, will you! [CHRISTY *comes in, in Jockey's dress, with* PEGEEN MIKE, SARA, *and other* GIRLS, *and* MEN.] (IV, 145)

The recapitulation of the motifs of Act II is very pronounced here. The

crowd repeat the offering of gifts to Christy. The gifts, symbolic of
his role as entertainer, are offered this time publicly by the men of
the village, after which, as in Act II, he is again left alone with
Pegeen.

> CROWD. Here's his prizes! A bagpipes! A fiddle was played by a poet in
> the years gone by! A flat and three-thorned blackthorn would lick the
> scholars out of Dublin town! (IV, 145)

In this last love-scene the incidence of metalanguage is at its most
concentrated. The use of language here has led many critics to detect a
stylistic exuberance, approaching self-parody, which has been variously
interpreted as either a direct satire on Irish romanticism or an ironic
qualification of the romantic vision of the play itself. The undercutting
of the poetic exuberance does not, however, depend on an *extrinsic*
location of the sense of irony in Synge himself. What is more
interesting is that both Christy and Pegeen refer to the linguistic
nature of their poetic utterances. They are aware of the precarious, at
times hyperbolical, yet creatively transfiguring, relationship between
word and referent: they are conscious, however transiently, of poetry
as making, and also of the limitations of such verbal constructs.
Christy's existential 'pity for the Lord God is all ages sitting lonesome
in his golden chair' (IV, 147), is inspired by his acceptance of the
waking, if passing, dream of love as something finer than the self-
enclosed static solitude of eternity. He opts for the time-bound
alternative to infinity, being

> astray in Erris when Good Friday's by . . . or gaming in a gap of sunshine
> with yourself stretched back into your necklace in the flowers of the earth
> (IV, 149).

Nicholas Grene comes close to identifying the play's dialectical
acceptance of finitude when he writes that 'Christy's description of his
emotion is vivid and genuine, and in no way denied by the incongruity
of object. Negative does not cancel out positive, but between the two
an electric current is set flowing'.[11] As they participate consciously in
the play of words, Christy's 'poetry talk' inspires in Pegeen real
tenderness and awakens rapture in himself:

CHRISTY [*with rapture*]. If the mitred bishops seen you that time, they'd be the like of the holy prophets, I'm thinking, do be straining the bars of Paradise to lay eyes on the Lady Helen of Troy, and she abroad pacing back and forward with a nosegay in her golden shawl.

PEGEEN [*with real tenderness*]. And what is it I have, Christy Mahon, to make me *fitting entertainment* for the like of you that has *such poet's* talking, and such bravery of heart? (IV, 149, my italics)

The conditional nature of their dream is acknowledged by the repetitive, stylised, formal placing of the 'if' participle at the beginning of several of their antiphonal exchanges: '*If* the mitred bishops . . .' '*If* I was your wife . . .' '*If* I wasn't a good Christian . . .' '*If* that's the truth . . .' (IV, 149). Neither of them ignores or tries to deny the element of gaming and entertainment in their projected lives together, nor do they gloss over the presence within the dream of the possibility of 'taking your death in the hailstones or the fogs of dawn' (IV, 149). The world they imagine is not a discrete, insulated Paradise: it is, rather, a continuation of life in the everyday world of 'jack straw roofing' and 'stony pebble' (IV, 149), but transfigured by the language of love. In its name Pegeen renounces the illusory quest for an exotic world beyond the seas and her desires of marrying 'a Jew-man with ten kegs of gold', in favour of the everyday world of the shebeen with 'the like of you drawing nearer like the stars of God' (IV, 151).

The drunken singing of Pegeen's father returning from the wake breaks in upon the psalmodic pledges of love. His prophetic song is a reminder of the darker side of the collective dream. It acts as a framing device, interrupting the action and recalling again that if Christy's heroic deed were a 'fact' it would be a crime punishable by death:

> The jailor and the turnkey
>   They quickly ran us down,
> And brought us back as prisoners
>   Once more to Cavan town.
> [*He comes in supported by* SHAWN.]
> There we lay bewailing
>   All in a prison bound . . . (IV, 151)

The father's speech prepares for the 'false ending' to the play, the

153

second mock wedding, and clears the ground for the 'real' finale. Drunkenly saluting Christy as 'a hardened slayer', Michael enviously compares him with Shawn, 'that shy and decent Christian I have chosen for my daughter's hand, and I after getting the gilded dispensation this day for to wed them now' (IV, 153). When Christy, for the second time on-stage, takes the loy into his hands, this time to claim Pegeen from Shawn, the dramatic irony again subverts the play-reality dichotomy. By merely lifting his weapon, our hero achieves a ritual victory over his opponent and wins the appropriate prize for the mock-slaying of his rival — a mock-wedding with his bride. But as Michael pronounces them man and wife in the name of the son who 'split his father's middle with a single clout' and blesses them in the name of 'God and Mary and St. Patrick' (IV, 157), the pseudo-resolution of the comedy is shattered by the violent eruption of Old Mahon onto the scene. Christy's final downfall is suitably literal:

> CHRISTY and PEGEEN. Amen, O Lord! [*Hubbub outside*. OLD MAHON *rushes in, followed by all the* CROWD *and* WIDOW QUIN. *He makes a rush at* CHRISTY, *knocks him down, and begins to beat him.*] (IV, 157)

As the crowd jeer him, 'There's the playboy! There's the lad thought he'd rule the roost in Mayo. Slate him now, Mister' (IV, 161), Pegeen rejects Christy *because* he has been story-telling and play-acting: to her he is 'an ugly liar was playing off the hero and the fright of men!'(IV, 163).

Just as we are promised action from Christy, Synge repeats his trick of playing with his audience: the second murderous blow of the father is also struck off-stage. But Christy has badly misjudged the nature of the social sanctions which will be brought to bear upon him by Pegeen herself for apparently daring to act out his deed — as she herself has encouraged him to do. The danger of his becoming the perpetual sport of his audience is made dramatically explicit by the villagers' attempts to dress him up once again — this time in a woman's petticoat and shawl:

> SARA [*runs in, pulling off one of her petticoats*]. They're going to hang him. [*Holding out petticoat and shawl.*] Fit these upon him and let him run off to the east.(IV, 167)

Pegeen leads the villagers towards their victim and they snare him in their noose. Christy's agonised question 'And what is it you'll say to me and I after doing it this time in the face of all?' (IV, 169) brings into the open at the crux of the drama the question of the relationship between word and action. Pegeen's answer is a betrayal of Christy as playboy, lover and poet. She is prepared to send the maker of images to his death once he becomes the doer of deeds:

> PEGEEN. I'll say a strange man is a marvel with his mighty talk; but what's a squabble in your back-yard and the blow of a loy, have taught me that there's a great gap between a gallous story and a dirty deed. [*To* MEN.] Take him on from this, or the lot of us will be likely put on trial for his *deed* today (IV, 169, my italics).

As she prepares her ultimate treachery, Christy gets ready to teach them all that a poet can bite as well as bark. He fights back, to regain his playboy status — but this time on his own terms. Revelling in the drama which will be enacted 'the day I'm stretched upon the rope with ladies in their silks and satins snivelling in their lacy kerchiefs, and they rhyming songs and ballads on the terror of my fate', he '*squirms round on the floor and bites* SHAWN's *leg*' (IV, 171). Laying claim with an astonished and astonishing delight to having slain his father twice, no matter what they all may choose to say or believe, he finally confounds their attempts to tie him down to their way of seeing him or his deeds:

> CHRISTY [*delighted with himself*]. You will then, the way you can shake out hell's flags of welcome for my coming in two weeks or three, for I'm thinking Satan hasn't many have killed their da in Kerry and in Mayo too (IV, 171).

At the moment when Christy bites Shawn's leg, Old Mahon, again seen only by the theatre audience, enters. Like Christy, he too is on all fours. For the stage audience his second resurrection is held in suspense until the point where Pegeen burns Christy's leg with a sod of turf. When their playboy's suffering is at its most intense, it is revealed to his tormentors that the very element of play which their words and actions deny has won through. Old Mahon is not-dead, and Christy's harrowing of hell brings them all face to face with the father's and his own resurrected image:

155

JIMMY [*seeing* OLD MAHON]. Will you look what's come in? [*They all drop* CHRISTY *and run left.*]
CHRISTY [*scrambling on his knees face to face with* OLD MAHON]. Are you coming to be killed a third time or what ails you now? (IV, 171)

Part of Christy's dramatic development has been concerned with freeing himself from fear of confronting the father — a fear which is widely shared by the society which sought to make of him the father-*slayer*. Christy, henceforth, will lay down the law. The elder shall serve the younger in his new world — and in this, Old Mahon finds a delighted sense of renewed identity:

CHRISTY. Go with you is it! I will then, like a gallant captain with his heathen slave. Go on now and I'll see you from this day stewing my oatmeal and washing my spuds, for I'm master of all fights from now. [*Pushing* MAHON.] Go on, I'm saying.
MAHON. Is it me?
CHRISTY. Not a word out of you. Go on from this.
MAHON [*walking out and looking back at* CHRISTY *over his shoulder*]. Glory be to God! [*With a broad smile.*] I am crazy again! [*Goes.*] (IV, 173)

As playboy, Christy became for the people a focus of their creativity as well as of their weaknesses and fears — but he refuses to be their fool. When they try to confine their hero to the Tempest island of illusion, giving him licence to exist as actor only within the context of a gallous story, he chooses to return to his Milan — but as gaffer now. His powers must be used in the service of living, and his judgement-day, like Prospero's, may well herald another dawn:

CHRISTY. Ten thousand blessings upon all that's here, for you've turned me a likely gaffer in the end of all, the way I'll go romancing through a romping lifetime from this hour to the dawning of the judgement day. [*He goes out.*] (IV, 173)

Christy's and Old Mahon's rehabilitation of each other is a *social* rehabilitation. It is the product of a vision rooted in the answer of the folk-imagination to the attenuated 'modern image of the individual body', where 'death is only death, it never coincides with birth; old age is torn away from youth; blows merely hurt, without assisting an act of

156

birth'.[12] In the folk-image 'death brings nothing to an end, for it does not concern the ancestral body, which is renewed in the next generation'. [13]

The coda to the play, the brief exchange between Michael James, Shawn Keogh and Pegeen Mike, looks forward to Brecht's epic theatre. Urged by the German Press in 1948 to rewrite the end of *Mother Courage* so that the central character would recognise the horrors of war, Brecht refused. He held that victims of catastrophe in life and in art do not always draw the necessary lessons from their experience. Moreover he was convinced that 'for as long as the masses are manoeuvred by politicians, everything that happens to them they look upon not as experience but fate.' . . . This explains why Brecht, remaining true to the logic and implications of historical truth of events, saw the dramatist's task not to lie in compelling Mother Courage to see the light at last, but in making sure the audience should see it.[14] Synge, too, opts for an open ending. He offers both reconciliation and a parting of the ways. Michael and Shawn have learnt little or nothing from their play-acting. They look upon what has happened fatalistically, as 'the will of God', and hope that the playboy will never again 'trouble us when his vicious bite is healed' (IV, 173). But it is to the painful loss of an alternative possibility that Pegeen's words passionately address us as she rejects the man who rejects the poet.

> PEGEEN [*hitting him* «SHAWN» *a box on the ear*]. Quit my sight. [*Putting her shawl over her head and breaking out into wild lamentations.*] Oh my grief, I've lost him surely. I've lost the only playboy of the western world (IV, 173).

Her cry is a 'damming of the stream of real life, the moment when its flow comes to a standstill, makes itself felt as reflux: this reflux is astonishment'.[15] Between Michael and Shawn who vainly try to rest on the petrified wave, and Pegeen who belatedly sees the dangerous but living waters thrust against the rock and longs to plunge into them, Synge leaves us, upon reflection, to make our choice.

NOTES

1. I use 'apotheosis' here both in its etymological and in its ironic sense; in the latter case, with the connotations of 'send-up' or 'come-uppance' which it has, for example, in the Oxford English Dictionary citation from Carlyle: 'Let us hope the Leave-alone principle has now got its apotheosis; and taken wing towards higher regions than ours'.

2. Thomas R. Whitaker, 'On playing with *The Playboy*', in Thomas R. Whitaker (ed.), *Twentieth Century Interpretations of* The Playboy of the Western World (Englewood Cliffs, New Jersey, Prentice-Hall Inc., 1969), pp. 1-20.

3. Dorothy Van Ghent has remarked on Dickens's use of this technique of characterisation in *Great Expectations*. She describes Estella and Miss Havisham as 'not two characters but a single one, or a single essence with dual aspects, as if composed by montage — a spiritual continuum, so to speak'. See W.J. Harvey, *Character and the Novel* (London, Chatto and Windus, 1965), p. 123.

4. Bertolt Brecht, 'Vorrede zu *Mann ist Mann*' from *Die Szene*, Berlin, April 1927, translated by Gerhard Nellhaus and published in John Willett and Rallph Mannheim (eds.), *Bertolt Brecht, Collected Plays*, Volume 2, Part I (London, Eyre Methuen, 1979), p. 100. Brecht describes the new human type, represented by Gayly Gay, as

> a great liar and an incorrigible optimist; he can fit in with anything, almost without difficulty. He seems to be used to putting up with a great deal. It is in fact very seldom that he can allow himself an opinion of his own . . . But this Gayly Gay is by no means a weakling; on the contrary he is the strongest of all. That is to say he becomes the strongest once he has ceased to be a private person; he only becomes strong in the mass (p. 100).

5. Nicholas Grene takes issue with critics who have seen Christy Mahon as a Christ figure. Grene argues that 'there is no evidence to support the idea that Synge intended to parody any of the figures suggested, Cuchullain, Christ or Oedipus . . . He had not the mind which could see and delight in endless ironic correspondences'. Nicholas Grene, *Synge: A Critical Study of the Plays* (London and Basingstoke, Macmillan, 1975), p. 135. It is our contention, however,

that just such a playful delight in the ironies of the human situation lies close to the essence of Synge's comic vision and informs his strategy and style.

6. Walter Benjamin, 'What is Epic Theatre?' (First version) in *Understanding Brecht*, translated by Anna Bostock (London, New Left Books, 1977), p. 8.

7. Ibid., p. 8.

8. The alternative endings are included in the drafts published in the *Collected Works*, Volume IV, *Plays*, Book II.

9. Harvey, *Character and the Novel*, p. 122.

10. Frye writes that

New Comedy normally presents an erotic intrigue between a young man and a young woman which is blocked by some kind of opposition, usually paternal, and resolved by a twist in the plot which is the comic form of Aristotle's discovery' and is more manipulated than its tragic counterpart
. . . The action of the comedy thus moves towards the incorporation of the hero into the society that he naturally fits.

Northrop Frye, *Anatomy of Criticism: Four Essays* (Princeton New Jersey, Princeton University Press, 1957), p. 44.

11. Grene, *Synge: A Critical Study of the Plays*, p. 135.

12. Mikhail Bakhtin, *Rabelais and his World*, translated by Hélène Iswolsky (Cambridge Massachusetts and London, Massachusetts Institute of Technology, 1968), pp. 321-2.

13. Ibid., p. 322.

14. Avner Ziş, *Foundations of Marxist Aesthetics*, translated by Katherine Judelson (Moscow, Progress Publishers, 1977), p. 129.

15. Benjamin, *Understanding Brecht*, p. 13. Benjamin derives his metaphor from the Widow Begbick's song in *Man equals Man*:

Don't try to hold on to the wave
That's breaking against your foot: so long as
You stand in the stream fresh waves
Will always keep breaking against it.

Brecht, *Collected Plays*, Volume 2, Part I, p. 50.

8.
TEXT AND CONTEXT IN
WHEN THE MOON HAS SET

THAT SYNGE'S first play, *When the Moon Has Set*, was rejected by Lady Gregory and Yeats is well known, as is the fact that his premature death left *Deirdre of the Sorrows* incomplete, with the task of preparing a text for performance and publication falling to these two Abbey colleagues assisted by his fiancée, Molly Allgood. Less well known are the various versions of the first work, especially the early two-act typescript (Item 4351, ff. 1-43 in the Trinity College Dublin Collection), believed by Ann Saddlemyer to be the version brought by the dramatist to Coole Park in September 1901. The text included in the Oxford University Press *Collected Works* is a conflation of two separate and later one-act drafts.[1] The title of the play does not occur in any of the typescripts. It appears in Synge's diary entry for 23rd May 1903, in relation to a one-act version completed in that month.[2] The one-act versions and the conflated text differ in many respects from the two-act play. Although she is referred to in the two-act typescript, Mary Costello does not appear therein as an on-stage character. The climax of the first act occurs when Columb Sweeny is shot by an off-stage character, assumed to be Stephen Costello, brother of Mary and uncle of the Sweenys' servant girl, Bride Kavanagh. Stephen, we are told, had taken an oath to 'shoot the next heir, cousin or descendant' (f. 7) of Columb's uncle. Yet a further distinguishing feature is the framing of the two-act play by substantial readings from a philosophical/aesthetic manuscript written by Columb Sweeny. This reflects on the relationships and affinities between music, art and

160

life. It draws heavily on passages in Synge's 'Autobiography', in the *Vita Vecchia* and in the *Etude Morbide*. The play is the most explicitly autobiographical of Synge's dramas. Indeed, we shall argue that the manuscript, together with the other metatextual devices, the letters from and to Columb's Parisian friend and fellow artist, O'Neill, and the letter from Columb's dead uncle to his heir, may be regarded as an inscription into the text of a life-history which the play attempts to explicate, or to release into dramatic action. It thus anticipates the metalinguistic and metadramatic features which are characteristic of all of Synge's later work.

The setting for the first play is the library of the Big House. The scene therefore foregrounds immediately the metatextual dimensions of the drama. As it opens, Sister Eileen is preparing a bow of crêpe, a sign of mourning for the dead master of the house. The first words are *read* from the aesthetic manuscript by Sister Eileen; they compare life with a symphony. As the play progresses, the traditional moral and ethical as well as religious values of the landlord family are called into question by the uncle's posthumously revealed love for a Catholic peasant woman, Mary Costello, and his self-confessed philosophical agnosticism. The challenge to the old values becomes even more explicit in the radicalism of his nephew and heir. Responsibility for the tragic outcome of the uncle's love does not rest solely with himself, or even with the family's traditional class attitudes or religious prejudices. Mary Costello, the poor woman whom he wished to marry, refused his offer because of her own Catholic faith and her inability to accept her lover's agnosticism. If we are to understand the more than purely autobiographical significance of this conflict, we need to note certain parallels between the women in the early play and Deirdre in *Deirdre of the Sorrows*.

By the time Synge came to write his last drama, Deirdre was already well established in the mythology of Irish nationalist aspirations as a typological figure whose tragic fate represented that of Ireland. Lady Gregory included the story of 'The Sons of Usnach' in her *Cuchulain of Muirthemna*. George Russell and Yeats had each written plays based on the legend and performed at the Abbey in 1902 and 1906 respectively. Indeed, there is evidence to suggest that Synge first began to consider his own version of the Deirdre legend in reaction against the treatment of the material in these earlier plays. Turning to *When the Moon Has Set*, we find that Sister Eileen, the object of Columb's matrimonial hopes, is a Catholic nun who plays the harp and sings the Gaelic song, the 'Cuilfhionn', and that she exchanges her nun's habit for a green wedding dress which was originally intended for Bride Costello. It would indeed be obtuse to ignore the political significance of these features and to see Sister Eileen as simply the distant cousin of the landlord family or a conflated analogue for Florence Ross and Cherrie Matheson.[3] She is as obviously a representation of Ireland as Deirdre, or as Yeats's Cathleen Ni Houlihan. There is a consistent, if formally unsuccessful, effort being made throughout to dramatise the auto-biographical material in such a way as to explore its social, historical, political and cultural determinants.

The society represented in *When the Moon Has Set*, like Conchubor's Emain in *Deirdre of the Sorrows*, is growing old and becoming painfully aware of its obsolescence.[4] With Columb's uncle lying on his death-bed, the atmosphere in the house and the surrounding countryside is one of degeneration, morbidity and incipient madness. Conchubor, likewise, is 'a man is ageing in his Dun, with his crowds round him and his silver and gold' (IV, 211). By his own confession, he brings to Deirdre as a marriage gift 'wildness and confusion in my own mind' (IV, 195). In both plays a form of escape into the natural world from the constricting paralysis of the respective dying generations is considered — although in neither case is this offered uncritically as a simple, or simplistic, alternative to life in society. Whereas, however, *When the Moon Has Set* insists on discovering an aesthetic order and pattern in the lives of its characters and imposing this on the historical and natural processes, the last play questions, and finally refuses, a too easily harmonious or aesthetically satisfying solution to the challenge of the 'filthy job — to waste and die' (I, 66).

In *When the Moon Has Set* the hero, Columb Sweeny, is a writer-musician with a mission. In personal terms, this takes the form of a proselytising determination to win his distant cousin from the celibate life which she regards as the highest form of religious expression. He attempts to convert Eileen from the asceticism of religious dogma to a dogmatic, if confused, aestheticism, which is expounded in the play's aesthetic manuscript. In the passage which Sister Eileen reads at the outset, life is envisaged as part of a cosmic work of art. The function of art is to make the playing of each part as perfect as possible and to reveal the ultimate perfection by expressing the abstract cosmic persona concealed beneath the impersonal, concrete deeds of a man's life-time. The debate continues when Columb reads to Sister Eileen a letter from his friend, O'Neill, in Paris. The friend, an *alter ego* of Columb and of Synge, emerges as one who has dedicated himself not just to writing about the fin-de-siècle romantic agony, but to living the part:

> He lives in a low room draped in black from the floor to the ceiling. He has a black quilt on his bed and two sculls [sic] on his Chimney-piece with girls hats on them. His matches are in a coffin, and his clock is a gallows. He sits there whenever he is not at work and drinks absinthe and vermouthe [sic] (f.9).

When Sister Eileen judges this behaviour as bordering on the insane, her cousin quickly points out that 'in the life of the cloisters and in this life of Ireland, men go mad every hour' (f.9). Decadence, aesthetic and religious, is thus provided with a local, and Irish, habitation.

The musical references throughout the play are at best inexact. At times they seem to assert an identity between the individual life, general life processes and a mystical, cosmic symphony; at others they suggest tropic analogies. Robin Skelton has described these philosophical passages as 'confused, over-emotional, and sloppy in terminology'.[5] The vagueness and imprecision of the language, the lack of any convincing testing out of the concepts through dramatic action, make it difficult to determine with any consistency Columb's philosophical/aesthetic position. Part of the play's weakness may be attributed to the tediously repetitive apostrophising of music's divine power and unifying impulse. The obsessive use of musical tropologisation to support, or to mask, the conceptual preoccupations of the drama is suspect, not just as a-historical music criticism. The emphasis on ultimate form is an attempt to transcend process and change. Ideal, discontented form offers an escape from the 'horrible' (f.26) concretions of history, time, and context-bound identity, which intrude upon the effort to express life, or the life-force, through media as uncomfortably referential as the language-using arts. The philosophical-aesthetic insight to which such a vague statement as 'every life is a symphony' (f.1) pretends remains unarticulated, and in *When*

163

the Moon Has Set the desire or motive to avoid articulation is strong.

The downgrading of language complements, throughout the main plot, the thematic elevation of form. It is part of the impetus towards dis-contentment which characterises the ascendancy sequence and is symptomatic of an effort to escape from the linguistically mediated, or the referential. In his final sermon to Sister Eileen, Columb dismisses the incarnate *logos* and celebrates instead a wordless metamorphosis:

> It is the beauty of your spirit that has set you free, and your emancipation is more exquisite than any that is possible for men who are redeemed by logic. You cannot tell me why you have changed, that is your glory (f.41).

The verbal expression of escapist metaphysics, with its risky praise of freedom from the necessities of logic or language, leads all too readily to the act of escape itself. Columb calls on Eileen to forsake history and tradition and to go with him to a green world of unadulterated arboreal beauty:

> COLUMB. The world of habit is diseased . . . We will go out among the trees. The red glow is faded and day is come . . . In the Name of the Summer, and The Sun, and the whole World I wed you as my wife (ff.41-2).

By an act of will, the forest world is made to become the whole World, but it fails to accommodate as part of its cosmology the diseased world of habit. Their departure is a solipsistic attempt to 'circumscribe all of objective reality with their own subjectivity'; retreat into this second world 'removes the ego from history' and 'protects the protagonists from historical change, from transformation'.[6] There is no trace, in Columb's final speech, of the compassionately ironic scepticism about ultimate solutions to the challenge of decay and mortality which may be detected in *Riders to the Sea* and *In the Shadow of the Glen*, nor any of the controlling self-reflective awareness of language and situation which subverts, in the later comedies, the impulse towards evasion or escape.

Yet the conclusion that *When the Moon Has Set* is totally committed to an escape from history into an aesthetically harmonised universe must be qualified. The play's embryonic sub-plots — the posthumously revealed affair between Columb's uncle and Mary Costello, and the relationship between Bride Kavanagh and Pat Murphy — are offered as contexts for the Columb-Eileen relationship. They are variations on the declared theme of the symphony, the dual 'facts of love and death' (f.13). As such, they attempt to restore a kind of contrapuntal content to the main sequence. The uncle-Mary Costello episode has as its theme the way in which love when denied leads to despair, insanity, violence and death. The relationship between Bride and Pat Murphy, by way of contrast, shows the couple accepting the death of the older generation and entering into their inheritance as the starting-point for the legitimisation of their life together as man and wife. Love and death are defined and discussed abstractly by Columb, as the subjects of the symphony. Yet once they are treated in the sub-plots in a partially successful dramatic, rather than generalised polemical, manner, they prove to be uncomfortable bedfellows of transcendental idealism. The open challenge to the guilt-ridden problems of inheritance and generation which are masked in the main plot by the musical terminology comes from the peasant-aristocrat Costello family, descendants of 'Old Castillian' (f. 5) stock. Stephen Costello both violates and absolves the House of Sweeny by his murderous attempt to shoot Columb because he is heir to the uncle. Stephen thus vicariously slays, but does not slay, the uncle/father, in the name or persona of Columb, who rises from this assault and is enabled to legitimate and successfully conclude his relationship with Sister Eileen. Eileen remains with the 'resurrected' Columb ostensibly to nurse him back to health, but in effect to enable him to pursue and consummate his courtship.

The continuum between plot and sub-plot is strengthened if we accept that Sister Eileen 'is' also both Mary Costello, the uncle's lover, and Bride. This is suggested by the fact that Eileen, persuaded by Bride's example to wed Columb, appears on-stage wearing Mary Costello's wedding dress at the end of the play. We can, then, observe a struggle in the play, through this complex net of relationships, to develop the theme of cathartic atonement, an attempt to dramatise the expurgation of the ascendancy sense of guilt through the transference of that guilt to Stephen Costello. Stephen is the mad twin brother of Mary. He also resembles, we are told, both Sister Eileen and Columb's *alter ego*, the 'cellist O'Neill. Stephen shoots Columb in revenge for a wrong presumed done, but not 'really' done, to Mary by the defunct landlord uncle. This same uncle 'really' intended marriage, which Mary's religious scruples, possibly Ireland's, or Eileen's, Catholicism, made impossible. 'If you love a woman', Columb's uncle writes, 'subdue her', but, he rapidly adds, 'you will not love a woman it is not lawful to love. No man of our blood has ever been unlawful' (f. 36). This posthumous, purely assertive, attempt at absolution from generational guilt clears the way, in terms of legitimacy, for Columb's union with Eileen. Removal of the shadow of guilt from the hero's association with the uncle-father facilitates the marriage between the ascendancy scion and his Catholic cousin.

The complex problematic of the relationship between generations and classes is treated in *When the Moon Has Set* in ways which suggest, however, that Synge was more than a little troubled by this easy absolution. The difficulty experienced by Columb in acknowledging a direct line of responsibility for the past suggests why in this play it is the uncle rather than the father who is the dying or dead paternal figure. Columb is his uncle's heir because an uncle, as Hamlet knew, is a father-usurper who is neither true father nor legitimate ruler. The uncle-father in Synge's first play rises vicariously into prominence in Act II, through the medium of his letter to his doubting heir. Communicating verbally to Columb in this highly literary drama, he inscribes himself *post mortem* into the text of his nephew's life. Their relationship, and the accompanying sense of guilt implicit in the absolution from it, is thereby simultaneously distanced and denied *and asserted*. The uncle's letter, referred to in a notebook which is taken from his death-bed, is hidden in a portfolio sealed with the two wedding rings of the marriage-which-never-was (or was it?). The portfolio and rings are enclosed in turn in a box which conceals the close-to-illegitimate family secrets (properties) of Mary Costello's wedding clothes, and, in later versions of the play, the infant garments of her babies who were never (or who were?) born.[7] The whole of this claustrophobic generational puzzle, stretching, like Banquo's line, to infinity, is, of course, contained within the House. Synge's society was 'patriarchal, hierarchical, and, ultimately, justified by God the Father, [it] depended at every level on the supremacy and potency of the male'.[8] By displacing the father-figure to the position of uncle, by giving this uncle an agnostic, radical past and by denying him

marriage/potency, Synge is seeking to strike, like Christy Mahon in
The Playboy of the Western World, a triple blow against a guilty past. The
guilt shows itself interestingly in O'Neill's letter welcoming Columb's
entering into his 'heritage' (f.9). 'My compliments', writes O'Neill, 'to
the little Irish pigs that eat filth all their lives that you may prosper'
(f.9). These words, we remember, are first recorded in Synge's Aran
notebooks

In *When the Moon Has Set* a resolution of the antinomic singularity of
the 'one mode' of existence (f. 19) which separates 'the dual puissance'
(f.21) of life exclusively into the virginal-matriarchal or the authoritarian paternal mode is attempted. 'We are not right', Columb tells
Sister Eileen, 'to distort the dual puissance of the mind' (f.21). This
power, which he has referred to earlier as 'the thought or the
unconscious will of reproduction. That is the symphony' (f.20),
becomes identified with the 'force' of 'a fertile passion that is filled
with joy' (f.21). The appeal here, however tentative and hedged about
with abstraction, is *away from* ideal form, towards content. In
evolutionary-aesthetic terms, it is in part a movement towards an
accommodation with the scientific naturalism which forced the poet to
live 'in the world of Darwin, not in the world of Plato'.[9] For Synge, as
for Yeats, the mechanistically interpreted post-Darwinian world
undoubtedly had its horrors. Chief amongst these was the apparent
denial of free will, or of any active creative role or autonomous identity
to the subject and therefore to the artist. Perhaps ontogeny was merely
the blind recapitulation of phylogeny, in which case, no purgatorial
fires could cleanse the present from the guilt of the past other than by a
going out of nature. Once this aesthetic preoccupation is historicised, it
suggests that for Synge, as for Yeats, the struggle for survival of the
ever-and-never dying generations, the nightmare of eternal recurrence,
would be all. At least a residual shudder of this fear is recorded in
Synge's *Autobiography*, and the vision of a universe in which this
deadly struggle seems total disturbs Columb also. In Act II, recovering
from the attempt on his life, he takes up again his discussion of survival
and reproduction. Despite the change from the frozen winter of Act I
to the splendour of June — or rather, because of it — Columb feels his
mortality. He is 'haunted by that appalling sensation in which we
realise the gulf of annihilation we are being whirled into', yet asserts

that 'through it all it is possible to find a strange impulse of joy' (ff. 26-7). In words taken almost directly from Synge's *Autobiography* he confesses to 'the envy I used to have of the wild plants that crush and strangle each other in a cold rage of growth' (f.26).

In *When the Moon Has Set* Columb seeks in music a way of expressing and confronting these rhythms of life and death. He claims that 'music is the only art that can express the first animal frenzy' (f.26), but hesitations and reservations about this non-representational solution creep in: 'In the orchestra it is a divine hymn, in literature, or painting it is horrible' (f.26). The downgrading of the more obviously referential arts is symptomatic of the deep unease in the play about the honesty of the play's musical, or aesthetic, argument itself. The unease is part of Synge's struggle to recognise and come to terms with the need to confront the generational process without being overwhelmed by feelings of horrible despair, or alternatively abstracting it out of existence. In relation to the ideas of Darwin, Spencer and Huxley, Yeats and Synge set out at first towards opposite poles. Yeats turned from them to Madame Blavatsky's theosophy — with a sense of critical irony which he never abandoned — and to the temporary attractions and consolations of Celtic mysticism. He claimed to have done so in reaction against his father's post-Darwinian unbelief. Synge, however, who never knew his father, found in science, and particularly in Darwin's *Origin of Species*, support, albeit disturbing and even at first traumatic, for his rebellion against his mother's literalising Christianity. It is possible to argue that he discovered the symbolic father in discovering the missing or absent historical principle of generation. In the theory of the origin of species is to be found the endorsement of the animal note, and the confirmation of the dual puissance of the body. But given this philosophical alternative, Synge was nonetheless faced with the need to forge a poetic for the creative writer, and an historical identity for himself, in what still appeared to be a closed, deterministic universe. Confronted by a related historical problem, Yeats saw himself and his fellow poets pushed, at least temporarily, into linguistic abstraction by being 'compelled to protect ourselves by such means against people and things we should never have heard of'.[10] The censoring connotations and abstract generalisations in this statement suggest that Yeats believed that the writers of his generation had access to information which they were too young — or immature — to know about. However disturbing Synge may have found his encounter with such people and things, he did not, as an artist, regret his acquaintance. We can certainly say that in *When the Moon Has Set* the abstracting motive in the main plot is very powerful and that it underwrites certain defensive-evasive features of the dramatic strategy and style. Nevertheless, there are clear and prophetic signs of the need to bring these abstractions to the bar of symbolic action and to test them out through and against the language and life of the play's 'peasant' characters.

The momentum of *When the Moon Has Set* is by no means exclusively in the direction of protecting the hero, the artist, his class or his society against change. Accepting, like Columb, that 'the Christian synthesis . . . has fallen' (f. 29), Synge recognised the crisis of European fin-de-siècle decadence as somehow necessary. He also traced a continuity between it and the problem of his own background, seeing in the one a response to the death of an old society and in the other the problems more often caused by a refusal to recognise, accept and accommodate to change. The struggle towards a critical understanding of these problems, and an attempt to relate the European to the Irish dimension, informs Columb's argument that with the breakup of the old Christian synthesis

> the imagination has wandered away to grow puissant and terrible again, in lonely vigals [sic] where she sits and broods among things that have been touched by madmen, and things that have the smell of death on them and books written with the blood of horrible crimes. The intellect has peered down into the tumult of atoms and up into the stars till she has forgotten her compliments [sic] in the personality, and the instinct for practical joy has taught anarchists to hate in the passion of their yearning for love (ff. 29 30).

What is regretted here is not the acquaintance with the new scientific theories and revelations, it is, rather, the inability, as yet, of the artistic intellect and sensibility to forge a complementary creative role for the human subject. The aesthetic dis-ease is shown to be grounded in time, place and history, and in the particular actions of individuals. The death of Columb's uncle, the attempted murder of Columb by the crazed Stephen, Eileen's (Columb's) life-denying celibacy, the prevalence of mental disturbance amongst the local people, all have their roots in the Irish political and social context, not in change as such, but in a perverse and doomed resistance to it. 'The old-fashioned

Irish conservatism and morality', Columb writes to O'Neill, 'seemed to have evolved a melancholy [sic] degeneration worse than anything in Paris' (f. 31).

Columb's attitude towards change, decay and death must be distinguished from that of O'Neill and Sister Eileen. O'Neill makes of mortality an obsessive aesthetic cult. Sister Eileen's particular obsession is with an outmoded religion which teaches mortification of the senses in this life in the name of spiritual life after death. For Columb, awareness of death, however horrifying, is a reminder of the need to embrace life here and now, and with it, history and change. The decay of religions and cultures, although 'an immense and infinite horror' (f. 29) to him, is preferable to the 'compromise with death and sterility' (f. 20). The death of the individual, or of societies, must be seen in relation to the 'cosmic faith' of Beethoven, Michelangelo, Rabelais and 'the magnificent Kermesse of Rubens' which 'expresses the final frenzy of existence' (f. 20). We can recognise in these statements, however strident or aesthetically inadequate, an attempt to relate artistic achievement to the artist's ability to wrestle with history and change and to accommodate the work of art to them.

The importance of the play's occasional Pyrrhic victories of action over schema lies partly in the way in which they point towards Synge's future achievements. Religion, art and literature cannot absolve history by explaining it away or by imposing upon it a spurious aesthetic teleology. There are signs of a desire to reformulate the question of historical role and identity in terms of the degrees and levels of integration and separation which can be established between the two central characters and the peasant community. We can detect these forces at work, for example, in the early scene which follows Sister Eileen's initial reading from the manuscript. Bride's attempts to relight the fading fire, and her lament about the wet turf, evoke, far more successfully than all of Columb's philosophising about change, degeneration and decay, the social crisis of the Big House and the dependence of its upper class occupants on their servants. The scene also manages to convey the depression and despondency caused among the peasants themselves by the decline of the social order which reciprocally defines their own identity — but it suggests, too, their greater resilience and resourcefulness, their tenacity of life, when faced with crisis. The dying down of the fire coincides with the announcement that Columb's uncle is dead. Bride kneels before the hearth, blowing on the fading embers of the turf:

> SISTER EILEEN [*going over to the fireplace where BRIDE is blowing the turf with her mouth*] — — You cannot light it?
>
> BRIDE [*talking with plaintive western intonation*] — — The turf's wet, Sister Eileen, for the roof has fallen in on the turf house with the weight of the snow on it, and I haven't a bit of sticks in the whole house. I told Murphy to bring some bogwood with him out of the town — — you can't find a stick here anyplace with the snow lying on the earth — — but he hasn't come back, the Lord knows what's keeping him (ff.2-3).

Columb and Sister Eileen have lost the art of making a turf fire. Columb 'throws it all about as if it was coal he had' (f.3). They rely for keeping alive the ancestral hearth on their peasant servants who in turn find fuel difficult to come by. Columb has even 'missed his way' to the Big House 'at the second crossing of the roads' (f.3). He has 'got stupid about the dark' (f.3) and has had to take directions from an old queer man — who turns out to be his would-be assassin, Stephen Costello. We have here, however briefly sustained, a much more satisfactory feeling, in theatrical terms, for the physical actuality of the world and a confidence in its capacity to carry dramatic meaning.

The contrast between the play's two styles — the abstract expository and the more substantially dramatic — emerges clearly if we compare any of the Columb-Eileen exchanges about mortality with Bride's account of the death of her father:

> SISTER EILEEN. What has happened?
>
> BRIDE. He is dead, Sister Eileen. Mrs Brady's husband was drunk, and he came up and took herself away before the Moon was set. Then I was there a while with the old man, and a little after twelve he gave a sort of a turn, and I went over, and he was dead in the bed. Then I was afeard to be there and no one along with me, so I came up to see would Mrs Byrne go down to keep me from being lonesome. I can't leave him altogether, and I can't stay there by myself (f. 37).

Instead of trying to *impose* an interpretation which closes in upon the complex reality of time, process and change, this passage offers as objective correlative of the theme the felt experience of a character acting in a particular context. Bride does not deny her sense of loss or try to translate it into an abstract philosophical gain. She responds to Columb's sympathy with words which are later spoken by Maurya in *Riders to the Sea* and which Synge first encountered in a letter written to him by his Aran friend, Martin McDonough:

> BRIDE. I'm destroyed crying: but what good is in it. We must be satisfied, and what man at all can be living forever (f. 37).

These words express her personal grief; they also acknowledge the impersonal inevitability of each man's life ending with death — the 'gulf of annihilation we are all being whirled into' (f.27) — and they recognise that only by accepting this as a necessity can we begin to be satisfied. The theme of commitment to present and future emerges again in Bride's reply to Sister Eileen's polite supposition that she will remain, as before, a servant at the Big House. Bride's answer asserts a limited, yet real, personal freedom. She wishes to marry Pat Murphy; now that she has inherited the farm and cows he will accept her. Nor has she waited for her father's death or the church's benediction or approval: she already bears the future within her, in carrying Pat's child.

It is, nevertheless, only rarely in *When the Moon Has Set* that Synge manages to bring about dramatically effective interplay between the two sets of characters and their respective linguistic registers. As Declan Kiberd points out, 'the rich dramatic potential inherent in the clash of character and of linguistic styles — between polite English and rustic dialect — is never developed, merely hinted'.[11] The problems with which he was attempting to deal in this first play proved too *immediate*, and for this reason at least in the main plot they are deeply repressed, and rarely achieve the dynamism of dramatic action. Synge's skills and confidence had not developed sufficiently for him to be able to control the dramatic strategy of symbolic language surely enough to use it as a shield in which to reflect and engage with the terrors of parentage and history without astonishment. Music becomes a substitute for the symbolic role which is played by language in the later works. One motive for the substitution has already been suggested: the main action is powerfully directed, on the surface, towards an attempt to stylise process and change, to admit them only as unlanguaged ultimate form.

The attempt to cope with life as language is, nevertheless, present in the metatextual devices of the manuscript and the various letters. This textualisation of life is an attempt to read back into time, to transform the history of the House of Sweeny. In terms of mediation, the manuscript and its epistolary supplements emerge as the play's central *dramatis persona*. If the texts within the text are seen as palimpsests, in both the Freudian and the Nietzschean sense, then the action becomes a dramatised *explication de texte*, with the sub-texts threatening, from time to time, to erupt into life. The first words of the play, which are read from the manuscript by Sister Eileen, refer to 'the real effort of the artist' (f.1) and to the relationship between this reality and biography and autobiography. As she handles and reads the manuscript, she waits for the 'real' Columb, who is absently represented to her through his writings. Yet when he appears, she awkwardly avoids him, leaving the room after a brief report on the uncle's death. When she returns, meaningful conversation again becomes possible only through the letter from O'Neill. The theme of the letter is art and eros. Vicariously, it expresses Columb's desire to possess Eileen and his fear of the act of possession. O'Neill writes of how he gazed on the aesthetic archetypal image of woman, Rodin's Eve, but when a real woman came to his studio, he 'could do nothing but talk' (f.8). He became a playboy, a 'Jester' (f.8) whose words were lost gems, thrown away on girls, not women. The business with the letter leads almost immediately to the next piece of mediating *écriture* — the notebook brought by Mrs Byrne from under the pillow of Columb's dead uncle. This notebook is a veritable treasure-house of palimpsests. It contains 'a little drawing of a girl' (f.10), again, we note, not a woman, which is variously said to resemble Bride, O'Neill, Columb's uncle, Stephen Costello and Eileen. It is 'in fact' a portrait of Mary Costello. A slip of paper refers the reader to 'the box between the library windows', which in turn contains 'my will and a letter to be read by my heir' (f.10). With the notebook are some keys. For the moment, Columb declines to unlock the family mystery, questioning his uncle's bid to implicate him in the past and to continue to project his patriarchal, testatory authority into the future. 'I do not know', declares Columb, 'that I am his heir' (f.10).

The episode which follows anticipates, for all its awkwardness, Synge's subversive use of religious rituals and sacramental rites in his later plays. Rejecting his uncle's attempt to inscribe himself into the text of his life, Columb goes to 'an old press' (f.11). He 'takes out two curiously formed wine glasses with a saucepan and decanter. Then he arranges the turf, pours some wine into the saucepan and puts it on the fire' (f.11). He is celebrating here a communion/wedding rite, in which the wine is to be changed to mingled blood on the focal altar of the house. The fire is a *turf* fire; not, we have been reminded, made of English coal. Columb spills a little of the wine onto the embers as he stirs the flames to life. This is the cue for Sister Eileen's (equally 'accidental') concelebration, as she, in turn, stains Columb's manuscript with the wine. We scarcely need to invoke Jacques Derrida's analyses to recognise the signification of this episode. Indeed, the ritual spillings are followed by a liturgical reading from the manuscript, the erotic connotations of which are barely concealed beneath the mask of the text's symphonic denotation:

> After dealing with the first movement that is filled with passion and excitement I go on to the next movement — — reading — — 'The position of the slow movement after the climax of the opening is also wonderfully suggestive. This sigh of beautiful relief, which comes as an explaination [sic] rather than a mere cessation of an excitement that is always pain, is the last utterance of man' (f. 13).

At the moment where the reading reaches the 'passion of relief' and 'the dissolution of the person' (f. 13) the wine obligingly boils over and Columb, pouring out two glasses, declares 'My wine is ready — — . . . Trinquez' (f.13). The drinking — 'C'est bien bon' (f.13) — is followed by the highly symbolic lighting of Columb's pipe from the fire.

The metatextual action continues in Act II when Columb dictates a letter to O'Neill, using Eileen as amanuensis. This is a further example of textual mediation between Columb and his cousin. The coming of spring becomes the almost Lawrentian referent for the displaced marital theme:

> A distant cousin of mine — a nun — who had been nursing my uncle stayed on here and took care of me. It has been a curious moment. I could look out from my bed into the woods and watch the spring beginning. I had

forgotten the marvelousness of the world. Soft grey days came first with quiet clouds, and the woods grew purple with sap, while a few birches that stood out before them like candle sticks with wrought silver stems, covered themselves with a dull mist of red. Then the hazels came out and hung the woods with straight ear-rings of gold that gave relief in their simplicity among the tangled boughs. One morning after rain spectres of pale green and yellow and pink seemed to be looking out between the trees (ff.31-2).

The letter is the medium through which Columb proposes marriage to Sister Eileen. When his cousin refuses to continue writing, Columb decides that the moment has come to read his uncle's letter, thereby *substituting it for his own unwritten/rejected text*. The box containing the letter also holds the wedding rings of Columb's uncle and Mary Costello, and Mary's wedding dress, soon to be used by the couple in their own wedding ceremony. The reading of the uncle's epistle is prefaced by a further liturgical speech from Columb, deriving in theme and style from his manuscript. The episode is solemnised — and scripturalised — by the lighting of oil-lamps and the references to the oil running out. The letter makes Sister Eileen want to leave. It is only when plot and sub-plot converge, when Bride Kavanagh enacts what the letter urges Columb and Eileen to do, that the main plot breaks through into action: Eileen puts on the wedding dress and yields to Columb's will.

Commitment to life is, however, ultimately denied to the two central characters in *When the Moon Has Set*, largely because they are assigned to an alternative which is removed from history and place. They are propelled, in the last instance, towards a musical requiem, the result of which is a withdrawal from the urgent problems of history, biography and time. The price exacted by the attempted transcendence of the diseased world of habit is a renunciation of the human condition. It leads inexorably to a relinquishing of identity and loss of personal freedom. Eileen acquiesces will-lessly and wit-lessly to being caught up in 'a dream that is wider than I am . . . I cannot help it' (f.41). Synge certainly struggles against paying the price, in this play, of what he was to characterise later as utopianism. Signs of the struggle are evident even in the closing lines, which, like Martin Doul's restored vision in *The Well of the Saints*, have one eye on the church and one on the greeny bits of ferns. Payment is nevertheless exacted by the idealism which results from the attempt to find in an escapist aesthetic

175

the ultimate answer to the challenge of history. In the diseased world in which the peasant characters, Bride and Pat, have to find their happiness, or not at all, Columb and Eileen would be little better than the pastoral playboys of O'Casey's *Purple Dust*, a play written partly as an affectionate parody of Synge. They become high comic equivalents of those renovators of the House of History who busk around in peasant smocks and sing pseudo-rustic songs. The most apt comment on such behaviour may be confidently left to O'Casey's First Workman:

> Well, God help the poor omadhauns! It's a bad sign to see people actin' like that an' they sober.[12]

NOTES

1. All references to the two-act version of *When the Moon Has Set* are given internally in the chapter. They follow the foliation of TCD MS 4351, ff. 1-43. This version has been published by the Friends of the Library of Trinity College, Dublin as a special edition of the journal *Long Room*, Double Number 24-25, Spring-Autumn 1982, with a critical introduction by M.C. King. For Ann Saddlemyer's comment on the conflated version offered in the Collected Works, Volume III, Plays II, see footnote number 2, p. 155.

2. The entry is as follows: 'Finished (?) one act Play "When the Moon Has Set (?)" .'

3. Robin Skelton describes Florence Ross, Synge's cousin, as 'the first girl to interest him emotionally'. See Robin Skelton, *The Writings of J. M. Synge* (London, Thames and Hudson, 1971), p. 9. Cherrie Matheson was a friend of the Synge family who came to stay at Castle Kevin as a companion for Florence. Synge proposed to her in 1895.

4. A similar awareness of decay permeates Synge's essay, 'A Landlord's Garden in County Wicklow', in which he remarks that

> if a playwright chose to go through the Irish country houses he would find material, it is likely, for many gloomy plays that would turn on the dying away of these old families, and on the lives of the one or two delicate girls that are left so often to represent a dozen hearty men who were alive a generation or two ago (II, p. 231).

5. Skelton, *The Writings of J.M. Synge*, p. 19.

6. Elliot Krieger, *A Marxist Study of Shakespeare's Comedies* (London and Basingstoke, Macmillan, 1979), p. 3.

7. See *Collected Works*, Volume III, pp. 171-3.

8. W.J. McCormack, *Sheridan Le Fanu and Victorian Ireland* (Oxford, Clarendon Press, 1980), p. 244.

9. Frank Lentricchia, *The Gaiety of Language*, Perspectives in Criticism, 19 (Berkeley and Los Angeles, University of California Press, 1968) p. 38.

10. W.B. Yeats, *Essays and Introductions* (London and New York, Macmillan, 1981), p. 145.

11. Declan Kiberd, *Synge and the Irish Language* (London and Basingstoke, Macmillan, 1979), pp. 147-8.

12. Sean O'Casey, *Purple Dust*, in *Three More Plays by Sean O'Casey* (London and Basingstoke, Macmillan, 1965), p. 123.

9.
MYTH AND HISTORY:
Deirdre of the Sorrows

WE HAVE argued that *When the Moon Has Set* is both circumscribed and impaired by Synge's attempts to ascribe an aesthetic teleology to nature and history. In deference to the demands of this programme, the central characters become mere pawns in the working out of a pre-determined game. Turning from Synge's first to his last play, we move from the realms of philosophically over-determined action to a plot the outcome of which is apparently controlled by the exigencies of fatal prophecy, or structured by the pattern of myth. In the story which forms the basis for the play, and which would have been familiar to most of Synge's audience not just through Yeats's and Russell's work, but also through the saga material and its translations, Deirdre's destiny is foretold at her birth. She is doomed to 'be the ruin of the Sons of Usna, and have a little grave by herself, and a story will be told forever' (IV, 209). In choosing to deal with what had become for his audience historical myth — or even heroic national history — Synge in some respects went against his own repeatedly expressed judgement of the potential dangers and pitfalls of the material for the modern dramatist. In the draft of an essay written on 18th March 1907 he argued that the very awakening of 'the sense of historical truth' in Europe made what he called historical fiction 'impossible' (IV, 393). His case is based on the difficulty of projecting onto characters from history 'our own language or feeling with perfect sincerity'; with our more sophisticated historical sense we know that such personages 'have been different from ourselves' (IV, 393).

178

If he was aware that the saga material might lead him away from the fundamental realities of life, why, then, did Synge turn for his own last work to the story of Deirdre? It is certainly true that he was attracted by the possibilities of creating a major dramatic role for Molly Allgood. About this, however, we have to be cautious, for there is evidence that he originally intended the play to centre on the Children of Usna. Undoubtedly the story struck a personal chord for the now all too often unwell dramatist: Deirdre challenges death by marrying Naisi, lives with him for seven years and then kills herself rather than survive him. As a dramatist, however, Synge was not inclined to view autobiographical material in terms of purely personal significance: 'no personal originality is enough to make a rich work unique' (II, 350). He also believed that the expression of a personality could reveal the movement of history itself. He may well have regarded his planned marriage to Molly as a more than merely private act. Like Sister Eileen's wedding with Columb, it would break through ascendancy and Catholic Irish social conventions and overturn the religious — and therefore political — expectations of both sides.

Deirdre, too, refuses to conform to society's plans for her future. She chooses to defy the warnings of the prophecy and she not only thwarts the personal wishes and desires of the ageing king, but also calls into question his regal authority. By refusing to become queen at Emain Macha, and deciding instead to wed Naisi, Deirdre rejects Conchubor as king, as suitor, and as surrogate father. Whatever may have been the social and political significance of any personally felt parallels between Deirdre's predicament and his own 'time, and locality and the life that is in it' (II, 350), we do have definite evidence also that before he began to work on *Deirdre of the Sorrows* Synge was worried by the opprobrium brought upon his Abbey friends and colleagues by the hostile reactions to *The Playboy of the Western World*. He was attracted, too, by the possibility of taking the kind of material used by Yeats and Russell and obviously in favour with the Abbey clientele, and treating it differently. On September 12th 1907 — shortly *after* his first draft of *Deirdre* — Synge wrote to Frederick J. Gregg:

The 'Playboy' affair brought so much unpopularity on my friends Lady Gregory, Mr. Yeats and the individual players of our company that I am placed in rather a delicate position. I am half inclined to try a play on

179

'Deirdre' — it would be amusing to compare it with Yeats' and Russell's — but I am a little afraid that the 'Saga' people might loosen my grip on reality (IV, xxvii).

An immediately obvious distinction between the two earlier 'Deirdre' plays and Synge's is linguistic: their high poetic style gives way to a modified version of the language of his 'peasant' drama. By having his 'Saga' people use this language, it is probable that he hoped to ensure for his play a degree of 'compatibility with the outside world and the peasants or people who live near it' (II, 351). Nor did he depend on language alone to counter the undesired tendency to utopian weakness. Declan Kiberd has shown that his version of the Deirdre story is closer to the hard, unromanticised Gaelic materials than either Yeats's or Russell's, who had to approach the sagas through translations and who were thus literally, as well as ideologically, at further remove from the original autochthonic sources.[1] The stylistic distinction of Synge's play points to a fundamental motive in the work — its recognition and critique of conflicting myths of history.

The dramatic tension generated by the disjunction between story and history in *Deirdre of the Sorrows* is deliberately foregrounded, a foregrounding adumbrated in the letter to Gregg, by the awareness, most acute in Deirdre herself, that the characters are actors, or pawns, in a story or game. The awareness of her status as the focus of a myth is a feature peculiar to Synge's play. But like Pirandello's *dramatis personae* in *Six Characters in Search of an Author*, she demands the right to act out, and even to emplot, her life and death — to show how it was. The play was a dual orientation, both towards and away from history and myth. The formal structural and linguistic strategies, by calling attention to their status and operations, establish the status of the text itself as a product of these tensions and the drama, viewed from this perspective, is metamythological. It is critically subversive of any escape into the formal consolations offered by promises of mystic, or artistic, immortality, while it acknowledges the influence of myth on consciousness and therefore on human history. As in *The Playboy of the Western World*, story acknowledges its debt to and its influence upon deed, without conceding any simple identification of the one with the other.

The play as it stands, and we must remember that it is unfinished, is in three acts. In Act I Deirdre is presented as a foster-child of nature who is foster-fathered, as well as wooed, by Conchubor. Like Mary Costello in *When the Moon Has Set*, she is dispossessed of her social birthright, which is to be offered back only through a marriage which above all else she wishes to avoid. It is one of the play's ironies that Deirdre begs Naisi to take her away from the woods of Slieve Fuadh to the woods of Alban in order to escape the very fate of marriage with Conchubor which the king plans as a means of gainsaying fate, or of turning myth to his own advantage. Conchubor is effectively the instigator of the events which lead to Deirdre's death — as Lavarcham repeatedly warns him. The king thus becomes the manipulator of the myth. Act II opens when Deirdre and Naisi and his brothers have been living in Alban for a seemingly idyllic seven years. History, however, has caught up with them, in the form of messengers from the king. Apparently persuaded by Fergus that Conchubor has forgiven them, they return, in Act III, to Emain and to their deaths. It is necessary to use the words 'seemingly' and 'apparently' because in many respects the detail of the action in Synge's play works against the broad narrative movement of the episodic plot.

From the outset there is an ambivalence about the status of the prophecy itself. Lavarcham doubts its determining power over human action when she asks

> Who'd check her like was made to have her pleasure only, the way if there were no warnings told about her you'd see troubles coming when an old king is taking her, and she without a thought but for her beauty and to be straying the hills (IV, 183).

As Lavarcham sees it, Deirdre's tragedy, if it is realised, will be the result not so much of fate, as of a deliberately engineered and obsessively pursued mismatch between an old and dying king and a young bride. By keeping Deirdre apart from society 'straying the hills', the ageing king intends her to save him, through her artificially cultivated and protected 'natural' innocence and youth, from a burden of guilt similar to that which afflicts the Big House in *When the Moon Has Set*. 'The like of me', he tells Deirdre, 'have a store of knowledge that's a weight and terror; it's for that we do choose out the like of yourself that are young and glad only' (IV, 193). By claiming

Deirdre for himself, Conchubor is, however, forcing upon her a living death. From the outset he treats her as his property. Fergus counts out the money the king has brought for her and Conchubor checks up on the 'mats and hangings and the silver skillets' (IV, 187) he has sent. Rather than accept such a fate, Deirdre chooses to go with Naisi and his brothers to the woods of Alban.

The lovers' withdrawal into the woods raises the critical issue of the idealising similarities between the sylvan alternative to existence in the diseased world offered to Sister Eileen, and the green world existence temporarily achieved by Deirdre and Naisi. The relationship between the action of the two plays at this point of withdrawal is signalled by Synge's use of the same ritual formula for the wedding ceremonies which are preludes in each case to the 'new' life. Yet although the temptation to escape is strong, Deirdre and Naisi are never presented in *Deirdre of the Sorrows* as totally integrated children of nature who, in Donna Gerstenberger's words, 'belong to the woods' as opposed to the court.[2] Deirdre does not wish to avoid marriage with the king merely that she may dwell forever in mountain or wood. Nor does she agree with Conchubor's suggestion that, kept apart from the social community, she must necessarily be 'gay and lively each day in the year' (IV, 193). 'There are', she tells the king, 'lonesome days and bad nights in this place like another' (IV, 193). Her fall into humanity and out of myth has already started when the play begins. She has dreamed of a man 'who'd be her likeness . . . a man with his hair like the raven maybe and his skin like the snow and his lips like blood spilt on it' (IV, 191). An essential paradox, however, is underlined by the highly conventional, stylised and derivative nature of this description. Taken from the source-material, it is immediately recognisable as a typical, indeed formulaic, account of the idealised prince or princess of many myths, legends and fairy-tales. Deirdre opposes to the king's ambition of using her to indulge his dream of escaping from the 'weight and terror' (IV, 193) of worldly knowledge a dream of her own making. Her aesthetic vision of Naisi, *the image which she is weaving into her tapestry*, is of 'a mate who'd be her likeness' (IV, 191). It is, therefore, a reflection, translated into art, of her mythologised self. It is also in a continuum with, and partly generated by, the self-deceiving vision of the ageing king. Deirdre weaves this image of ideal beauty into the form of a picture of Conchubor's nephew as the ideal prince, thus projecting into the next generation the myth of perfection for which Conchubor longs. 'All say', Lavarcham tells the king, 'there isn't her match at fancying figures and throwing purple upon crimson and she edging them all times with her greens and gold' (IV, 187).

The link between Conchubor's coveted escape from his nightmare of age and death and Deirdre's desiderated escape into her dream of life is forged through the metaesthetic medium of the unfinished tapestry. The king examines the web as he questions Lavarcham about Deirdre; Deirdre herself defiantly continues to weave her picture as she rejects the king's plans for her future. The life which she figures for herself and the 'three young men, and they chasing in the green gap of a wood' (IV, 191) is opposed to his design. Yet the opposed visions are interdependent and they have a remarkable affinity with each other — an affinity which is underlined by the lexical and syntactic parallelism:

CONCHUBOR [*now almost pleading*]. It's soon you'll have dogs with silver chains to be chasing in the woods of Emain, for I have white hounds rearing up for you, and grey horses, that I've chosen from the finest in Ulster and Britain and Gaul.

DEIRDRE [*unmoved, as before*]. I've heard tell in Ulster and Britain and Gaul, Naisi and his brothers have no match and they chasing in the woods (IV, 191).

Deirdre's counter-statement is framed within the context of *story*, of what she has 'heard tell'. Beauty, and life, have assumed in her fancy an heroic form. The tale she is translating into tapestry has made her dissatisfied with the life to which she is confined. Like Tennyson's Lady of Shalott, as long as she remains within the imprisoning confines of the myth, Deirdre sees life only through images and texts. She is suspended between two related shadow worlds, the living death of Emain Macha if she marries the old king, and the threat of a 'little grave by herself' (IV, 209), if she weds Usna's son.

When Deirdre decides to follow her vision, to break from the web-and-loom picturing of Naisi and his brothers and go with them towards her dream of life, she does not appear dressed in her peasant's clothes. She arrays herself in the full courtly splendour of a queen about to claim her worldly kingdom and power:

DEIRDRE [*gathering her things together with an outburst of excitement*]. I will dress like Emer in Dundealgan or Maeve in her house in Connaught. If Conchubor'll make me a queen I'll have the right of a queen who is a master, taking her own choice and making a stir to the edges of the seas . . . Lay out your mats and hangings where I can stand this night and look about me. Lay out the skins of the rams of Connaught and of the goats of the west. I'll put on my robes that are the richest for I will not be brought down to Emain as Cuchulain brings his horse to its yoke, or Conall Cearneach puts his shield upon his arm (IV, 199).

Her dramatic, and self-dramatising, transformation is motivated by her angry determination not to be treated as a mere piece of the king's property. There is, again, a paradox at the heart of Deirdre's defiant gesture. She asserts her identity by dressing up, by assuming the role of a queen and comparing herself with Emer and Maeve. By so doing, she seeks to escape from myth through myth: Emer and Maeve, both of them queens with an historical identity, are also figures who, in the Irish nationalist context, are antitypes of Ireland as a nation.

The expectation aroused by Deirdre's appearance as a queen powerful enough to rival Emer and Maeve *in their courts* is not, however, fulfilled. Even when in Act I Deirdre exhorts Naisi to defy Conchubor, she introduces, in place of any explicit political or social challenge to her bondage, the theme of choosing death as an alternative not just to her enforced marriage, but to the common fate of growing old. 'Isn't it a small thing is foretold about the ruin of ourselves, Naisi,' she asks, 'when all men have age coming and great ruin in the end?' (IV, 211). This theme of a personalised romantic agony is developed in Act II alongside an attempt to assert the harmony and sense of identity which Deirdre and Naisi have found with the natural world. Their life in Alban, however, unlike the political intrigues and battles depicted in the sagas, is not very dissimilar from Deirdre's a-social existence on Slieve Fuadh. The conjunction of two related escapist tendencies, the choice of death as an alternative to age and the opting for the life of 'nature' in place of social life, certainly threatens to weaken the play in the very way Synge feared — by loosening its grip on reality. The dramatic problems to which this tendency gave rise were to grow enormously in the constantly reworked — and for Synge himself, never satisfactory —

second act. Related problems continue to threaten the credibility of the action in Act III, which leaves largely unresolved the question of Deirdre's and Naisi's reasons for returning to Emain. Some of the resulting inconsistencies were noted by Darrell Figgis as early as 1911, when he pointed out that, having returned to Ireland to seek death rather than allow old age to destroy their love, Deirdre begs the king to forgive Naisi and herself, asking him to

> let call Ainnle and Ardan, the way we'd have a supper all together, and fill that grave, and you'll be well pleased from this out having four new friends the like of us in Emain (IV, 253).[3]

The extent of Synge's own dissatisfaction with Act II may be judged by a report he made on 29th August 1908 to Lady Gregory:

> I have been fiddling with Deirdre a little. I think I'll have to cut it down to two longish acts. The middle act in Scotland is impossible (IV, xxix).

One of the major problems which he faced was that of convincing himself, his characters and his audience that the seven years which Deirdre and the Sons of Usna have spent in the woods of Alban have sufficient substance — or reality — to be acceptable as a credible, not to mention desirable, alternative to Emain Macha, with all its challenges and threats. The problem may lie in Synge's reluctance to admit that the abstract idealism, which so powerfully attracted him in his first play, offers no real alternative to the decay of Conchubor's court. Yet the suspicion is never far away that the woodland existence of Deirdre and the Children of Usna is a form of living death. For all its alleged harmony with nature, its quest for biological warmth, 'pressing the lips together, going up and down, resting in our arms, Naisi, wakening with the smell of June in the tops of the grasses, and listening to the birds in the branches that are highest' (IV, 231), it has deprived Deirdre, and Naisi and his brothers, of the social dimensions of reality.

The personal temptation of falling half in love with death, of trying to see it as a means of escaping from old age, must have been great for Synge. It very probably contributed to the attraction which such a solution is made to present to Deirdre and Naisi. That it had its

185

political and ideological attractions also for an ascendancy which had begun to glimpse the spectre of its own demise is amply attested by the powerful appeal of Nietzsche to the Anglo-Irish imagination. Nietzsche's myth of eternal recurrence seemed to offer the hope, eventually to turn nightmare for Yeats, that death-as-mythical-rebirth was at least a way to being enabled to go on living. Synge, however, was too conscious of the social and historical dimensions of myth not to question these 'solutions' even when he was drawn towards them. Lavarcham pours scorn on Deirdre's and the poets' assertions that dying is always to be preferred to growing old:

> If it's that ails you, I tell you there's little hurt getting old, though young girls and poets do be storming at the shapes of age. [*Passionately.*] There's little hurt getting old, saving when you're looking back, the way I'm looking this day, and seeing the young you have a love for breaking up their hearts with folly (IV, 219).

The word 'shapes' suggests here that such railings are directed more often against fancied shadows than realities.

The problem nevertheless remains that Deirdre's and Naisi's determination for love and life, because of the exclusively naturalised form which it takes, has become unnatural. It is as much an evasion of human historical reality, and therefore a falsification of nature, as Columb's escape into the trees. Alban threatens, for Synge, to become a utopian dream turned dramatist's nightmare. In the woods Naisi and Deirdre do nothing because few, if any, opportunities are open to them for meaningful human activity. Their lives are 'sleepy' and 'a game'. Ainnle and Ardan scarcely exist as dramatic characters. They are mere shadows, ghostly reminders of the attenuated, atrophied nature of social bonds which are starved of any possibility of, or context for, growth. This development — or lack of it — worried Synge. He tried in a draft dated 28th November 1907 to give more scope for action to Ainnle, even allowing him to raise the disconcerting question of what their way of life has to offer himself and his brother:

> AINNLE. There have been strange things done in Alban and strange things done in Ireland, but this is the strangest, Deirdre, that myself and Ardan should be well pleased and we living bachelors and servants for yourself and Naisi (IV, 377).

No answer is forthcoming, beyond an unconvincingly strident panegyric to the power of Deirdre's beauty.

We must conclude, therefore, that Synge's own dissatisfaction with the lack of meaningful action in the second act of *Deirdre* does him greater justice as a dramatist than any premature acclamation of the unfinished work as a masterpiece. His repeated attempts to redraft it show how far he had come from that too-easy yielding to unearned unity with nature which concludes *When the Moon Has Set*. A more thorough-going development of the formal potential offered by metalinguistic and metadramatic strategies might have enabled him to come to grips with this challenge of a world of idealising abstraction. It is through such strategies, for example, that Shakespeare exposes the ideological implications of the retreat of Duke Senior into the woods in *As You Like It*, showing us how the Duke 'not only translates nature into style . . . but also appropriates Nature as the occasion for his style'.[4]

Even in the unsatisfactory Alban sequence Synge does not suppress completely the potentially subversive elements of his material. Declan Kiberd recognises this when he suggests that the lovers' 'passion was failing precisely because of the artificial nature of their life in Alban. There, the very fact that their love meant everything was itself a threat to its survival'.[5] Yet it is not the fact that Deirdre's and Naisi's love means everything that threatens it: the problem, rather, is that the everything which Alban offers is nothing. So withdrawn is it from reality that it allows no scope for love to develop. The lovers' relationship can only be at best asserted; it is never tested out. The tragedy of Deirdre and Naisi is that the natural qualities of life have been rendered artificial by their alienation from their social nature. However much the text might contradict Synge's stated intention of making Deirdre's and Naisi's flight to Alban an escape from an indifferent existence into a determination for life, he was surely right, then, to characterise their return to the king's court at Emain, however threatening or corrupt, as an 'inevitable sweeping into «the» current of life' (IV, 370).

In the third act of the play the prophecy of the ruin of the sons of Usna and the death of Deirdre is realised. Almost half the act, however, is taken up with the proposing of alternatives to the predicted end. These critical perspectives on fate help to restore a context of choice to the action. They make it possible for us to compare what is with what might have been, and go some way towards converting the vague, narrative *Angst* of Act II into an at least partially successful and socially contextualised tragic action. The structure of the act divides into two movements. The turning-point occurs when Conchubor's men attack Ainnle and Ardan, and Naisi, leaving Deirdre, goes to their aid. The opening of the act looks back, in terms of character, setting and theme, to the beginning of the play. The setting, a *'tent below Emain, with shabby skins and benches'* (IV, 241) recalls the small house on Slieve Fuadh where Conchubor tried to cultivate and keep Deirdre for himself. In place of the rich tapestries and hangings, with which he first sought to purchase her love, this time he has provided only 'frayed rugs and skins are eaten by the moths' (IV, 247). As before, Lavarcham tries to persuade Conchubor of the perverse nature of his possessive will to own Deirdre for himself. The tone of her argument now is much more elegiac than in the first act. She reminds the king of their mutual old age and their subjection to nature:

> It's a poor thing the way me and you is getting old, Conchubor, and I'm thinking you yourself have no call to be loitering this place getting your death, maybe, in the cold of night (IV, 241).

But the king is not simply a private person, and so she warns him also of the trouble he will bring 'this night on Emain and Ireland and the big world's east beyond them' (IV, 243). She tries to counter his obsession by claiming that Deirdre, too, will have changed:

> Ah, Conchubor, my lad, beauty goes quickly in the woods, and you'd let a great gasp, I tell you, if you set your eyes this night on Deirdre (IV, 243).

The equalising familiarity with which Lavarcham addresses the king, calling him 'my lad', probably owes a stylistic debt to the euhemerised folk versions of the myth which, according to Declan Kiberd, Synge very possibly heard during his visits to Aran and Connemara.[6] The significance of this process is not, however, purely stylistic. When a society, or its institutions, officially endorses a myth, it requires of the artist 'that he transform the spiritual creative function of the myth (and hence of faith) into the external function of idolatry'.[7] It requires him to treat it reverentially, as a sanctified and unchangeable dogma. Euhemerisation is subversive of such official acts of appropriation. Just as his interest in the social and economic roots of folk tales alerted Synge to the strikingly modern preoccupations with problems of price, rent, evictions and land ownership in the Aran islanders' retellings of stories and poems, so too he 'grasped the relationship between the heroic world of the ancient legend and the peasant Ireland in which the story still lingered. Conchubor and the other leaders of the Ulster Cycle were euhemerised gods who had been reduced by the storytellers to the status of mortals'.[8] The tension which in the original autochthonic myths led to the creation of the gods and the fates finds expression in our century in 'the earthly tension between men and commodities', and it is precisely to Conchubor's treatment of Deirdre as a purchased property that the play returns us in Act III.[9]

The king remains, throughout Act III, obstinately indifferent to Deirdre's human status. Awareness of his own mortality merely intensifies his determination to grasp the object he regards as his prize in the game of life:

> CONCHUBOR. You think I'm old and wise, but I tell you the wise know the old must die, and they'll leave no chance for *a thing* slipping from them, they've set their blood to win (IV, 243, my italics).

Believing that power confers upon him the right to control the destiny of others in his own interest, he alienates himself and the class he represents — Naisi and his brothers are his nephews — from the natural and the humanised world. That all of Conchubor's military energies and statecraft are directed towards the fetishisation of Deirdre, his foster daughter, is part of the play's *leitmotif* of crisis and decline, relating it closely to the generational obsessions of *When the Moon Has Set* and the transformations attempted therein between *eros* and *thanatos*. This is, in Volosinov's words, a 'motif old in and of itself' which reappears in new guises at moments when 'a social class finds itself in a state of disintegration and is compelled to retreat from the arena of history'.[10] The supreme tragic irony of Synge's play lies in the fact that the king's treatment of Deirdre turns story into a history of destruction. His obsessive pursuit of his desire to possess her burns

189

Emain to ashes and, by destroying his own nephews, it destroys the succession also. When his men carry out his murderous commands, death comes between himself and his object, making reconciliation impossible.

The possibility of a change in the destructive relationship between Deirdre and the king is raised as soon as Deirdre and Naisi make their appearance. In place of seeing their return to Emain as an acceptance of death which will protect their love against decay, Deirdre looks now for full social recognition and self-realisation. She sees them claiming their 'right to Emain', their 'having curtains shaken out and rich rooms put in order; and . . . great state to meet us' (IV, 247). Just as she attributes the discrepancy between her dream of social integration and the alienating reality which surrounds them to Conchubor's lack of 'a queen like me in Emain' (IV, 249), Deirdre uncovers the next stage of the king's scenario for action — the grave he has dug for his own nephews:

> [*She pulls hanging, and it opens.*] . . . There's new earth on the ground and a trench dug . . . It's a grave Naisi, that is wide and deep (IV, 249).

Confronted thus with the reality of death, her immediate reaction is to opt for life:

> DEIRDRE [*in a faint voice*]. Take me away . . . Take me to hide in the rocks, for the night is coming quickly (IV, 249).

The grave, now that it has materialised, is 'a hard thing', which their 'days in Alban that went by so quick' (IV, 249) cannot soften or make attractive. The fact of death intrudes upon the imagery of transfiguration and forces a reassessment of the myth of immortality. To die is no longer a desired consummation or means of escape from age, although life without Naisi — the life the king intends — seems 'things . . . worse than death' (IV, 251).

In *Deirdre of the Sorrows*, the drawing back of the curtain on the grave is the epiphany of death — of death entailed by life, but also brought about by the historic actions, in time and by an act of will, of those with power over the lives of others. In Nicholas Grene's words, the grave is 'the reality which makes everything else fade into insubstantial illusion'.[11] More accurately, perhaps, it is the dramatic representation of a reality which challenges illusion and self-deception, from the mystical nature-illusions forced upon and fostered by Deirdre and Naisi to the related calculating self-deception of Conchubor which turns love into an investment against age and people into manipulated objects. The grave is at the very centre of Conchubor's society, and it becomes the main challenge to his authority. In its presence, on its very edge, Conchubor, Deirdre and Naisi briefly discover a human kinship which offers a fragile and fleeting glimpse of a possible alternative to their tragic relationship. This alternative is not an escape from dying, but a turning away from the deformed and deforming possessiveness which allows Deirdre and Naisi only the desperate choice of living in order to die, or dying because they have chosen to live.

The tragedy of Deirdre and Naisi is not that no outcome other than the prophesied tragic end is conceivable; it is, rather, that their tragedy is unavoidable within the constraints imposed upon the lovers by the king. Conchubor has played a game of ownership with Deirdre for so long that seeming has come to dominate word and deed. He is only half convinced of the earnestness of her appeal for an alternative ending to their story:

> CONCHUBOR [*looking at her for a moment*]. That's the first friendly word I've heard you speaking, Deirdre. A game the like of yours should be the proper thing for softening the heart and putting sweetness in the tongue, and yet this night when I hear you, I've small blame left for Naisi that he stole you off from Ulster (IV, 253).

The king remains trapped in the language of gaming and stealing. Cries of betrayal and sounds of battle break in on his deliberations and the mortal price which he pledged as part of his wager for Deirdre is exacted; characteristically, his acknowledgement of this is expressed yet again in terms of gambling:

> CONCHUBOR. I was near won this night, but death's between us now (IV, 255).

The anguished quarrel between Deirdre and Naisi which follows has been both praised and criticised — criticised because of the inconsistency of Deirdre's desperate appeal to Naisi to stay with her and save her from death and praised for the tragic irony which supposedly shows Deirdre and Naisi losing, on the edge of the grave, the love they resolved to preserve by dying. Neither the praise nor the criticism fully recognises the dramatic significance of the emphasis on the conflicting emotions and attitudes which divide Deirdre against herself. Deirdre pleads with Naisi to save them both from death — but any refuge, under Conchubor's dispensation, would be a condemnation to 'the darkness behind the grave' (IV, 255). The final stripping of any remaining illusions from Deirdre comes when, recognising that they have 'had a dream, but this night has waked us surely' (IV, 255), she sends Naisi to fight for Ainnle and Ardan:

> DEIRDRE. Let you go where they are calling! [*She looks at him for an instant coldly.*] Have you no shame loitering and talking and a cruel death facing Ainnle and Ardan in the woods? (IV, 255).

Naisi's failure to share her anguished insight is the highest price, in personal terms, which Deirdre pays for her tragic recognition of the real nature of the gap between individual need and social responsibilities. The division between her love for Naisi and the obligations of brotherhood is, in Conchubor's kingdom, rendered absolute. Naisi is almost on the point of recognising the kindness of Deirdre's cruelty, but he goes to his death missing the implications of his own insight:

> NAISI [*frantic*]. They'll not get a death that's cruel and they with men alone. It's women that have loved are cruel only, and if I went on living from this day I'd be putting a curse on the lot of them I'd meet walking in the east or west, putting a curse on the sun that gave them beauty, and on the madder and the stone-crop put red upon their cloaks.
> DEIRDRE [*bitterly*]. I'm well pleased there's no one this place to make a story that Naisi was a laughing-stock the night he died (IV, 257).

No sooner is Naisi slain than Conchubor returns. Vainly attempting to cover up the untidy reality of death, closing the tent '*so that the grave is not seen any more*' (IV, 257), he claims Deirdre as his prize:

> CONCHUBOR. They've met their death, the three that stole you Deirdre, and from this out you'll be my queen in Emain (IV, 257).

Her '*bewildered and terrified*' (IV, 257) reply underlines the destructive impact of the king's murderous words: 'It is not I will be a queen' (IV, 257). Conchubor persists with his crude determination to buy the love to which he has denied the right to give itself freely — but the very words he uses betray the empty folly of his bid. The word 'rooms', with its tomb-like associations, the references to gold and bronze, and the negative force of 'never', cancelling out queenship and dwelling, all conspire to reveal the implications of his bargaining talk:

> CONCHUBOR. I've let build rooms for our two selves Deirdre, with red gold upon the walls, and ceilings that are set with bronze. There was never a queen in the east had a house the like of your house, that's waiting for yourself in Emain (IV, 259).

The play does not permit Deirdre to escape quickly or easily from the final confrontation between the mercenary possessiveness of Conchubor's disintegrating world and her own bid for integrity. Left briefly to herself, she finds little consolation from the natural world. The night which once seemed to befriend Naisi and herself is now pitiful for want of pity:

> DEIRDRE. To what place would I go away from Naisi? What are the woods without Naisi, or the seashore? (IV, 261).

Grieve though she may, Lavarcham reminds her, the sunny places will remain, summer itself will continue to come and human life will persist.

> CONCHUBOR [*furiously*]. Fergus cannot stop me . . . I am more powerful than he is though I am defeated and old (IV, 265).

Her grief ignored by Fergus and Conchubor alike, Deirdre is treated almost to the end as an object, to be guarded 'all times' (IV, 267). Conchubor's society, of which Fergus is a product, if now a rebellious one, is pathologically incapable of according to her her human value. By isolating her initially from society so that he might have her as queen over his kingdom, Conchubor condemned Deirdre to a life deprived of the social action and identity essential to human fulfilment. Her last speeches bear tragic witness to the loss of an integrity to which she can only bear witness in death. She is 'broken up with misery' (IV, 267) as she looks on 'the flames of Emain starting upward in the dark night' (IV, 267). The seat of Conchubor's civilisation will be razed to the ground, and in its place untamed predatory nature will rule: 'there will be weasels and wild cats crying on a lonely wall where there were queens and armies, and red gold' (IV, 267).

Deirdre turns from her lament over Emain to an elegiac address to a nature which is bereft now of its comradeship with the lovers who slept so sweetly with each other but who could never fully waken into action in sunlit or in moonlit woods:

> I see the trees naked and bare, and the moon shining. Little moon, little moon of Alban, it's lonesome you'll be this night, and tomorrow night, and long nights after, and you pacing the woods beyond Glen Laid, looking every place for Deirdre and Naisi, the two lovers who slept so sweetly with each other (IV, 267).

It is appropriate that she should locate part of the greatness and the glory of the lovers' drama in the harmony and delight, however partial, which Naisi and she sought and found in the natural world. It is appropriate, and necessary too, if the play is to avoid the retreat from history which weakens *When the Moon Has Set*, that she should recognise a complementary greatness in her social role, however partial or abortive it has been:

> DEIRDRE [*in a high and quiet tone*]. I have put away sorrow like a shoe that is worn out and muddy, for it is I have had a life that will be envied by great companies. It was not by a low birth I made kings uneasy, and they sitting in the halls of Emain. It was not a low thing to be chosen by Conchubor, who was wise, and Naisi had no match for bravery (IV, 267).

Her tragedy lies in the historical irreconcilability between these two roles. It resides in the alienation which arises between the two natures, the primary and the social, when forced into conflict with each other. The play remains true to this tragic dilemma to the end. While claiming that 'great joys were my shares always' Deirdre acknowledges that 'it is a cold place I must go to be with you, Naisi, and it's cold your arms will be this night that were warm about my neck so often' (IV,

194

269). Turning to Conchubor, she reminds him of his responsibility for their fate:

> It's a pitiful thing, Conchubor, you have done this night in Emain, yet a thing will be a joy and triumph to the ends of life and time (IV, 269).

Deirdre's fate is symptomatic of a society which makes it impossible to survive without prostituting herself. In an earlier version of the play, Lavarcham tells her that if she stays in the court she will become the king's 'concubine' (IV, 262, note 3). Neither, however, can she grow into full humanity by retreating into the private sphere of communion with nature. This new-found realism is tragically incisive. The play does not dismiss the fictional dream as an escapist illusion. Rather, it contextualises the prophecy and the dream, showing us that Deirdre's taking of her life is the only formal gesture by which, *in Conchubor's world*, she can affirm that life's value. The story and the act, entering into our consciousness, share in the human tragedy and triumph of the historical process. As Fergus throws his sword into the grave, the drama of the 'fate of Deirdre and Naisi next the Children of Usna' draws to a close — but the war between Fergus and Conchubor ends only 'for this night' (IV, 269).

Although incomplete and dramatically flawed, *Deirdre of the Sorrows* attempts that movement 'out beyond the personal into the wider reaches of history' which Joseph Frank attributes to the work of Pound, Eliot and James Joyce.[12] By encouraging his audience to experience the plot as a network of possible meanings, Synge has produced that something different from Russell's and Yeats's plays, and from the saga material, which he set himself as an objective. It was to take Yeats as dramatist until 1938 to achieve, in 'Purgatory', by related metadramatic strategies, what W.J. McCormack has described as an 'exposure of his inauthentic tradition' — the self-deceived tradition of a dying generation or class condemning itself to sterility by refusing to accept its mortality.[13]

NOTES

1. See Declan Kiberd, *Synge and the Irish Language* (London and Basingstoke, Macmillan, 1979), p. 178: 'The fundamental differences between Synge's play and the other works may be explained by the fact that, unlike Yeats and Russell, Synge did not rely on nineteenth-century English translations. Instead, he went back to the original texts of the legend in the Irish language'.

2. Donna Gerstenberger, *John Millington Synge*, Twayne's English Authors Series, 12 (New York, Twayne Publishers, 1964), p. 101.

3. Darrell Figgis, 'The Art of J. M. Synge', in *Studies and Appreciations* (London and New York, J.M. Dent and Dutton, 1912), p. 56.

4. Elliot Krieger, *A Marxist Study of Shakespeare's Comedies* (London and Basingstoke, Macmillan, 1979), pp. 77-8.

5. Kiberd, *Synge and the Irish Language*, p. 194.

6. Ibid., p. 190. Kiberd notes here that 'the popularity enjoyed by the legend at all levels of society made it inevitable that it would enter the folk tradition . . . Synge must have heard many . . . versions during his sojourns in Connemara and Aran'.

7. Max Raphael, *Proudhon Marx Picasso: Three Studies in the Sociology of Art*, translated by Inge Marcuse (New Jersey and London, Humanities Press and Lawrence and Wishart, 1980), p. 92.

8. Kiberd, *Synge and the Irish Language*, p. 191.

9. Raphael, *Proudhon Marx Picasso*, p. 140.

10. V.N. Volosinov, *Freudianism: A Marxist Critique*, translated by I.R. Titunik (London, Academic Press, 1976), p. 11.

11. Nicholas Grene, *Synge: A Critical Study of the Plays* (London and Basingstoke, Macmillan, 1975), p. 168.

12. Joseph Frank, 'Spatial Form in Modern Literature: An Essay in Two Parts', in *Sewanee Review* (1945), Part II, p. 652.

13. For a discussion of Yeats's treatment of this theme in 'Purgatory', as well as of his use of metadrama in that play, see W.J. McCormack, 'Yeats's "Purgatory": A Play and a Tradition', in *Crane Bag* Volume 3 No 2 (1979), pp. 33-44.

10.
NOT MARBLE NOR THE GILDED
MONUMENTS: Synge Reassessed

OUR PRINCIPAL concern in this analysis has been to demonstrate that
Synge's drama, while it derives much of its material from the folk
tradition of the Irish people, offers a complex and extremely relevant
exploration of the relationships between word and referent, between
language and action, between myth and history and between text and
world. The tracing of this theme to its origins has involved a return to
Synge's autobiographical drama, *When the Moon Has Set*. It has also
entailed a close concentration on *The Aran Islands*, in an attempt to
establish that this work is not a journalistic exercise, or an antiquarian
record of Synge's impressions of a doomed way of life. Now, in
conclusion, we may, perhaps, with greater discrimination, take up the
theme of the ways in which his major prose work reflects the
preoccupations and strategies of the dramatic writings. We shall look
at how Synge's critical attitude towards Loti's *Pêcheur d'Islande*, which
he had by him while writing *The Aran Islands*, points towards an
awareness of the relationships of these works to developments in late
romantic European literature which is much more perceptive, and
relevant to his own situation, than most interpretations of either Loti's
writings or his own. The parallels and distinctions between Loti and
Synge will lead us to consider briefly his affinity with modernist writers
such as Beckett and Joyce. Furthermore, we will suggest that the
relationship between their shared metatextual strategies and the
metadrama of Shakespeare's last comedies suggests a continuity
between Elizabethan and Jacobean literature and modernism which,

197

at least in the Anglo-Irish context, might be as significant as any emphasis on discontinuity. Such comparisons will allow us an opportunity also to reassess Eliot's famous dictum on the use of myth in Joyce and Yeats, and to raise the question of whether it is sufficient, or appropriate, to regard 'the mythical method' exclusively, or chiefly, as a strategy for imposing an aesthetico-political order on the anarchy of the age.[1]

In his correspondence with James Patterson and Spencer Brodney, Synge's concern about the importance of *The Aran Islands* as a work of art is obvious. To Brodney he wrote 'I look on *The Aran Islands* as my first serious piece of work' (II, 47). In the letter to Patterson he expressed 'a great relief that *The Aran Islands* is thought well of after all' (II, 47). The final typescript of the work contains a note, later crossed out, that 'the general plan of the book is . . . largely borrowed from Pierre Loti, who has, I think, treated this sort of subject more adequately than any other writer of the present day' (II, 48). The reference here is to Loti's *Pêcheur d'Islande*, ostensibly a study of the lives and fate of Breton fisher-folk woven around the story of Gaud, Yann and Sylvestre Gaos. Yann, the fisherman who weds Gaud (she wears a black funeral gown) is finally wedded to the sea when he is drowned on a fishing-trip to Iceland. On the surface, the two works might indeed appear to have much in common. Synge, however, seems to have realised that the differences between *Pêcheur d'Islande* and *The Aran Islands* were at least as significant as any similarities. The key to his decision to eliminate the reference to Loti from the typescript may well lie in a critical essay which he wrote for *The Speaker* on 'Loti and Huysmans'. The article appeared on 18 April 1903. It offers a useful perspective from which to consider the need for a reassessment of Synge's work, and in particular of the ways in which technique and style offer a critique of the myths of ascendancy and nationhood to which he has been accused of contributing and succumbing. In the article, Loti is described as

> a man who is tormented by the wonder of the world . . . till at last his one preoccupation becomes a *terrified search for some sign of the persistence of the person.* Like most wanderers, he fears death more than others, because he has seen many shadowy or splendid places where he has had no time to live, and has lived in other places long enough to feel in breaking from them a share of the desolation which is completed in death (II, 395, my italics).

We have noted in our analysis of *The Aran Islands* the recurrent theme of Synge's own sense of alienation. This finds expression from time to time in a preoccupation with the *dissolution* of the person, and is often consequent upon or followed by attempts to create an illusion of identity with the people and/or the landscape, or the sea. The fear of solipsistic loss of identity is, perhaps, most powerfully communicated in the dream sequence in Part I, when the writer endures the terrifying experience of being forced to dance to the music of dislocated time and place, become the music of his own nerves and blood. With his comment on Loti before us, it is illuminating to compare Synge's treatment of this theme of dissolution with the last chapter of *Pêcheur d'Islande*. Loti is describing Yann's death, some six months after the 'actual' catastrophe:

> Une nuit d'août, la-bas, au large de la sombre Islande, au milieu d'un grand bruit de fureur, avaient été célébrées ses noces avec la mer.
>
> Avec la mer qui autrefois avait été aussi sa nourrice; c'était elle qui l'avait fait adolescent large et fort, — et ensuite elle l'avait repris, dans sa virilité superbe, pour elle seule. Un profond mystère avait enveloppé ces noces monstrueuses. Tout le temps, des voiles obscurs s'étaient agités au-dessus, des rideaux mouvants et tourmentés, tendus pour cacher la fête; et la fiancée donnait de la voix, faisait toujours son plus grand bruit horrible pour étouffer les cris.[2]

Whereas Loti yields to the 'profond mystère' — Yann, we are told, struggled mightily, but in the end, 'il s'était abandonné'[3] — Synge fights back successfully from the nightmare of total submersion in the introspective and against the consequential loss of self, struggling back to consciousness and externality, or objectivity:

> At last with a moment of uncontrollable frenzy I broke back to consciousness and awoke.
>
> I dragged myself trembling to the window of the cottage and looked out. The moon was glittering across the bay, and there was no sound anywhere on the island (II, 100).

What is being evoked in Loti's prose-poem is a yielding to death as to an incestuous nuptial consummation, 'ces noces monstrueuses'. In the dream sequence from *The Aran Islands*, Synge dances with the even more monstrously inbred partner of 'my own person or consciousness' (II, 100). In both passages, there is a similar evocation of a horrible agitated music. Synge is 'swept away in a whirlwind of notes' (II, 100); Yann is caught up in the theatrical agitation of 'rideaux mouvants et tourmentés, tendus pour cacher la fête'. The maternal-bridal-mortal embrace is accompanied by a terrible chant of the sea crying out to smother the bridegroom-son's cries for Gaud, for 'sa femme de chair'.[4]

The characters in *Pêcheur d'Islande* avoid death by never rising into life. It would indeed be foolhardy to deny the attractions of a related hermeticism, in which life is equated with death, to the author of *Riders to the Sea, In the Shadow of the Glen, When the Moon Has Set* and *Deirdre of the Sorrows*. Attraction, nevertheless, should not be construed as either connivance or consent. Loti tries to deny the reality of death by blurring, or annihilating, the distinctions between death and life. His Breton fishermen are never the men of Brittany in the sense in which Synge's Aran islanders are the people of Aran. They are citizens, or ghost subjects, in the ice-bound kingdom of the dead. In the opening tableau of *Pêcheur d'Islande* they are already entombed:

> De grosses poutres passaient au-dessus d'eux, presque à toucher leurs têtes; et, derrière leurs dos, des couchettes qui semblaient creusées dans l'épaisseur de la charpente s'ouvraient *comme les niches d'un caveau pour mettre les morts*.[5]

Yann Gaos never succeeds in breaking from the maternal embrace of the sea. He remains after birth, as Jeanne A. Flood has said of Patrick Pearse, 'reciprocally linked . . . to the maternal figure'.[6] To this union Synge, as well as Joyce, refused to give his blessing. In Loti's work Synge detected

> a feeling of unreality, a feeling that one is outside what is vital in the growth of European thought, and that an appeal is being made to young men without health, and to women without occupation, rather than to those who count, singly or collectively, in contemporary intellectual life (II, 395).

In *The Aran Islands*, while he acknowledges and explores his own feelings of unreality, he successfully locates the subjective experience of alienation and loss of identity in an objective, though of course fictional, social context. While the structure and style of his prose, therefore, reflect those processes of dissolution which were part of the

200

psychic experience of his class, the temptation to universalise this experience, to internalise and dissolve all objectivity, is repeatedly resisted. The people themselves, their way of life and their use of story and legend, refuse to conform to the idealising wishes of the artist, just as the young boy of Aran resists the artist narrator's attempts to take, or make, a picturesque, aesthetically pleasing, photograph of him in his island clothes.

It is, of course, the writer himself who records, or presents, the youth's reluctance to make such concessions. He thus acknowledges the recalcitrance of his material — of the life beyond the work — to the aestheticising impulse. The episode of the photograph focuses attention, characteristically, on the problematic relationships and distinctions between art and life, and the symbolic moment is located firmly in a specific historical context. The modern artist is represented, appropriately perhaps, as a photographer. The mechanised maker of images, the great artificer, wrestles, here, with the scion of Stephen Dedalus's old man of the mountain cabin. But it is Synge who is able to acknowledge in the youth from the west as, perhaps, Mulrennan never could have done, the will exerted, against the artist's wishes, to struggle towards the future. The portrait-making narrator wants to compose the youth into a primitivised artefact yet the text insists that to live beyond the frame — or the proscenium arch — the boy must 'step out into the world' (II, 134). The work of art, as Lukacs observed, leads to a great door through which there is no passage, no continuation of the aesthetic universe.[7] We, the reader or the audience, must turn away from that door back to life. The boy of Aran will discover — and here the writer's knowledge goes beyond that of his subject on the threshold — that the Sunday clothes on the island become the everyday garments of the labourer in the wage economy of mainland life.

The Aran Islands addresses itself both to and from men and women to whom occupation is a necessity. It also sets out to encourage in its readers a response to 'the newer thoughts which come together near the real activities of life' (II, 395). The work certainly has many features, both formal and thematic, which associate it with modernism. These include the musical approach to structure, characterised by the juxtaposition of theme and countertheme, and the use of *leitmotif*. These devices cut across the chronological linearity of the basic journalistic, or diary, sequencing. Consequent upon this type of structuring is the dislocation, but not the disappearance, of the diachronic dimension. If we turn from *The Aran Islands* to Synge's fragmentary attempts at novel-writing along conventional nineteenth-century lines, we find the style is inert and the content shows signs of that attenuation of the socio-historical imagination which Lukacs detects in works where 'the hero is strictly confined within the limits of his own experience . . . The narrator, the examining subject is in motion; the examined reality is static'.[8] Had Synge continued with these experiments, the result, we suspect, would have been 'decomposed' autobiography. The release of the examined reality into action in his writing is crucially related to his discovery of the symbolic nature of the relationship between word and referent and between text and world, and to his ability to build this dialectic into the work of art. The development of the necessary strategies was part of the essential struggle away from solipsistic subjectivity and total relativism into a situation in which, as in the highly self-referential work of Beckett, solipsism itself becomes the subject of objective representation, and is brought under the historically grounded scrutiny of language and form. A major role in this development from aesthete to dramatist was played by the fluid state of language in Ireland and by Synge's Aran experiences, which prepared the ground for his exploration, in his dramatic writings, of the nature of drama and of dramatic form.

Synge's plays are complex investigations of 'literature and art as social phenomena of importance in a dynamic interrelationship with man's social and moral existence'.[9] Any reassessment of his work as the symbolic product of his class, or as a form of modernism leading back to the European tradition, including Shakespeare, and forward to the achievements of the later Yeats, and of Joyce, O'Casey and Beckett, must take account of their metatextual character. The dramatic works are not just 'peasant plays' any more than *The Aran Islands* is the chronological record of an antiquarian, or a journalist with an interest in 'folk-life'. They are, rather, 'extraordinarily profound theoretical disquisitions on the aesthetics of drama, and even more, on the relationship of art to reality' — and it is this fact, we suspect, which made Synge very much a dramatist's playwright long before critics began to recognise his more than provincial significance.[10] The world of *The Well of the Saints* or *The Playboy of the Western World* might seem to be at some remove from that of Beckett's *Endgame*, or *Waiting for Godot*, yet they are connected by a related preoccupation with the nature of language and the nature of play. The characters in *Waiting for Godot* act out their play, like the villagers in *The Playboy of the Western World*, while waiting for life, or is it death, to begin. They are actors doomed to wait on the stage rather than in the wings. The greatest fear of Estragon and Vladimir is the fear that there is, perhaps, beyond the stage, or even on it, 'Nothing to be done'; they may be left entangled in 'The Net' and 'squirming like an aesthete'.[11] Ironically, they therefore fill the vacancy of waiting with play acting, in an effort to convince themselves of their reality. Trying desperately to open the closed door, they always turn in the wrong direction. They fear most of all that if one or other of them leaves the stage, that 'charming spot', like Pegeen's playboy he will be gone for ever — although as Estragon points out to Pozzo when he protests imperiously about Vladimir's departure, Didi had to leave the stage to piss: if he'd stayed 'he would have burst'.[12]

Whenever Estragon and Vladimir peer out beyond the proscenium arch they retreat in horror, seeing there only 'that bog'.[13] Yet although the stage may close off, for the characters, the darkness beyond, the comic horror of their plight is just as surely intensified by their inability to escape from the stage. The rhetorical effect on the audience is to create a desire for the breaking of the self-perpetuating pseudo-order of playing the aesthetic game, with its apparently unending capacity for the 'composition of decompositon'.[14] The order which Estragon and Vladimir endlessly reconstruct has its heroism in their resolutely histrionic world, but it has its horror too, which breaks out in Lucky's demented shouting of his text, the 'result of the labours left unfinished crowned by the Acacacacademy of Anthropopopometry of Essy-in-Posse of Testew and Cunard'.[15] *Their* unwillingness, or inability, to end the game makes *us* urgently aware of the need for an ending, for the movement outward from the paralysed action to the activity demanded by 'hills are waiting for the spade and plough' (III, 141).

Because of their shared Anglo-Irish Protestant background, their common interest in languages and in European literature and philosophy, and their proximity in time, it is, perhaps, only to be expected that one should discover thematic and stylistic parallels

203

between the works of Synge and those of Beckett. Of greater interest for any attempt to trace the modernist preoccupation with the relationship between the word and deed and between text and world, as well as for an assessment of the centrality of Synge's work as opposed to its provincialism or its supposed peculiarly Irish delight in words for their own sake, are the close affinities between his complex and sophisticated deployment of metalanguage and metadrama and Shakespeare's dramatic practice. In *The Winter's Tale*, for example, the very title invites us to see the work as a dramatisation, a projection into action, of Mamillius's whispered tale 'of sprites and goblins' haunting 'a man . . . Dwelt by a churchyard'.[16] Camillo and Paulina, the two authors of the redeeming action, make use of art to enable Polixenes and Leontes to break from the spell-binding, yet constitutive, power of art mistaken for reality. They are able to break the spell *through the spell*, precisely because they recognise art for what it is — a double-edged weapon which can turn us either to morbid distraction from living or to engagement with life. Awareness of the dialectic between play and life, and between word and deed, distinguishes the characters who live in the world of reality from Leontes, and later, Polixenes, and the moribund and spectral churchyard world. Leontes fatally identifies Hermione's 'entertainment' of Polixenes with 'the agent' of adultery, just as Pegeen at the end of *The Playboy of the Western World*, or the Douls at the outset of *The Well of the Saints*, mistake the word for the deed, the game for the reality, failing therefore to recognise — or acknowledge their responsibility for the making of — their true identity and relationships.[17] Again, the terminology is very precisely metadramatic. The king sees himself as acting out in reality

> so disgrac'd a part, whose issue
> Will hiss me to my grave.[18]

His confusion of role-playing with reality is inescapably linked with fears for his own legitimacy and succession. His fundamental error of judgement, the inability to distinguish between, and therefore rightly to relate, entertainment and act, does *in deed* cause Leontes to act out a disgraced part, and like the Old Man in Yeats's 'Purgatory', to destroy his heir. It is given to Perdita to express most succinctly this double-edged nature of the dramatic, when Florizel and Autolycus exchange garments to act out the 'scene' devised by Camillo as 'medicine' for the two charmed monarchs:[19]

> CAMILLO. Unbuckle, unbuckle [*Florizel and Autolycus exchange garments*]
>   Fortunate mistress — let my prophecy
>   Come home to ye! — You must retire yourself
>   Into some covert: take your sweetheart's hat
>   And pluck it o'er your brows, muffle your face,
>   Dismantle you, and (as you can) disliken
>   The truth of your own seeming . . .
> PERDITA. I see the play so lies
>   That I must bear a part.[20]

Leontes learns, in the end, the lesson which is relearned in *The Well of the Saints, The Playboy of the Western World* and *Deirdre of the Sorrows*: the need for each not just to play a part, but to be able, and willing, to stand outside the performance and to answer for his actions:

> LEONTES. Good Paulina,
>   Lead us from hence, where we may leisurely
>   Each one demand, and answer to his part
>   Perform'd in this wide gap of time, since first
>   We were dissever'd: hastily lead away.[21]

In Synge's plays also, metaliterary, or more comprehensively, metaesthetic, techniques are developed, which call attention to the power of art to cut into chronological or ' historical' time and to exert its influence upon men's actions as well as their dreams. This power is shown to relate closely to, even to derive from, the capacity of words to objectify, and to realise, states, conditions and acts which have their origins, or authorship, in the subjectivity of language-using man. Words, and works of art, have a generative force which can operate to construct or destroy, to strengthen, or to dissolve or suppress, the mediations of reality. As Martin and Mary Doul and Christy Mahon discover, and as Leontes recognises when it appears that his words have indeed condemned his wife to death and his line to destruction, language can be used both to generate 'a non-referential discourse . . . that is quite unrelated to, and unchecked against, reality and all plausibility', and to cause the 'unreal' to become an effective influence upon reality.[22] The word once spoken, Hermione reminds her husband, cannot be cancelled out simply by a process of unsaying. Since language is a social product and process, it also has the disconcerting habit of revealing the hidden referentiality of the apparently non-referential, and of expressing the repressed. Nor can the word as word ever give way totally to the pressures of solipsism (as Beckett knows) because it is simultaneously 'both subjectivity and communication, or better . . . intertextuality'.[23] This necessary — and unavoidable — ambivalence of the dialogic (or dramatistic) word 'implies the insertion of history (society) into a text and of this text into history'.[24] Language is, from this perspective, essentially metonymic, for 'inasmuch as *metonymy* implies the part for the whole, language is always giving us the part of the whole and is thus always making us aware of a gap between the signifier and what might be being signified'.[25] The uncovering of this gap, and the exploration of its historically catastrophic dimensions, is a major theme, though not always consciously pursued, of what Tony Tanner has called

post-Viconian society: the society that *knows* that it makes itself, even if it does not always know how, or always wish to know how.[26]

Indeed, as our analysis of *When the Moon Has Set* suggests, the gap sometimes yawns most widely in works which try to avoid or conceal its existence.

In his last play, *Deirdre of the Sorrows*, Synge chose to return once again to the problem of dramatising the decline of a Great House and of a ruling class in crisis, divided against itself. By his choice of the 'Deirdre' story, he made it inevitable that this drama would not only be compared with Yeats's treatment of the subject, but would also be considered in relation to the political aspirations and images of the Irish nationalist movement. Indeed, such a play could scarcely avoid becoming a statement about, or an exploration of, the relationships between history and myth. Yeats, the great myth-maker of a certain powerful version of Irish national consciousness, repeatedly asks us to believe that his myths of history do, in fact, constitute a *reading* of history — a reading which makes history itself 'almost indistinguishable from aesthetics'.[27] A similar aestheticising approach to the present, which sees it as a formless chaos requiring the imposition of an order from a more stable age which obeyed and accommodated its myth-makers with due deference to their superior wisdom, informs the thinking behind T.S. Eliot's essay, ' "Ulysses", Order and Myth'. In this essay Eliot describes Joyce's use of the Odyssean parallels as 'simply a way of controlling, of ordering, of giving a shape and a significance to the immense panorama of futility and anarchy which is contemporary history'.[28] 'It is a method', Eliot helpfully adds, 'already adumbrated by Mr. Yeats, and of the need for which I believe Mr. Yeats to have been the first contemporary to be conscious . . . Instead of narrative method we may now use the mythical method'.[29] Eliot's use of the word 'simply' is a small fig-leaf used to conceal some very large ideological and critical assumptions, and to enable him to pass off as statements about technique sweeping value judgements upon the rebellious naughtiness of the times. His approach to myth, at least in his critical and polemical writings, is to see it as a restorer and guarantor, as well as generator (preferably Christian) of

> continuity and coherence in politics . . . reliable behaviour on fixed principles persisting through changed situations . . . continuity and coherence in literature and the arts . . . and a positive distinction — however undemocratic it may sound — between the educated and the uneducated.[30]

With the devastating send-up of learning 'how to see the world as the Christian Fathers saw it' in *The Well of the Saints* and the comic apotheosis of the process of 'reascending to origins' in *The Playboy of the Western World* in mind, we might, however, be forgiven for enquiring whether Synge's dramatic technique, and, we hasten to add, Joyce's not dissimilar use of metatextual strategies, has much in common with Eliot's invocation of myth as an aid to and legitimator of the imposition of a socio-aesthetic order on recalcitrant history.[31] Synge's use of myth in *Deirdre* is not designed to impose an order on a chaotic world; indeed, it is closer to the spirit of the play to suggest that Conchubor brings the prophesied chaos on Emain Macha because of a ruthless determination to impose his will on Deirdre, to possess her as his booty and his prize. His behaviour is a classical example of what happens when a man in power acts 'on fixed principles persisting through changed situations'.

The dialectic between history and myth in *Deirdre of the Sorrows* offers a deeper exploration of their nature and their relationships than either the attempts to replace history by myth, or the efforts of a mechanistic realism to ignore or deny the very real part played by myths in the making of history. In *Ulysses*, Joyce frequently invokes myth to demystify the mythological, while at the same time according full recognition to its immense power to structure — and to mediate — our versions of history. In her essay on 'James Joyce, Patrick Pearse and the Theme of Execution', Jeanne Flood examines this process in operation upon one of the most sacred stories which is used to legitimate the ideology of yet another powerful version of Irish nationalist consciousness — the execution of Robert Emmet. At the end of the 'Sirens' sequence in *Ulysses*, Bloom 'looks in the window of Lionel Marks's antique shop, sees Emmet's picture and thinks of Emmet's last words which, via a mistaken reference to Meyerbeer, he associates with Christ's'.[32] Joyce is using the mythical method not to impose order on anarchy, but to undermine the Emmet myth, with its siren-like capacity to seduce the Irish patriot with the attractions of the *dulce et decorum* ideal of laying down one's life for the mother- (or father-) land. Bloom

> deals with his flatulence, while in his mind reciting the famous conclusion of Emmet's speech from the dock . . . Pearse called these words 'the most memorable ever uttered by an Irish man'. Joyce's comic and degraded use of them immediately precedes the 'Cyclops' episode in which he presents the great parodic version of Emmet's execution.[33]

This 'structuring' use of the Odyssean parallel is, we suspect, a far cry from the kind of imposition of order on an age which has lost all form, which Eliot believed he detected in *Ulysses* and in Yeats. It is, rather, a strategic protest against the imposition of a specific, mystifying version of the past on the present and the future, which is very close indeed, in soul and in form, to the mood and manner of Synge's antithetical dramatic vision. Joyce's 'factification' of a version of history, his rewriting, or representation, of the archetypal story of Emmet's death, has much in common with the Rabelaisian behaviour of Mary Byrne with the parish priest in *The Tinker's Wedding* — and the multitude attending Bloom's nuptial ceremony are also treated to a performance of the old tinker woman's subversive anthem, 'The Night Before Larry Was Stretched'.

Although *Deirdre of the Sorrows* undoubtedly shows, particularly in its second act, the powerful attractions of the heroic aristocratic myth for Synge, his last play nevertheless testifies to his struggle to establish a social context with which the myth interacts. That he was more successful in finding an objective correlative for his personal and historical drama in 'folk tale' and 'peasant' settings and characters may well be symptomatic of a related need to conceal from himself the psychic implications of his artistic insight into the necessary dialectics of history. It may also be due, partly, to the fact that he found, in the stories and legends of the people of Aran, a form of transfigured realism which enabled him to

discipline [his] subjectivity and [his] artistic individuality within the objective requirements of art, within the objective social currents unconsciously demanding expression in the people.[34]

Synge rejected the temptation to deny the reality of death by identifying it with, or substituting it for, life. Such an identification of opposites attempts to cancel out opposition; it strives to accomplish the impossible task of circumscribing the dialectic of history or replacing it by the false equilibrium of stasis, the fixating power of the eternal *fiat*. A short, untitled poem, written by Synge in November 1908, condenses the drama of these contending claims into six brief lines which enact the temptation offered by Joyce to Stephen Dedalus to accept the perfection of the text in place of the work of life, and which also offer Synge's answer to the invitation. In the opening lines, the poet presents himself as reader, author and work. He is reading, or has just read — the ambiguity of the verb form is important — his own work, into which is inscribed a version of his 'I':

I read about the Blaskets and Dunquin
The Wicklow towns and fair-days I've been in
I read about Dunmanway, Aran Mor
And men with kelp along a wintry shore (I, 66).

The movement from the self-absorption of the speaking-reading-written 'I' to the other — to the 'men with kelp along a wintry shore' — begins to dissolve the literary solipsism of the initial situation. The line which follows, taking its cue from the latent death-imagery in line 4, cuts across the dreamlike ambivalence of tense and tenselessness with a sudden, stressed, adverb of time:

> Then I remember that that 'I' was I (I, 66).

But the stammering attempt to capture identity in the instant serves only as a reminder of the impossibility of holding fast, through contextualisation, to a static point in or out of time which can be identified with a stasis of the self. That the work of living entails the task of dying is acknowledged in the concluding line. Synge, too, has a job to do which is not deferred or cancelled out by his reading or writing:

> And I'd a filthy job — to waste and die (I, 66).

There is, here, no sentimental indulging in the *frisson* of the grave, no Loti-like aestheticising of death, nor any attempt, either, to shut it up within, or out of, the covers of the book.

The description of death as a 'job' is characteristic of a man who was able to recognise that historical as well as personal fullness of life necessitated an acceptance of death, but that this was no reason for succumbing to a fear of life which would paralyse action. In his *Autobiography* Synge recalls how

> an aunt of mine died in our own house. My mother asked me the day after if I was not sorry. I answered with some hesitation . . . that I feared not . . .
>
> The sense of death seems to have been only strong enough to evoke the full luxury of the woods. I have never been so happy. It is a feeling like this makes all primitive people inclined to merry making at a funeral (II, 7).

It is possible to detect even here a tendency to experience death, vicariously, as the guarantor of life. The theme reappears in the poem 'Queens', which offers an interesting contrast to Yeats's 'Under Ben Bulben'. Yeats begins his poem by asking us to take an oath of belief in, or fidelity to, the power of the word to prophesy and to confer immortality on the heroic:

SWEAR by what the sages spoke
Round the Mareotic Lake
That the Witch of Atlas knew,
Spoke and set the cocks a-crow.
Swear by those horsemen, by those women
Complexion and form prove superhuman.[35]

The starting-point of Synge's poem is also a performative act, but one which is placed in the past. The poet and his addressee have been engaged for seven days in the god-like game of conjuring up existence by the act of naming — a mimesis of the Genesis-myth. But the activity, it is suggested, is also an attempt to search out time past, to hold it fast — and possibly, therefore, a waste of time on words alone:

Seven dog-days we let pass
Naming Queens in Glenmacnass
All the rare and royal names
Wormy sheepskin yet retains (I, 34).

Is there, we wonder, a Joycean process of profane reversal at work in the reference to 'dog-days'? The deflating mood of the opening lines hints that there may well be. The lines which follow focus, through the metalinguistic act of naming, on the interface between art and life. The poem brings to bear on this interface the concentrated light of the broad spectrum of literature, history, myth, biblical lore, legend, folk tale and religion, whose colours are diffused throughout Synge's dramatic world. It ransacks history and art with a democratic eclecticism which beats Yeats's aristocratic selectivity in 'Ben Bulben' at its own aesthetic game. The two actors in the drama — only one speaks — have named queens renowned for their names, for their lack of names, for their beauty, for their ugliness, for their finery, for their power, for their poverty:

Queens whose finger once did stir men,
Queens were eaten of fleas and vermin . . .
Queens who cut the bogs of Glanna,
Judith of Scripture, and Gloriana (I, 34).

No one in Synge's poem is denied the right to be named: the litany is all-embracing. In its very comprehensiveness, and its topsy-turvydom, it creates a carnival atmosphere where order and hierarchy are set aside and every woman is a queen.[36] The naming creates a sense of an on going, living-and-dying community, which is the very antithesis of Yeats's monumental 'pale, long-visaged company'.[37] His queens, like Mary Byrne, like Mary Doul, like Nora Burke and the Widow Quin, come momentarily, briefly, even riotously to life, to answer gaily to their calling. They are not, however, conjured up like the Witch of Atlas, to be thrust 'back in the human mind again'.[38] Rather, they are vigorously, comically, unsentimentally, thrust back into their graves, or firmly consigned to their decaying sheepskin texts. In the end, the players turn from their naming game, acknowledging mortality and welcoming life:

> Yet these are rotten — I ask their pardon
> And we've the sun on rock and garden
> These are rotten — so you're the queen
> Of all are living, or have been (I, 34).

The poems, like the dramas, cast a warm, laughter-loving eye on life, on death. They remind us constantly of the necessary distinction between the corporeal and the aesthetic. Synge's work is open to history because it attends to the fact that the relationship between world and text is neither identity nor exclusiveness, yet it asks us to recognise the important paradoxical truth, for artist and audience alike, that

> one can play only at what is there: one cannot play at anything without it somehow becoming part and parcel of one's life.[39]

NOTES

1. T.S. Eliot, ' "Ulysses", Order and Myth', in *Selected Prose of T.S. Eliot*, edited by Frank Kermode (London, Faber, 1975), p. 178. This essay first appeared in *The Dial*, November 1923.

2. Pierre Loti, *Pêcheur d'Islande* (Paris, Ancienne Maison Michel Levy Frères, 1895), p. 343. The quotations from *Pêcheur d'Islande* are given in French because the text loses in translation the incantatory rhythm of the original and the dream-like assonance and alliteration which are essential components of Loti's aestheticising style. The following translation is from the English edition of the work which was published in London around 1900 by Collins. The translator is unnamed and the publication date is not given:

> One August night, out off gloomy Iceland, mingled with the furious clamour of the sea, his wedding with the sea was performed. It had been his nurse; it had rocked him in his babyhood and had afterwards made him big and strong; then, in his superb manhood, it had taken him back again for itself alone. Profoundest mystery had surrounded this unhallowed union. While it went on, dark curtains hung pall-like over it as if to conceal the ceremony, and the ghoul howled in an awful deafening voice to stifle his cries (p. 253).

3. Ibid., pp. 343 and 344.

4. Ibid., p. 343 ('his fleshly wife').

5. Ibid., p. 2, my italics. The following translation is from the Collins version:

> Thick beams ran above them, very nearly touching their heads, and behind them yawned the berths, apparently hollowed out of the solid timbers, like recesses of a vault wherein to place the dead (p. 10).

6. Jeanne A. Flood, 'James Joyce, Patrick Pearse and the Theme of *Execution*', in *Irish Studies*, Volume I (1980), p. 112.

7. 'Every written work, even if it is no more than a consonance of beautiful words, leads us to a great door — through which there is no passage'. Georg Lukacs, *Soul and Form*, translated by Anna Bostock (London, Merlin Press, 1974), p. 113.

213

8. Georg Lukacs, *The Meaning of Contemporary Realism*, translated by John and Necke Mander (London, Merlin Press, 1963), p. 21. Synge's attempts at novel-writing include some pages of a novel about nurses, TCD MS 4382, ff. 2-5, and the first chapter of a projected novel, 'Flowers and Footsteps', TCD MS 4382, ff. 39v-42v. This material dates from the period 1897-8. It echoes many of the themes of *When the Moon Has Set*.

9. Georg Lukacs, *Writer and Critic and Other Essays*, edited and translated by Professor Arthur Kahn (London, Merlin Press, 1978), p. 205.

10. Ibid., p. 204.

11. Samuel Beckett, *Waiting for Godot: A Tragicomedy in Two Acts*, second edition (London, Faber, 1979), p. 40.

12. Ibid., pp. 13 and 15.

13. Ibid., p. 15.

14. John P. De Sollar, 'Sound and Sense in Samuel Beckett's Drama and Fiction', in *Irish Studies*, Volume I (1980), p. 135.

15. Beckett, *Waiting for Godot*, p. 43.

16. William Shakespeare, *The Winter's Tale*, edited by J.H.F. Pafford, The Arden Shakespeare, fourth edition (London, Methuen, 1963), II. 1.26, pp. 29-30.

17. Ibid., I.2.111, 114.

18. Ibid., I.2.188-9.

19. Ibid., IV.4.594, 588.

20. Ibid., IV.4.647-56.

21. Ibid., V.3. 151-5.

22. Tony Tanner, *Adultery in the Novel: Contract and Transgression* (Baltimore and London, Johns Hopkins, 1979), p. 50.

23. Julia Kristeva, *Desire in Language: A Semiotic Approach to Literature and Art*, edited by Leon Rondiez and translated by Thomas Gora, Alice Jardine, and Leon S. Rondiez (Oxford, Oxford University Press, 1980), p. 68.

24. Ibid., p. 68.

25. Tanner, *Adultery in the Novel*, p.95.

26. Ibid., p. 52.

27. Seamus Deane, 'The Literary Myths of the Revival: A Case for their Abandonment' in Joseph Ronsley (ed.), *Myth and Reality in Irish Literature* (Waterloo Ontario, Wilfred Laurier University Press, 1977), p. 319.

28. Eliot, ' "Ulysses", Order and Myth', p. 177.

29. Ibid., p. 177.

30. T.S. Eliot, *The Idea of a Christian Society* (London, Faber, 1939), p. 40.

31. Ibid., p. 62.

32. Jeanne Flood, 'James Joyce, Patrick Pearse and the Theme of Execution', p. 115.

33. Ibid., p. 115.

34. Lukacs, *Writer and Critic*, p. 207.

35. W.B. Yeats, 'Under Ben Bulben', in *Collected Poems of W.B. Yeats* (London and Basingstoke, Macmillan, 1950), p. 397.

36. 'Carnivalesque discourse breaks through the laws of language censored by grammar and semantics, and, at the same time, is a social and political protest. There is no equivalence, but rather, Identlty between challenging official linguistic codes and challenging official law'. Kristeva, *Desire in Language*, p. 65.

37. Yeats, 'Under Ben Bulben', p. 397.

38. Ibid., p. 398.

39. Georg Lukacs, *Soul and Form*, translated by Anna Bostock (London, Merlin Press, 1974), p. 37.

BIBLIOGRAPHY

1. THE WRITINGS OF J.M. SYNGE

(a) Published Material:

 J.M. Synge: Collected Works, general editor Robin Skelton (London: Oxford University Press, 1962-68)

 Volume I : *Poems*, edited by Robin Skelton (1962)

 Volume II : *Prose*, edited by Alan Price (1966)

 Volume III: *Plays*, Book I, edited by Ann Saddlemyer (1968)

 Volume IV : *Plays*, Book II, edited by Ann Saddlemyer (1968)

(b) Unpublished Material:

 All references are to The Synge Manuscripts in the Library of Trinity College, Dublin. They follow the itemisation and foliation of the collection, as set out in the catalogue prepared on the occasion of the Synge centenary exhibition, 1971, and published by Dolmen Press for the Library of Trinity College Dublin.

2. WRITINGS ABOUT J.M. SYNGE

Bushrui, S.B., editor, *Sunshine and the Moon's Delight: A Centenary Tribute to John Millington Synge 1871-1909* (Gerrards Cross, Bucks.: Colin Smythe; Beirut: The American University, 1972)

Donoghue, Denis, ' "Too immoral for Dublin": Synge's *The Tinker's Wedding*', *Irish Writing* 30 (1955) 56-62

Gerstenberger, Donna, *John Millington Synge*, Twayne's English Authors Series, 12 (New York: Twayne Publishers, 1964)

Greene, David H. and Stephens, Edward M., *J.M. Synge, 1871-1909* (New York: Macmillan, 1959; Collier Books, 1961)

Grene, Nicholas, *Synge: A Critical Study of the Plays* (London and Basingstoke: Macmillan, 1975)

Kiberd, Declan, *Synge and the Irish Language* (London and Basingstoke: Macmillan, 1979)

McCormack, W.J., 'Politics and Dramatic Setting: the Experience of Oscar Wilde and J.M. Synge'. Paper presented at the British Sociological Association Conference, University of Sussex (1978) Unpublished

Skelton, Robin, *The Writings of J.M. Synge* (London: Thames and Hudson, 1971)

Stephens, Edward, *My Uncle John: Edward Stephens's Life of J.M. Synge*, edited by Andrew Carpenter (London: Oxford University Press, 1974)

Synge, Reverend Samuel, *Letters to My Daughter: Being Intimate Recollections of John Millington Synge* (Dublin and Cork: The Talbot Press, 1931)

Whitaker, Thomas R., editor, *Twentieth Century Interpretations of* The Playboy of the Western World (Englewood Cliffs, N.J.: Prentice-Hall, Inc., 1969)

3. GENERAL

(a) Books:

Bakhtin, Mikhail, *Rabelais and His World*, translated by Hélène Iswolsky (Cambridge Massachusetts and London: Massachusetts Institute of Technology, 1968)

Beckett, Samuel, *Waiting for Godot: A Tragicomedy in Two Acts* (London: Faber, 1979)

Benjamin, Walter, *Understanding Brecht*, translated by Anna Bostock (London: New Left Books, 1977)

Berger, John, *Ways of Seeing* (London: BBC and Penguin Books, 1972)

Brecht, Bertolt, *Man Equals Man* and *The Elephant Calf, Collected Plays*, 2, Part I (London: Eyre Methuen, 1979)

Brown, Richard H., *A Poetic for Sociology: Towards a Logic of Discovery for the Human Sciences* (London: Cambridge University Press, 1977)

Burke, Kenneth, *A Grammar of Motives* (New York: Prentice-Hall, Inc., 1945)

Burke, Kenneth, *Language as Symbolic Action: Essays on Life, Literature, and Method* (Berkeley and London: University of California Press, 1966)

Downer, Alan S., editor, *The Art of the Play: An Anthology of Nine Plays* (New York: Holt, 1955)

Eliot, T.S., *The Idea of a Christian Society* (London: Faber, 1939)

Eliot, T.S., *Selected Prose*, edited by Frank Kermode (London: Faber, 1975)

Frye, Northrop, *Anatomy of Criticism: Four Essays* (Princeton, New Jersey: Princeton University Press, 1957)

Harvey, W. J., *Character and the Novel* (London: Chatto and Windus, 1965)

Heilman, Robert B., *Tragedy and Melodrama; Versions of Experience* (Seattle:

University of Washington Press, 1968)

Henn, T.R., *The Harvest of Tragedy* (London: Methuen, 1956)

Henry, P.L., *Language, Culture and the Nation: Two Lectures* (Dublin: Comharchumann Chois Fharraige, 1974)

Jameson, Fredric, *The Prison-House of Language: A Critical Account of Structuralism and Russian Formalism* (Princeton and London: Princeton University Press, 1972)

Krieger, Elliot, *A Marxist Study of Shakespeare's Comedies* (London and Basingstoke: Macmillan, 1979)

Kristeva, Julia, *Desire in Language: A Semiotic Approach to Literature and Art* (Oxford: Blackwell, 1980)

Lentricchia, Frank, *The Gaiety of Language*, Perspectives in Criticism, 19 (Berkeley and Los Angeles: University of California Press, 1968)

Levitt, Paul M., *A Structural Approach to the Analysis of Drama* (The Hague and Paris: Mouton, 1971)

Lodge, David, *The Modes of Modern Writing: Metaphor, Metonymy, and the Edward Arnold, 1977)*

Loti, Pierre, *Pêcheur d'Islande* (Paris: Ancienne Maison Michel Levy Frères, 1895)

Loti, Pierre, *An Iceland Fisherman* (London: Collins, n.d.)

Lukacs, Georg, *Soul and Form*, translated by Anna Bostock (London: Merlin Press, 1974)

Lukacs, Georg, *The Meaning of Contemporary Realism*, translated by John and Necke Mander (London: Merlin Press, 1962)

Lukacs, Georg, *Writer and Critic and Other Essays*, translated by Arthur Kahn (London: Merlin Press, 1978)

McCormack, W.J., *Sheridan Le Fanu and Victorian Ireland* (Oxford: Clarendon Press, 1980)

McCormack, W.J., and Alistair Stead, editors, *James Joyce and Modern Literature* (London, Boston, Melbourne and Henley: Routledge and Kegan Paul, 1982)

Nietzsche, Friedrich, *We Philologists*, translated by J.M. Kennedy (Edinburgh and London: T. N. Foulis, 1911)

O'Casey, Sean, *Three More Plays by Sean O'Casey* (London; Macmillan, 1965)

Pratt, Mary Louise, *Toward a Speech Act Theory of Literary Discourse* (Bloomington and London: Indiana University Press, 1977)

Raphael, Max, *Proudhon Marx Picasso: Three Studies in the Sociology of Art*, translated by Inge Marcuse (New Jersey: Humanities Press; London: Lawrence and Wishart, 1980)

Ronsley, Joseph, editor, *Myth and Reality in Irish Literature* (Waterloo Ontario: Wilfred Laurier University Press, 1977)

Shakespeare, William, *The Winter's Tale*, edited by J.H.P. Pafford, *The*

Arden Shakespeare (London: Methuen, 1963)

Tanner, Tony, *Adultery in the Novel: Contract and Transgression* (Baltimore and London: Johns Hopkins, 1979)

Trench, Richard Chevenix, Archbishop, *On the Study of Words*, twenty-sixth edition (London: Kegan Paul, Trench, Trübner and Co., 1899)

Volosinov, V.N., *Freudianism: A Marxist Critique*, translated by I.R. Titunik (London: Academic Press, 1976)

Volosinov, V.N., *Marxism and the Philosophy of Language*, translated by Ladislav Matejka and I.R. Titunik (New York and London: Seminar Press, 1973)

White, Hayden, *Metahistory: The Historical Imagination in Nineteenth-Century Europe* (Baltimore and London: Johns Hopkins, 1973)

Williams, Raymond, *Marxism and Literature* (Oxford: Oxford University Press, 1977)

Worth, Katharine, *The Irish Drama of Europe from Yeats to Beckett* (London: Athlone Press, 1970)

Yeats, W.B., *Autobiographies* (London and Basingstoke: Macmillan, 1955)

Yeats, W.B., *Essays and Introductions* (London and New York: Macmillan, 1961)

Yeats, W.B., *The Collected Poems of W. B. Yeats* (London and Basingstoke: Macmillan, 1950)

Zis, Avner, *Foundations of Marxist Aesthetics*, translated by Katharine Judelson (Moscow: Progress Publishers, 1977)

(b) Articles in Journals:

Delargy, J.H., 'The Gaelic Story-teller. With Some Notes on Gaelic Folktales', *Proceedings of the British Academy* (1945), 177-221

De Sollar, John P., 'Sound and Sense in Samuel Beckett's Drama and Fiction', *Irish Studies*, 1 (1980), 133-52

Flood, Jeanne A., 'Synge's Ecstatic Dance and the Myth of the Undying Father', *American Imago*, 33.2 (1976), 174-96

Flood, Jeanne A., 'James Joyce, Patrick Pearse and the Theme of Execution', *Irish Studies*, 1 (1980), 101-24

Frank, Joseph, 'Spatial Form in Modern Literature: An Essay in Two Parts', *Sewanee Review* (1945), 221-653

McCormack, W.J., 'Yeats's "Purgatory": A Play and a Tradition', *Crane Bag*, 3.2. (1979), 33-44

Mitchell, Jack, 'The Role of Emotion in the Theatre of Sean O'Casey', *Irland: Gesellschaft und Kultur*, 2 (1979), 121-9

Richter, Dieter, 'History and Dialectics in the Materialist Theory of Literature', translated by Vicki Hill and Charles Spencer, *New German Critique*, 6 (1975), 31-47

Zipes, Jack, 'Breaking the Magic Spell: Politics and the Fairy Tale', *New*

German Critique, 6 (1975), 116-35

4. BIBLICAL REFERENCES

All references are to the King James Version of the Holy Bible, published by Oxford University Press

INDEX

221